JESUS AND MAGIC

Jesus and Magic

FREEING THE GOSPEL STORIES
FROM MODERN MISCONCEPTIONS

Richard A. Horsley

CASCADE *Books* • Eugene, Oregon

JESUS AND MAGIC
Freeing the Gospel Stories from Modern Misconceptions

Copyright © 2014 Richard A. Horsley. All rights reserved. Except for brief quotations in critical publications or reviews, no part of this book may be reproduced in any manner without prior written permission from the publisher. Write: Permissions, Wipf and Stock Publishers, 199 W. 8th Ave., Suite 3, Eugene, OR 97401.

Cascade Books
An Imprint of Wipf and Stock Publishers
199 W. 8th Ave., Suite 3
Eugene, OR 97401

www.wipfandstock.com

ISBN 13: 978-1-4982-0172-8

Cataloging-in-Publication data:

Horsley, Richard A.

    Jesus and magic : freeing the gospel stories from modern misconceptions / Richard A. Horsley.

    xiv + 178 p. ; 23 cm—Includes bibliographical references.

    ISBN 13: 978-1-4982-0172-8

    1. Bible. Gospels—Criticism, interpretation, etc. 2. Magic—Ancient. 3. Healing in the Bible. 4. Miracles—Biblical teaching. 5. Exorcism—Biblical teaching. I. Title.

BS2545 M5 H66 2014

Manufactured in the USA

Contents

Introduction | vii
Abbreviations | xi

PART 1: Miracles

Introduction to Part 1 | 3

1. A Missing Concept: (Elite) Judean and Hellenistic Culture | 7
2. The Concept of Miracle and Jesus' Healings and Exorcisms | 20

PART 2: Magic

Introduction to Part 2 | 35

3. Modern Construction of Ancient Magic | 37
4. Construction of Jewish Magic | 53
5. Construction of Jesus as Magician | 63
6. The Magician—and Jesus—as Sociological Type | 75
7. Discourse, Ritual Practices, and Healing | 92

PART 3: Jesus's Healings and Exorcisms

Introduction to Part 3 | 103

8. The Gospel Stories as the Sources | 107
9. Healing Episodes | 119
10. Exorcism Episodes | 143

Conclusion | 163
Bibliography | 169

Introduction

INTERPRETERS OF JESUS SEEM to be stuck when it comes to dealing with the healings and exorcisms. They are stuck in old terms and phrases that long ago became frozen into standard scholarly concepts and assumptions. The Gospels are full of episodes of healing and exorcism. In the Gospel of Mark they compose most of Jesus's ministry in Galilee. In the recent spate of books on Jesus, however, interpreters devote little or no attention to their interpretation. Why?

The development of the New Testament studies branch of theology in the age of Enlightenment is surely part of the reason. When critical theologians and biblical scholars finally tried to come to grips with the nascent culture of science in evaluating the Gospel accounts as sources for the historical Jesus, they dismissed most narratives as unreliable. The infancy narratives involved angels. The passion narratives were clearly testimonies of Easter faith. To Enlightenment reason it was clear that the healings and exorcisms—like multiplying food, walking on water, and raising the dead—did not happen by natural causes but must have involved supernatural causes (God). That is, they were "miracles," perhaps even with elements of "magic."[1] Modern scholars, of course, couched their interpretation in modern terms. Since modern, scientific people could not believe in spirits and miracles or magic, interpreters of Jesus tended to avoid the "miracle stories." They focused largely on the more reliable sayings in the Gospel sources and presented Jesus mainly as a teacher. This left Jesus's healings and exorcisms classified as "miracles" or "magic," along with raising the dead and "nature miracles," and left skeptical interpreters with little or nothing to offer by way of illuminating discussion.

---

1. Since recent translations of healing and exorcism episodes in the Gospels and other relevant passages often use the language of biomedicine or other historically problematic terms, I have usually presented my own translations—sometimes as a deliberate alternative.

INTRODUCTION

In recent decades the grip of Enlightenment reason on what counts as reality has loosened considerably. Even the natural sciences are seen to operate according to certain models or paradigms. Yet even in the resurgence of research on the historical Jesus in the last generation, interpreters are stuck in what have become standard scholarly concepts. It somehow has not occurred to Jesus interpreters, who claim to be investigating Jesus in his historical context, to inquire how ancient people understood healing and exorcism. They were "amazed" or "astounded" at incidents of healing. But did they share our modern concepts of miracle or magic? Perhaps it would be appropriate to question key terms and assumptions that became standard in the field of New Testament more than a century ago.

The way interpreters of Jesus and the Gospels deal with Jesus's healings and exorcisms has not changed much since the highly influential scholar Rudolf Bultmann's important analysis nearly ninety years ago. Treating the Gospels as mere containers or collections of discrete sayings and stories that had circulated separately, contemporary interpreters following Bultmann dismantle the Gospels to isolate the individual sayings and stories. Such analysis then classifies the stories into different kinds, the most extensive category being "miracle stories," under which scholars lump all of the stories that focus on healing or exorcism or "raising the dead / resuscitation" or "nature miracles / wonders." Then, partly because "the sayings-tradition" also attests healings and exorcisms, contemporary scholars such as Meier and Funk (and the Jesus Seminar)[2] repeat Bultmann's conclusion from 1926, that while most of the miracle stories are legendary, "there can be no doubt that Jesus did the kind of deeds which were miracles . . . , that is, deeds which were attributed to a supernatural, divine cause."[3]

These same scholars, however, then ignore Bultmann's other conclusion from 1926, that there is "no great value in investigating more closely how much in the gospel miracle tales is historical."[4] They devote great energy and hundreds of pages to searching through the isolated individual miracle stories for fragmentary "historical facts" or elements that "have a chance of going back to some event in the life of . . . Jesus."[5] Meier devoted twice as much space (530 pages) to the "miracle stories" as to Jesus's message, and Funk and the Jesus Seminar devoted five years of research,

2. Meier, *Mentor*; Funk and the Jesus Seminar, *Acts*.
3. Bultmann, *Jesus*, 173.
4. Ibid., 174.
5. Meier, *Mentor*, 648, 652, 726.

discussion, and voting (1991–1996) and five hundred pages to the "acts of Jesus." As the result of this painstaking analysis of the miracle stories, however, they find precious few elements that they deem authentic.

While scholars define the types of stories ostensibly by (literary) form (e.g., as pronouncement stories or controversy stories), modern Western rationalist criteria are determinative for "miracle stories." The concept of miracle came into prominence in the European Enlightenment. Recent interpretation of Jesus's healing and exorcism is thus solidly embedded in two major controlling modern assumptions. The most determinative is that the healings and exorcisms were miracles and that miracle is a concept appropriate to social-cultural life in antiquity. The other, which is reinforced by the first and in turn strongly reinforces it, is that the sources for the historical Jesus are individual sayings and Jesus-stories. Accordingly, Jesus-interpreters isolate healing and exorcism stories from the literary context that might provide indications of their meaning context. Focused narrowly on the miraculous (that they find difficult to believe really happened), giving little or no attention to social interaction, scientific-minded modern interpreters then focus even more narrowly on whether any particular elements in these stories might possibly go back to Jesus.

This severely narrow focus, however, is limiting for investigation of (the Gospels' portrayal of) Jesus's healing and exorcism in historical context. Little or no attention is paid to the significance of healings and exorcisms in Jesus's mission as portrayed in the Gospels. And little or no attention is given to the historical social-political context of the sicknesses and healings and the spirit-possession and exorcisms in which Jesus was reportedly engaged. The underlying question, however, is whether the two modern assumptions on which this narrow focus is based are valid: the assumptions that healings and exorcisms constitute miracles, and that authentic Jesus-material most likely takes the form of sayings.

The recent scholarly resurgence of interest in "magic" in the ancient world a generation ago has only compounded the problems of standard interpretation of Jesus's healing and exorcism. In the twentieth century, history-of-religions scholars, among others, had constructed a synthetic concept of magic in the ancient Greek and Roman world from a variety of ancient sources, mostly from late antiquity. Without justification from ancient sources, New Testament scholars then expanded the concept of ancient magic to include healing and exorcism, and it became standard for interpreters of Jesus to find certain features of magic in healing and exorcism stories. Morton Smith made a bold and far-reaching argument that Jesus himself was a magician, based mostly on an uncritical use of passages from the "magical papyri" of late antiquity.[6] In yet another argument that Jesus was a magician, John Dominic Crossan further broadened the concept of ancient magic on the basis of Bryan Wilson's abstract sociological typology developed during the 1950s and 1960s.[7]

Those of us interested in further exploration of Jesus's healing and exorcism are thus faced with controlling concepts that have not been subjected to critical review. Such a review would seem to be required prior to further research into and interpretation of (stories of) Jesus's healings and exorcisms. This book aims to begin such a critical review of the scholarly constructs of miracle and magic that have come to focus and even control investigation and interpretation of (stories of) Jesus's healing and exorcism.

Part 1 examines whether the concept of "miracle," rooted in Enlightenment rationalism and now embedded in the field of New Testament studies, is attested in ancient sources and applicable to the healing and exorcism stories in the Gospels.

Part 2 attempts a critical review of the modern scholarly concept of ancient magic and addresses whether it is applicable to the ancient texts and practices that are adduced as evidence. Because ancient "magic" is the result of successive steps of scholarly construction—and carries considerable modern Western cultural baggage—its critical deconstruction requires several steps. The steps of critical review taken in part 2 suggest that what became the standard concept of ancient magic is not attested by or applicable to the texts and practices adduced as evidence, and that the broadened construct of magic by New Testament scholars is not applicable to the healing and exorcism (stories) of Jesus.

Part 3 begins with a brief summary of why and how the Gospels, which have been increasingly recognized as sustained narratives and not as mere containers of sayings and stories, are the historical sources for Jesus in historical context, and why isolated stories are not. Then a critical reexamination of the healing episodes and the exorcism episodes as components of the Gospel stories—while noting in passing that they do not fit the modern concepts of miracle or magic—finds that the healings and exorcisms are portrayed as relational and interactional.

---

6. Smith, *Jesus the Magician*.
7. Crossan, *Historical Jesus*; Wilson, *Magic and Millennium*.

Abbreviations

Ancient Sources

Ant.	*Antiquities* (Josephus)
Helen.	*Helennic Enkomion* (Gorgias)
Hist.	*History* (Herodotus)
Is. Os.	*De Iside et Osiride* (Plutarch)
L.A.B.	*Liber Antiquitatum Biblicarum* (*Biblical Antiquities* [Pseudo-Philo])
Leg.	*Legum allegoriae* (Philo)
Mut.	*De mutatione nominum* (Philo)
PGM	*Papyri graecae magicae: Die griechischen Zauberpapyri.* Edited by K. Preisendanz. Berlin, 1928
POxy	Oxyrhynchus Papyri. Edited by B. P. Grenfell and A. S. Hunt. 1898ff
Philops.	*Philopseudes* (Lucian)
Prob liber sit	*Quod omnis probus liber sit* (Philo)
Rep.	*Republic* (Plato)
Spec. Leg.	*De specialibus legibus* (Philo)
Geogr.	*Geography* (Strabo)
Vit. Apoll.	*Life of Apollonius of Tyana* (Philostratus)
War	*Jewish War* (Josephus)

ABBREVIATIONS

Contemporary Sources

ABD	*The Anchor Bible Dictionary*. Edited by D. N. Freedman. 6 vols. New York, 1992
ABRL	Anchor Bible Reference Library
ANRW	*Aufstieg und Niedergang der römischen Welt Geschichte und Kultur Roms im Spiegel der neueren Forschung*. Edited by H. Temporini and W. Haase. Berlin, 1972–
CBQ	*Catholic Biblical Quarterly*
CBQMS	Catholic Biblical Quarterly Monograph Series
GR	*Greece and Rome*
HDR	Harvard Dissertations in Religion
HR	*History of Religions*
HTR	*Harvard Theological Review*
JAAR	*Journal of the American Academy of Religion*
JBL	*Journal of Biblical Literature*
JSJ	*Journal for the Study of Judaism in the Persian, Hellenistic, and Roman Period*
JSNTSup	Journal for the Study of the New Testament: Supplement Series
JSPSup	Journal for the Study of the Pseudepigrapha: Supplement Series
LCL	Loeb Classical Library
LNTS	Library of New Testament Studies
NDST	Notre Dame Studies in Theology
NovT	*Novum Testamentum*
NTS	*New Testament Studies*
RRelRes	*Review of Religious Research*
SBLDS	Society of Biblical Literature Dissertation Series
SBLRBS	Society of Biblical Literature Resources for Biblical Study
SBLSymS	Society of Biblical Literature Symposium Series
SBLTT	Society of Biblical Literature Texts and Translations

ABBREVIATIONS

SBT	Studies in Biblical Theology
SJLA	Studies in Judaism in Late Antiquity
STDJ	*Studies on the Texts of the Desert of Judah*
TSAJ	Texte und Studien zum antiken Judentum
WUNT	Wissenschaftliche Untersuchungen zum Neuen Testament
ZPE	*Zeitschrift für Papyrologie und Epigraphik*

PART 1
Miracles

Introduction to Part 1

THE CONCEPT OF MIRACLE is deeply embedded in modern biblical studies, particularly in interpretation of Jesus and the Gospels. While many interpreters of Jesus allow that stories of his healings and exorcisms include some elements of magic, nearly all interpreters simply assume that the healing and exorcism stories are miracle stories, and (correspondingly) that the healings and exorcisms were miracles. Interpreters are thus applying to Jesus, the Gospels, and antiquity generally a concept developed in the European Enlightenment, articulated most influentially perhaps by David Hume.[1] Voltaire and other eighteenth-century philosophers understood miracles as supernatural phenomena (as opposed to natural phenomena), as violations of "the divine, immutable, eternal laws" of Nature and Reason. A concise definition of *miracle* from Jacob Vernet exemplifies the understanding that became standard in the Enlightenment: "a striking work which is outside the ordinary course of Nature and which is done by God's all-mighty will, and such that witnesses thereof regard it as extraordinary and supernatural."[2]

After centuries of discussion and debate in theological circles, interpreters of Jesus and the Gospels still assume and work with an understanding of miracle that bears a close resemblance to that of Enlightenment theologians. John P. Meier, who has devoted considerable critical review and reflection to the miracles of Jesus, while attempting to avoid distracting

---

1. See Keener, *Miracles*, ch. 5, for extensive recent discussion of Hume's argument and epistemology, and ch. 6 for the effects of Hume and recent shifts.

2. Jacob Vernet's treatment, as discussed by Craig, "Problem of Miracles." For a recent survey of how the miracles in the Bible were understood by key theologians and philosophers from the Reformation through the Enlightenment and after, see Zachman, "Biblical Miracles."

debate about "laws of nature," still defines miracle as "(1) an . . . extraordinary event . . . , (2) that finds no reasonable explanation in human abilities or in other known forces that operate in our world of time and space [i.e., Nature], and (3) [that hence is] . . . the result of a special act of God, doing what no human power can do."[3] That Meier's definition represents the view standard in the New Testament field can be seen in the opening of Harold Remus's article on "Miracle: New Testament" in the *Anchor Bible Dictionary*: "an extraordinary phenomenon," which is "inexplicable in terms of familiar, everyday causation, and so is ascribed to a superhuman force or agency."[4] Although Meier offers his definition in the chapter on "Miracles and Modern Minds," he clearly thinks this definition pertains to miracles in the ancient Mediterranean world, where "most people readily granted the possibility and reality of miracles,"[5] and to Jesus and his followers, as in the phrase he uses repeatedly: "extraordinary deeds deemed by himself and others to be miracles."[6]

Moreover, belief in miracles or in spirits and the like seemed irrational to scientific moderns in contrast to their own enlightenment. Although not always articulated, the attitude that belief in miracles is irrational continues to carry this baggage in interpretation of the healings and exorcisms of Jesus. This was vividly evident a generation ago in the judgment that miracle stories were the product of a quasi-animistic, rural attitude from the border areas of Syria and Palestine, which contrasted with the more civilized urban origins of the ethically oriented sayings-tradition of Jesus.[7] Directly in the rationalist tradition of Bultmann, Theissen continued to understand miracle stories as "an expression of an irrational, childish state of humanity."[8] Indeed, he viewed "belief in miracles and superstition" as having increasingly bubbled up from popular culture so that "even educated people" took up "irrational attitudes far removed from good common sense," and he judged "primitive Christian belief in the miraculous [as] one of the catalysts of the general belief in the miraculous in late antiquity."[9]

---

3. Meier, *Mentor*, 512.
4. Remus, "Miracle," 857.
5. Meier, *Mentor*, 511, 535.
6. Ibid., 536, 617, 622, 630.
7. Trocme, *La formation*, 37–44.
8. Alkier, "'For Nothing Will Be Impossible,'" 7–8.
9. Theissen, *Miracle Stories*, 231–32, 269, 276. He uses the story of the hemorrhaging woman in a highly questionable way to illustrate a "connection between socio-economic

INTRODUCTION TO PART 1

As Albert Schweitzer and others have discussed at length, theologians and interpreters of Jesus have devoted endless discussion to whether Jesus performed miracles and to how they should be understood.[10] But they have given little attention to whether the Judean and Galilean contemporaries of Jesus or the Hellenistic culture into which early Jesus movements spread had a concept of miracle, much less the same understanding of miracle as modern theologians and biblical scholars do. More important, specifically, do the Gospel sources for Jesus have a concept of miracle? Recent interpreters of Jesus give virtually no critical attention to this question. Even Meier, who devotes a lengthy chapter to "Miracles and Ancient Minds," never gets around to examining the question.[11] Rather he simply assumes that "miracles were accepted as part of the religious landscape," and that the problem for the historian is "the all-too-ready acceptance of them by ordinary people."[12] Even a recent collection of essays that probes the "concepts of reality" in the "miracle stories," for which the "rationalist hermeneutics" prominent in New Testament studies since David Hume, is inappropriate, nevertheless still works on the assumption that miracle is the appropriate classification.[13] And in New Testament studies more generally it is simply assumed that the categories of miracle and miracle story are appropriate for classifying and interpreting a wide range of phenomena and/or stories, including of healing and exorcism.[14]

Exploration of the Gospel accounts of Jesus's healing and exorcism, therefore, requires an investigation of whether there was something like the modern concept of miracle in Jewish and/or Hellenistic culture at the time of Jesus, including in the Gospel sources, and whether healings and exorcisms were included within this concept.

---

status and belief in miracles" (251).

10. Albert Schweitzer was one of the few interpreters of Jesus in his generation to give serious attention to how problematic the miracle stories of Jesus had been for modern (theological) scholars. Much of Schweitzer's famous survey in *Quest* is devoted to this issue. See also Meier's chapter on "Miracles and Modern Minds" in *Mentor*; Craig, "Problem of Miracles"; Zachman, "Biblical Miracles."

11. Meier, *Mentor*, ch. 18, focuses instead on "Pagan and Jewish parallels to Gospel materials," and the relation of miracle and magic, both of which he simply assumes were realities in the ancient world.

12. Ibid., 535; this is yet another illustration of how scholarly assumptions are often rooted in modern Western elite culture.

13. Alkier and Weissenrieder, *Miracles Revisited*.

14. For example, Cotter, *Miracles*; Cotter, *Miracle Stories*; Labahn and Peerbolte, *Wonders*; Watson, *Miracle Discourse*.

1

A Missing Concept: (Elite) Judean and Hellenistic Culture

IT IS STANDARD IN New Testament studies both to assume that the modern concept of miracle is applicable to a widespread phenomenon, and to assume that "several [ancient] terms, variously translated, denote this phenomenon."[1] Whether the modern term and concept of miracle is appropriate to ancient accounts that refer to *dynameis* or *terata* or *paradoxa* or *semeia*, however, requires investigation. It should not be imagined either that our investigation can establish what the vast majority, or what most people, believed. Nearly all Judean and Hellenistic literary sources were produced by the cultural elite. We have few or no direct sources for most ordinary people in antiquity. Most of our survey will thus necessarily focus on elite culture.[2] The Gospels, however, which consisted primarily of traditions and stories about ordinary people that emerged from ordinary people, provide sources at least for the villagers of Galilee and perhaps nearby areas into which the early Jesus movements spread. In the survey of chapter 2 and the analysis of healing and exorcism stories in part 3, we will thus be dealing with popular Galilean and nearby culture.

---

1. As exemplified in the article by Remus, "Miracle," 857.

2. See the more extensive surveys of "the ancient evidence" in Keener, *Miracles*, chs. 1–3; and in Eve, *Jewish Context*.

Elite Judean Culture

To ascertain whether an equivalent to the modern concept of miracle was operative for elite Judeans contemporary with Jesus, we may best examine Judean texts contemporary or nearly contemporary with Jesus and the Gospels. Our task has been facilitated by studies that examine "the concept of miracle" in one or more of these texts, that is, simply assuming the concept and then looking for its equivalent or appearance in the ancient Judean text(s). Eric Eve's recent survey is particularly useful insofar as, while still claiming that most second-temple Jews did believe in miracles, he must admit that he does not find very clear evidence of an ancient equivalent of the modern concept of miracle in most of the texts he examines.[3]

One might reasonably imagine that the most obvious texts in which to look for an ancient Judean equivalent of the modern concept of miracle—for a concept of or term for an extraordinary happening inexplicable in ordinary life, hence due to divine or supernatural agency—would be texts produced by ancient Judean intellectuals, learned scribes, such as the book of Sirach. And indeed, sages such as Ben Sira not only taught instructional wisdom to their protégés but cultivated cosmological wisdom about the governance of the universe and reflective or speculative wisdom about wisdom itself as a transcendent force involved in that divine governance. They had learned the traditional, shall we say international, scribal lore about the correlations between earthly phenomena and events and the heavenly forces involved in divine governance.[4] In contrast with modern Enlightenment philosophers, however, the ancient sages constructed no sharp division between Nature and the supernatural. In the ancient Near East the divine powers of the universe were directly and regularly involved in earthly affairs; or, in the case of Judea, "the Most High," or God, was involved in earthly governance either directly or through one of the many semi-divine forces or spirits (messengers or angels).

Ben Sira's speech about physicians and their medicines offers a good example of the divine–human synergism (Sir 38:1–15). Just as the Lord created medicines out of the earth, so the physician's healing also comes from the Most High. The ill person should pray to the Lord (who will heal) and make the appropriate sacrifices but also resort to the physician and pray for the success of his diagnosis and healing. The modern concept of

3. Eve, *Jewish Context*.
4. Fuller treatment in Horsley, *Scribes, Visionaries*.

miracle seems quite foreign to Ben Sira's understanding of healing and of the governance of the world generally by the Most High and Wisdom.

Little of Ben Sira's wisdom (in the book of Sirach) is devoted to the divine agency in Israelite/Judean history. But he does devote a long hymn of praise of the ancestral officeholders, particularly Aaron in the covenant of the (high) priesthood, to the legitimation of the Oniad dynasty that he served as adviser and propagandist (Sirach 44–50). All those officeholders were extraordinary and were established or blessed by the Most High. But that hardly leads us to apply the modern concept or miracle to their divine appointment. Included in the litany of praise are, interestingly enough, Moses's wondrous acts that countered the acts of the Egyptian wise men at Pharaoh's court—but with no mention of Moses's even more wondrous acts of deliverance in the exodus and wilderness (Sir 45:1-4). And when Ben Sira comes to the prophet Elijah (and his protégé Elisha), his knowledge and transmission of prophetic lore is patently evident (48:1-14). He selectively summarizes the tradition of Elijah's prophetic acts known (to us) in 1 Kings 17–19, 21, with emphasis on Elijah's pronouncement of the word of the Lord in the drought and with particular emphasis on the destruction of predatory kings (as commissioned on Sinai), and finally with emphasis on Elijah's future role in the restoration of Israel. Included among the wondrous deeds of Elijah (in two of the twenty-six lines) is Elijah's resuscitation of the widow's son by the word of the Lord (48:5), which in effect downplays the role of healings and multiplication of food in Elijah's renewal of Israel (in 1 Kings 17–19, 21). This hardly provides a basis for suggesting that miracles "could come to be seen as the most important activity of the prophet."[5] In Ben Sira's paean, the most important activity of the prophet Elijah in his general renewal of the people was in political pronouncement and agitation commissioned by God.

Insofar as Jesus-interpreters often find his miracles closely related to his supposedly eschatological orientation, we might expect to find interest in miracles in the apocalyptic texts usually cited as expressions of Jewish eschatology. Apocalyptic texts such as Daniel 10–11; the Book of Watchers (1 Enoch 1–36); and the Animal Vision (1 Enoch 85–90) are surely important for comprehending the learned scribal understanding of the origins of the heavenly forces now locked in struggle for control of history as a key aspect of the historical context in which Jesus worked.[6] But one looks in vain in

---

5. Vs. Eve, *Jewish Context*, 113.
6. Critical analysis of these texts in historical context in Horsley, *Scribes, Visionaries*;

apocalyptic texts such as Daniel 7, 8, 10–11; *1 Enoch* 1–36; 85–90; and *4 Ezra* for interest in inexplicable, extraordinary happenings due to divine agents, and one finds in particular no healings and exorcisms.

The discovery of the Dead Sea Scrolls provided not just previously unknown Judean texts, but a previously unanticipated variety of texts, a few of which seemed to offer parallels to the miracles of Jesus. The *War Rule* (1QM) presented a highly schematized doctrine of two opposed sets of spiritual forces locked in a struggle for control of human life and history. Other texts seemed to offer a parallel to Jesus's exorcism and to Jesus's supposedly eschatological miracles. Abraham's driving off of the spirit that God had sent to afflict Pharaoh in the *Genesis Apocryphon* 20:11–34, however, is hardly a miracle, insofar as it was accomplished by the well-known and widespread religious practices of prayer and the laying on of hands. Nor does the inappropriately titled *Messianic Apocalypse* (4Q521, which is hardly an apocalypse) present divine actions that could appropriately be labeled miracles.[7] Liberating captives and bringing good news to the poor have not usually been classified as miracles. Healing the wounded and lifting up the crippled and even restoring sight to the blind are not necessarily miraculous. All of these actions, along with reviving the dead, are allusions to the people's long-standing expectation that God would restore the people still living under circumstances of imperial conquest—expectation articulated in prophetic texts such as Isa 29:18–19; 35:5–6; and 61:1; and in Ps 146:7–8 (and even in the Eighteen Benedictions). The text in 4Q521, in what had become common language of deliverance, does not refer to individual miracles of healing and raising the dead, but to the restoration of the whole people that had been languishing under imperial rule.

The *Liber Antiquitatum Biblicarum* (*L.A.B*), usually taken as contemporary with Jesus and the Gospels, narrates the events in which God has repeatedly delivered the people. Eve claims that the three most common words (in the Latin translation of the Greek translation of an apparently Hebrew original) for *miracle* (which all occur together in *L.A.B.* 9:7) are *mirabilia, signa,* and *prodigia*. Fairly clearly these correspond to the standard terms that referred to the wondrous incidents ("signs and wonders") of the exodus and wilderness accounts in many Judean texts, some of which were later included in the Hebrew Bible. Survey of the occurrence of these terms, however, shows that the *L.A.B.* applies these terms "to a rather diverse

---

Horsley, *Revolt of the Scribes*.

7. Versus Eve, *Jewish Context*, 192, following others.

range of phenomena" and "often narrates what we might consider to be a miracle without attaching any particular term to it."[8] The narrative seldom calls attention explicitly to how extraordinary or humanly impossible the deeds are that it attributes to God. What links these events is not so much how unusual or supernormal they are, but how significant they are in the deliverance of God's people, or in the salvation of the righteous and the punishment of the wicked.[9] That is, what have been taken as miracles in the *L.A.B.* do not fit the modern definition of *miracle* that Eve and others assume.

The histories of Josephus are probably the most important texts from which to discern whether elite Judean culture had some equivalent of the modern concept of miracle. His corpus is extensive; he interprets many episodes from Israelite tradition that modern scholars view as miracles; and his accounts are some of the principal sources for beliefs, practices, figures, and events around the time of Jesus. As interpretations of the miracle stories of Jesus do, so surveys of Josephus's view of miracles simply assume that miracle was an operative concept in ancient culture.[10] They focus on the terms *semeia* ("signs"), *paradoxos* ("amazing" or "wondrous"), and *epiphaneia* ("manifestation") as Josephus's "vocabulary" or "language of miracle."[11] In Josephus's histories, however, these terms are not comparable to the modern concept of miracle.

Semeia Josephus uses in reference to a variety of things, including passwords, Roman military standards, signals, and symbols. He frequently uses *semeion* for an omen or portent of a future event, including those that preceded Vespasian's acclamation as emperor and the Roman destruction of Jerusalem (*War* 1.23, 28; 3.404; 4.623; 6.296, 315).[12] A derivative but more specialized usage is for the "signs" God provides to convince people

---

8. Ibid., 120.

9. Ibid., 124.

10. Delling, "Josephus und das Wunderbare"; MacRae, "Miracle"; Otto Betz, "Wunder bei Josephus."

11. Since Josephus does not use *dynamis* for the unusual occurrences or events themselves, he provides no direct terminological comparison with the Gospels' representation of Jesus's "acts of power." Similarly Eve, *Jewish Context*, 33.

12. *Semeion* in Josephus's histories is often somewhat synonymous with *teras* (or *terastion*), another term for *omen* or *portent*, which he uses more frequently in the *War* than in the *Antiquities*. In suggesting that Josephus uses *teras* in the sense of *miracle* at *War* 1,331; 5.411, Eve, *Jewish Context*, 33, may be depending on Thackeray's 1927 translation in the Loeb Classical Library.

that prophets are indeed delivering divine messages or carrying out divine commands. In his narrative of Moses's commission on Sinai and his first steps toward leading the exodus from Egypt, Josephus mentions repeatedly the three *semeia* (Moses's staff turning into a snake, his hand becoming white when placed in his bosom, and water from a stream turning into blood) that God gives Moses to convince himself, then the Hebrews, and later Pharaoh to recognize that he is sent by God and does all at God's command (*Ant.* 2.272–284). Although these "signs" do not include the event(s) of actual deliverance from Egypt (2.237; and evidently do not include the plagues), they have been done "for [the people's] liberation." Some of these "signs" are hardly what modern scholars would classify as miracles: Saul is to meet certain people on the road, including an assembly of inspired prophets, and a sudden hailstorm comes upon the Israelites (6.54–57, 91–94; 10.24–29).

Josephus presents certain occurrences mentioned in Israelite tradition as God-given omens or portents of key events in the deliverance of Israel or of Israel's heroes or kings. What makes them "signs," however, is not their occurrence beyond what is humanly or naturally possible (what characterizes the modern concept of miracle) but their relation to those future events, and often a prophet's role in announcing and/or petitioning God for them. Josephus and other elite Judeans, like Tacitus and other ancient Romans, understood prophecy, dreams, omens, and portents as among the means by which God (or the gods) governed the world and communicated with humans.[13] Such prophecy and portents, however, were "not regarded as miracles."[14] After recounting Elijah's prophecies about king Ahab, Josephus concludes in a typical, moralizing fashion: "nothing is more beneficial than prophecy and the foreknowledge which it gives, for in this way God enables us to know what to guard against" (*Ant.* 8.418).

Paradoxos is claimed as another key term in Josephus's "vocabulary of miracle." Josephus uses the term, however, mostly in the sense of "unexpected" or "amazing" or "wondrous," in reference to occurrences that modern readers would not classify as miracles. While he does refer to the dividing of the Red Sea as an "amazing deliverance" and to the manna as "divine and wondrous food," (*Ant.* 2.295, 345; 3.1, 30, 38), he uses the same term for how "amazingly" Moses was raised, for the "wonder" by which Moses was saved by being placed in a basket, and for the "unexpected" gifts

---

13. Delling, "Josephus," followed by MacRae, "Miracle."
14. MacRae, "Miracle," 132.

and favors the Israelites had received from God prior to the manna and the water from the rock (2.216, 221–223; 3.14). God delivers the people in several "(divine and) wondrous" victorious battles (5.28; 9.14, 58, 60). Daniel in the lion's den "amazingly" escapes death (10.214). Like the "signs," the "wonders" of deliverance are also done by the providence (*pronoia*) of God. Josephus, however, does not seem to make much of a distinction between the "wonders" or the "signs" and other manifestations of God's power and providence.

Epiphaneia, which scholars also include in Josephus's supposed language of miracle, occurs in connection with certain of the wonders in Israel's history of deliverance. Moses observes the withdrawal of the sea, after it had been struck by his staff, as "the manifestation of God" leading to their "wondrous deliverance" (*Ant.* 2.339). Some other "manifestations" of God are the fire darting out of the air onto Solomon's altar and Isaac's marriage to Rebecca (8.119; 1.255; cf. 3.310). Close to the time of Jesus, Petronius, the Roman governor of Syria, took the unexpected rain that fell following his decision to disobey Caligula's order to install his statue in the Jerusalem Temple as an indication of God's "presence" or "manifestation" in protection of the Judeans (18.286). The *epiphaneia* (of God) stands parallel to the power of God as what is revealed in such amazing events. But *epiphaneia* does not correspond to the modern concept of miracle.

Josephus, finally, does not include healings and exorcisms among either the "signs" or the "wonders."[15] In his account of the healing of Hezekiah, the sign may have led to the healing by evoking the king's trust in Isaiah's promise. But the sign, a repetition in the sun's path, preceded the healing. The healing of Jeroboam's hand, withered when he gave the signal to arrest the prophet, is a new development after the sign about the future desecration of Jeroboam's altar and is God's response to the prophet's prayer to God (8.232–234, 244). Hezekiah and his people are "amazingly" delivered from conquest by Sennacherib, and the "wonder" of Isaiah's promise that he will be healed is too much to believe (10.24, 28). But the healing itself, while immediate, is not "amazing." Elijah's raising of the widow's son to life is "beyond all expectation" but not called a sign or a wonder. In his account of Elisha's actions, Josephus omits several mentioned in the scriptural narrative (2 Kings 1–13), including healings, focusing evidently on political events. The exorcism of a demon by Eleazar before the future emperor Vespasian and his entourage, often cited as evidence of Jewish magic

---

15. Cf. Eve, *Jewish Context*, 51.

and miracle, is neither a "sign" nor a "wonder," but a "healing" (*therapeia*; *Ant*. 8.46–48). For Josephus, healings and exorcisms were evidently *not* "signs" or "wonders," much less miracles.

The Judean historian understands prophecies accompanied by "signs," and events that were "amazing" portents—whether in the history of Israel or in contemporary affairs—within his overall theology of history as some of the ways that God governs the world. In contrast with the modern Enlightenment worldview, Josephus found omens, portentous events, and prophetic signs compatible with the (rational) nature of the universe. As he says regarding his historiography in his introduction to the *Antiquities*, "nothing will appear unreasonable, nothing incongruous with the majesty of God and his love for humanity; everything, indeed, is here set forth in keeping with the nature of the universe (*tei ton holon physei*)" (*Ant*. 1.24).[16] He does not hesitate to draw "lessons" from his own prophetically interpreted historiography in arguing, for example, against the errors of the Epicureans, that divine providence governs human affairs (e.g., *Ant*. 10.277–280).[17] Josephus and other such Judean elite contemporary with Jesus thus evidently had no concept corresponding to either the modern, Western notion of miracle or the related dichotomy of natural (or historical) and supernatural.

Elite Hellenistic Jewish Culture

With the *Wisdom of Solomon* and the treatises of the mystic Jewish philosopher Philo of Alexandria we move outside the Judean and Galilean context of Jesus and the origins of the Gospels, and into the cultural influence of Hellenistic enlightenment theology. Among the sections of the *Wisdom of Solomon* are a reflection on the personified semidivine force of Wisdom and on her role in the universe (chs. 6–9), a litany (without names) of how Wisdom had been guiding the people's affairs since the creation (Wis 10:1—11:4), and a long poetic discourse on how the Egyptians were punished in the same events and elements in which the Israelites were delivered (11:5—19:22). What had long become the stereotyped terms for the events of the exodus (*semeion, teras, thaumastos*, and *paradoxos*) appear

---

16. MacRae, "Miracle," 131.

17. See further ibid., 138–41, for his broader explanation of Josephus's seemingly apologetic "rationalistic" statements regarding the events he narrates; and, more generally, on Josephus's understanding of the history of the Judeans, see Attridge, *Interpretation*.

A MISSING CONCEPT: (ELITE) JUDEAN AND HELLENISTIC CULTURE

at a very few points in these sections. For example, personified heavenly Wisdom knows both the past and the future, knows "turns of speech," and has foreknowledge of "signs and wonders" as well as of seasons and times (8:8). By entering the soul of a servant of the Lord, she "withstood dread kings with wonders and signs," and "guided [the people] along a marvelous way" (10:17). Because of God's all-powerful hand, the Egyptians were troubled by "monstrous specters" (17:15); but his children gazed on "marvelous wonders" in the course of their exodus and wilderness way (19:6–9). Insofar as these passages lay no stress on how the events of deliverance were "amazing or seemingly impossible,"[18] the modern concept of miracle does not seem to fit. There is "no clear-cut miracle vocabulary that would indicate a conscious awareness of a distinct class of events . . . There is no emphasis on these events *as* miracles."[19]

From his survey of Philo's nonallegorical treatises Eve claims that for him "miracle is a special act of God (possibly through an intermediary) that accomplishes something that would otherwise be impossible."[20] Eve thus makes the ancient Jewish enlightenment theologian sound like the modern Enlightenment philosophers. The survey of terms, however, results in ambiguities. Like Josephus, Philo uses the term *thauma* and its compounds with reference to things that are wonderful or marvelous but hardly miraculous in the modern sense. Only the passive form of "wonder-working" (*thaumatourgeo/ema*) appears to resemble what modern interpreters call miracle working. Caution is in order, however, since Philo at one point refers to "a wonderful piece of nature's handiwork (*hupo physeos tethaumatourgetai*; *Mut. Nom.* 162). Philo uses the standard terms "signs" and "wonders" both with reference to the exodus-wilderness events and in connection to matters that moderns would not consider miraculous. In a distinctive contrast with the Synoptic Gospels (where Jesus refuses to give a sign), he has Moses perform "signs" as proof that he is God's chosen agent. Philo deploys the passive form of *megalourgeo* ("mighty work") with reference to "enormities" as well as to the great works of God.

Completely missing in Philo's treatises is any suggestion that healing happens in an extraordinary and inexplicable way. He frequently discusses both physical and spiritual healing.[21] He values the physician as the means

---

18. Eve, *Jewish Context*, 90.
19. Ibid., 92.
20. Ibid., 61.
21. Ibid., 79.

through which God effects healing (*Leg.* 3.178). Similarly, Philo has no need for exorcism, since he knows of no maleficent spirits.

Philo's treatises come the closest to touting God's wondrous deeds (through Moses) as proofs of divine providence and deliverance. He finds "wondrous" particularly deliverance from human threats, unusual demonstrations of God's providence, and God's punishment. Like Josephus and Hellenistic philosophers, however, Philo understands God or the divine as directly involved in worldly and human affairs, with no separation between Nature or Reason and the supernatural—a separation so central to modern Enlightenment thinking. Indeed, for Philo Reason (*Logos*) was not only divine but was God's Reason.

Elite Hellenistic-Roman Culture

Like Josephus and other Jewish intellectuals, the Hellenistic-Roman cultural elite had no concept that corresponds to the modern Western concept of miracle. As in Josephus's histories, so in Greek or Latin it is difficult to find terms that might correspond to the modern concept of miracle. There are several that refer to wonders, omens, portents, prodigies, or signs, often ominous events or strange occurrences that bode well or ill for city-states or public figures or hopes and fortunes. The extraordinary phenomena or events to which *semeia* or *terata* or *paradoxoi* or *prodigiai* referred were sometimes attributed to divine agency and sometimes not. Developing usage of the Latin term *miraculum* in late antiquity provides the link to the later Christian and then modern concept of miracle. In early usage, *miraculum* usually meant merely something that aroused wonder (frequently in Livy, *Hist.*, 1.47.9; 2.13.13; 4.35.9; 5.46.3), although by the second century CE it could also be used for wondrous events attributed to a deity (Apuleius, *Met.* 2.28). Unusual healings were not prominent among such "wonders" or "portents," moreover, presumably because unusual healings were not usually thought of as wonders or portents. While it had no such meaning at the time of Jesus himself, however, by late antiquity Christians came to use the term for the wonders Jesus worked, as well as for the acts of the martyrs.[22]

Ancient intellectuals, in contrast to modern so-called scientific thinkers, did not make a sharp distinction between divine causation and reason or nature, between the supernatural (miraculous) and the natural. The divine was rational and natural, the gods an integral part of nature, the

---

22. Remus, *Pagan-Christian Conflict*, 52, and 234n16.

cosmos. The healings of Asclepius were understood as caused by the god, but also in accordance with human healing practices. As illustrated by the philosopher Celsus, precisely because of their use of reason the cultural elite could understand and affirm, for example, that the healings of Asklepios were done by divine agency (and that Asklepios was divine) through the incubations and other rituals at temples, while Jesus's healings were shams. The famous physician Galen thought that God and nature belong to one and the same continuous reality, in which universal rules pertain. The significant dreams he sends were not miraculous in the sense of interrupting the natural course of things. They did not come from some supernatural realm but from a higher level in a continuum of reality.[23]

The Roman historians Tacitus and Suetonius provide accounts of healings that modern scholars habitually classify and discuss as miracles.[24] In both accounts, after the death of Nero, when the Roman general directing the devastation of Galilee and Judea, Vespasian, was waiting in Alexandria to sail to Rome to consolidate his advent as the new emperor, a blind man and a disabled man sought healing from the new Caesar. The Hellenistic-Egyptian god Serapis had advised or promised that the emperor could heal the blind man by moistening his cheeks and eyeballs with his spittle, and could heal the lame man by touching his leg or arm with his foot. Vespasian's hesitation, the advice he was given, and his decision to proceed may be particularly illustrative of the attitude of the Roman elite. The emperor-to-be was uneasy that he still lacked the numinous *auctoritas* (prestige or divinity) of an emperor, or that he might exhibit a certain *vanitas* (the term can mean "vanity" or "failure"). Suetonius says that although he lacked faith (*fides*) that he could succeed, his "friends" prevailed upon him. Tacitus has him asking the opinions of physicians whether such blindness and infirmity could be healed by human skill. Persuaded that he might be the chosen minister of the divine will and that all things were possible by his good fortune, Vespasian attempted both healings in public before a large crowd—successfully.

---

23. Tieleman, "Natural Cause," 112. On ancient intellectuals such as Galen and Celsus, see more broadly Martin, *Inventing Superstition*, who emphasizes that they did not have a category of the supernatural in which divine forces were separated from nature (13–14).

24. Tacitus, *History* bk. 4, ch. 81; Suetonius, *Vespasian* 7. See discussion in Morgan, *Year of Four Emperors*, 170–255; Luke, "A Healing Touch" (with a very broad concept of miracles); and Leppin, "Imperial Miracles."

These are vivid accounts of how such healings happened in a network of relations between the person seeking healing, an agent in whom they believed healing power to be working or available, and the divine or the gods (both Serapis and the gods of the Romans). The ancient Alexandrians and Romans, including the elite friends, Vespasian, and the historians Tacitus and Suetonius—as well as the ordinary people—believed or understood that special power (or at least divine favor) was involved in the healing of the blind and disabled who sought healing from the nascent emperor. But all looked to Vespasian himself as the agent of the healing. To abstract (the accounts of) such healings into the concept of miracle sweeps them up into a broad, general modern category inapplicable to the accounts of Tacitus and Suetonius.

Since ancient intellectuals, not sharing the modern distinction between the natural and the supernatural, believed that extraordinary events and incidents such as wondrous healings were possible and happened, they often did not resort to divine agency. Ironically this can be illustrated by an episode of "raising from the dead" by Apollonius of Tyana as portrayed by Philostratus—one of several that have been standardly cited in comparison with the miracle stories about Jesus (*Vit. apol.* 4.45).[25] Contrary to the way that the widely used Loeb Classical Library translation has it[26] ("a miracle which Apollonius worked"), however, the episode begins rather less ominously: "And here is another of Apollonius's wonders" (*thauma*). And contrary to the modern concept of miracle, the unusual occurrence is not inexplicable (by nature), nor is it attributed to divine causation. The account begins, "The girl seemed to have died," and with his touch and whisper, Apollonius "woke the girl up (from sleep) from seeming death." The episode ends with two alternative (possible) explanations, neither of which involves the divine: he restored a dead girl by the warmth of his touch, *or* he detected a spark of life in her, "for it was said that although it was raining at the time, a vapour went up from her face." Thus one of the principal episodes that form-critics and other Gospel interpreters have used as a prime example of a Hellenistic miracle story that helps explain (so to speak) the development of the miracle stories about Jesus simply does not fit the concept of miracle presupposed by modern interpreters.

25. Since at least the foundational form-critical work of Bultmann, *History of the ynoptic Tradition*. Recent review of issues and scholarly treatments in Koskenniemi, "Function of the Miracle Stories," with broad uncritical concept of "miracles/miracle stories."

26. Philostratus, *Life of Apollonius*.

A MISSING CONCEPT: (ELITE) JUDEAN AND HELLENISTIC CULTURE

This brief survey should be sufficient to indicate that ancient Judean and Hellenistic-Roman texts do not have terms and a concept that correspond to the modern concept of miracle. The key difference is evidently that ancient elites understood divine or heavenly powers or God to be involved in earthly or historical life. This contrasts with modern Enlightenment or scientific culture, in which the supernatural or miraculous became separated from Nature and Reason. In Judean culture, that God had repeatedly delivered the people from subjection or suffering was wondrous. In both Judean and Hellenistic culture it was recognized that certain figures might exercise special, unusual powers. But there was no special classification of miracle or the supernatural.

2

The Concept of Miracle and Jesus's Healings and Exorcisms

THE INFLUENTIAL GERMAN PHILOSOPHER Lessing exemplified the Enlightenment understanding of and skepticism toward miracles: "I live in the eighteenth century, in which miracles no longer happen." A century and a half later, Rudolf Bultmann, arguably the most influential New Testament theologian of the twentieth century, declared that "now that the laws of nature have been discovered, we can no longer believe in spirits." Being consistent in his thinking, he insisted that it was impossible to avail oneself of modern medical discoveries "and at the same time believe in the New Testament world of spirits and miracles."[1]

During the last century, however, enlightened people in the Western world have become much more aware of human realities in their own and in other cultures. Whether they believed in them or not, Western anthropologists lived and conversed with people whose culture included spirits. After the discovery of the Dead Sea Scrolls, biblical scholars could read in the *Community Rule* and the *War Scroll* from Qumran that some of their ancient intellectual counterparts were convinced that their life and that of their society were subject to a sustained struggle between two opposed Spirits (1QS 3–4; 1QM 13, 15–19). At least some of the intellectuals who produced the texts inscribed on those scrolls evidently experienced communication with heavenly spirits. Even if they do not believe in spirits (or perhaps by "suspending their disbelief"), biblical interpreters can

---

1. Bultmann, "New Testament and Mythology," 4–5.

appreciate how both ancient Judean intellectuals and Galilean peasants may have interacted with spirits, including with what they thought of as the Holy Spirit.

With miracles, the situation of modern Jesus-interpreters appears to be different. These heirs of Lessing and Bultmann, while skeptical of miracles, nevertheless work on the assumption that Jesus, his followers, and other ancient people did believe in miracles as understood and defined in modern scientific culture (as discussed at the beginning of chapter 1). They read the Gospels and other sources through the lens of Enlightenment philosophy and theology. In the belief that the episodes of healing and exorcism in the Gospels are miracle stories thick with supernatural overlays (and folkloristic motifs and Easter faith), the interpreters work to sort through them for possible elements that might go back to Jesus's ministry.[2] They do not first ask whether the modern definition of *miracle* is appropriate to the healing and exorcism stories they are analyzing as sources for data on the historical Jesus.

A crucial first step in historical investigation is to evaluate the sources critically. An important consideration in using the sources, then, is to discern interpretive concepts and language appropriate to the sources in their historical, cultural context. To discern whether the modern concept of miracle is applicable to the Gospel presentations of Jesus's healings and exorcisms, we carry out a brief critical review of the episodes and summaries in Gospel narratives and of statements in the Gospel speeches of Jesus. This will anticipate and prepare the way for the fuller and closer examination of the healing and exorcism episodes in the Gospel stories in part 3, below.

The consensus in Gospel studies continues to hold that the Gospel of Mark and the Jesus speeches parallel in Matthew and Luke (thought to be from their common source, Q) are the earliest sources. The Gospels of Matthew and Luke, it is believed, followed and adapted both Mark's narrative and the Q speeches in shaping more complex Gospels. The Gospel of John is distinctive in its long dialogues and discourses, includes no exorcism stories, and finds some of Jesus's healings as among the "signs" that Jesus performed in his mission to the people.

To anticipate the results of the following survey, the Gospel sources give no indication that a classification of some of Jesus's actions as miracles is appropriate—as if certain of his actions were so extraordinary as to be inexplicable by either human abilities or known forces operative in the world

---

2. Meier, *Mentor*; and Funk and the Jesus Seminar, *Acts*, are typical.

(Nature) and hence the result of a special act of God or other supernatural force.

Terms and Concepts in the Gospels

Interpreters still working on the assumption that the modern concept of miracle is applicable to the Gospel accounts claim that the Gospels "have a number of words to designate Jesus's miracles (e.g., *dynamis, semeion, teras, paradoxon*)."[3] But that is simply not the case.[4] The Gospels have no special term that refers specially to the healings and/or exorcisms of Jesus—certainly no term that could be appropriately translated as "miracle." They do not utilize the terms, for example, that Josephus uses for extraordinary and/or highly significant events, some of which are taken by modern interpreters as miracles.[5]

Most significant, perhaps, is that the Synoptic Gospels (Mark, Matthew, and Luke) do not compare Jesus's healings and exorcisms to the exodus events by referring to them as "signs and wonders." Signs and wonders are what false messiahs and prophets will do in the future (Mark 13:22 // Matt 24:24). Jesus is adamant both in Mark and in a Q speech followed by both Matthew and Luke that he will give no sign to satisfy his elite opponents (Mark 8:11–12 // Matt 12:38–39; Luke/Q 11:(16), 29–30; Matt 16:1–4; Luke 23:8)—except for "the sign of Jonah," which is presumably his prophetic warning. These references to "signs," moreover, indicate that the term may not refer specially to a healing or exorcism at all, but perhaps to some omen or portent. Luke presents the child Jesus laid in the manger as a "sign" to the shepherds (Luke 2:12, 34). "Sign" refers to the great significance of an event in its context, and not to some action by itself. This is true of "sign" in the Gospel of John as well, which elaborates on the significance

---

3. Meier, *Mentor*, 600.

4. *Teras* does not occur at all; *paradoxon*, which appears only at Luke 5:26, is how all of what happens, evidently including the forgiveness of sins, in the episode in Luke 5:17–25 strike all of the amazed onlookers, evidently including the scribes and Pharisees who charged Jesus with blasphemy. That *dynamis* and *semeion* are not "designations" of miracles in the Gospels will be discussed further below.

5. Alkier, "'For Nothing Will Be Impossible,'" 8, discerns clearly that "what we call miracle is not the same as what biblical texts call *dynameis, paradoxon, semeia kai terata*, and so on," yet continues to project the modern concept of "miracles/miracle stories" onto Gospel stories and other ancient texts.

of key events (however extraordinary they may be) that Jesus catalyzes at key places and times.

That terms such as "signs and wonders" appear in reference to healings and other phenomena in Paul's letters and in the book of Acts suggests that the ways texts later included in the New Testament draw on language of Israelite tradition should be one of the key steps in interpretation of those texts. Recent rhetorical criticism of so-called miracle discourse divides Israelite tradition into broad categories derived from modern scholarship that do not correspond to categories in ancient Judean texts themselves. (So, for example, scholars speak of apocalyptic texts, priestly texts, or wisdom texts).[6] Yet how particular key terms from Israelite tradition are used differently in particular texts, such as in Paul's letters and in the Gospels, remains unexplored. Ironically as well, such rhetorical criticism also perpetuates the projection of the modern concept of miracle onto healing, exorcism, and other stories. Miracle discourse, like apocalyptic or wisdom discourse, is a broad modern scholarly classification.

That at least some of Jesus's healings and exorcisms were wondrous or marvelous is indicated in some but by no means the majority of the episodes in the Gospel stories. That some appeared as wondrous is indicated by how the onlookers or crowds are "amazed" or "astounded" (*thaumazo, ekstasis, existemi*), although no term of "wonder" is applied to the healing or exorcism itself. This motif, however, is less prominent in the healing and exorcism episodes than commonly imagined. In Mark it occurs only at the end of the episodes of the healing of the paralytic, of the exorcism of the spirit named Legion, and of the resuscitation of the twelve-year-old woman (2:12; 5:20; 5:42, and some parallels in Matthew and Luke). Nor is amazement confined to responses to healings and exorcisms. In Mark, Jesus himself is amazed at the lack of trust he encounters in his home town, and Pilate is amazed at Jesus (6:6; 15:5). Matthew has the disciples frequently amazed, and the Pharisees are amazed at how Jesus responds to their entrapment over the tribute to Caesar; and Luke has people amazed at what happened to Zechariah (Matt 8:27; 21:20; Luke 1:21, 63).

The term *dynameis* ("powers") is used in some summaries and discussions of Jesus's healings and exorcisms, and of other incidents in general (Mark 6:2, 5, 14; 9:39 and parallels). The English translations of the term as "acts/deeds of power" and "mighty acts" may have been misleading in

---

6. See especially the articles of Robbins, "Miracle Discourse"; Bloomquist, "Role of Argumentation"; and Watson, "Miracle Discourse."

shifting the focus to actions of Jesus rather than to the power that flows from or through him to others. The different referents of *dynamis/eis* and connections in which it operates is a prime indicator of how the people among whom the Gospels originated experienced life as a field in which powers were operative, often in conflict. The ultimate power, of course, was God, and a key aspect of the good news (gospel) that Jesus was preaching was that God was using power for the deliverance of the people (Mark 9:1; 12:24; 14:62). It is significant to note that those references to the power of God are not connected to healings and exorcisms but to the more general crisis in the governance of history.

In the cultural world presupposed and articulated by the Gospel stories, however, other powers (some of them associated with the heavenly bodies) were active in the heavenly governance of the world and in the lives of people (13:25–26; as in elite scribal culture). The "unclean spirits" or "demons" (such as Legion), which might possess the people, wielded power in, among, or over them, so that power was necessary to expel or defeat or "overpower" them (as in the exorcisms). And people who were suffering various illnesses or disabilities, such as the hemorrhaging woman and many others, were eager to come into contact with power that would heal or liberate them from their illness or disability.

This field of powers indicated in the Gospel narratives generally may help us understand the reference to healings or exorcisms by Jesus or by others as *dynameis*. The term "powers" is not used in and for particular healing or exorcism episodes. The case of the hemorrhaging woman is the only episode in which the term "power" is used, as Jesus feels "power" go forth from himself. Mention of "powers" is made, and relatively rarely, in reference to incidents in summaries and discussions. In his hometown (Mark 6:1–6), the people hearing Jesus in the local village assembly were astounded, exclaiming, "What is this wisdom that has been given to him? What *powers* are being done by his hands!" The narrator adds "he could do no *power* there, except that he laid his hands on a few sick people and healed them." When Herod Antipas hears of Jesus and his disciples casting out many demons and healing many sick people, he imagines that "these powers are at work in him" (or perhaps rather "through him") because John the Baptist (whom Antipas had beheaded) has been raised from the dead (Mark 6:15). Jesus admonishes the disciples not to stop someone from using "power" in his name to exorcize demons (Mark 9:39). In the mission speech in Q (Luke/Q 10:2–16), after Jesus commissions the disciples to live and work in villages, healing the sick and proclaiming the kingdom of God, he pronounces woes on unresponsive villages because they had not turned around their collective lives in response to "the (acts of) power(s)" that had been done for them. In all of these summary or discussion passages in Mark and Matthew and Luke, "powers" refers generally to healings or exorcisms or other incidents (manifestations of power[s]) that happen in the interaction among people (see further discussion in ch. 9, below).

Agency and Interaction

As I noted in the introduction to part 1, the modern scholarly understanding of miracle, as reflected upon by interpreters of Jesus and the Gospels, involves "an . . . extraordinary event . . . that finds no reasonable explanation in human abilities or in other known forces that operate in our world of time and space [i.e., Nature], and [that hence is] . . . the result of a special act of God, doing what no human power can do."[7] This understanding or definition does not fit the healings and exorcisms portrayed in the Gospels. The Gospel stories show no concern for explanation beyond the interaction of people in their social-cultural world, and give little or no indication of special acts of God in the healings and exorcisms.

The episodes of healing and exorcism in the Gospel of Mark show little or no indication of any cause or agency other than Jesus or the interaction between Jesus and the healed person who comes in trust, sometimes with supporting relatives or friends. In the healing episodes in Mark, Jesus takes the hand, forgives the sins, asks the paralytic to extend his hand, or commands the young woman to "get up." The "leper" says "you can make me clean," the hemorrhaging woman reaches out to touch him and power goes forth. In a summary, people touch his cloak. All these episodes are interactions in the social world of time and space, with no suggestion of divine or supernatural agency. It is the same in the Markan exorcism episodes. In the first, the unclean spirit recognizes Jesus as exercising superior power as "the holy one of God," but the witnessing people in the village assembly do not identify the power as God's or as supernatural, yet do recognize that Jesus is "teaching" (operating) with "authority/power" (1:22–28). In two other exorcism episodes, Jesus commands the spirit to "come out," with no overtone of divine or supernatural agency. Even in Jesus's response to the accusation of having Beelzebul (with its political analogies for "household"

7. Meier, *Mentor*, 512.

or "kingdom" of Satan), even if one infers that God (not Jesus) must be the agent who has bound Satan, it seems clear that it is in the exorcisms of Jesus that Satan's goods are being plundered. (This is discussed further in ch. 10.)

The portrayal of Jesus's healings and exorcisms is much the same in the Gospel of Matthew, with perhaps more emphasis on the people's trust in Jesus (or in the power working through him). In the healing of the two blind men, for example, Jesus asks them pointedly, "Do you trust that I am able to do this?" (Matt 9:28). Again in the Gospel of Luke the portrayals of Jesus's healings and exorcisms are much the same as in Mark, happening through the words and gestures of Jesus and the disciples, in interaction with the healed ones, whose trust has been a key factor.

It is mainly or only in the beginning of Gospels, particularly at Jesus's baptism, that the Spirit of God plays a role. Luke also states pointedly that Jesus began his mission "filled with the power of the Spirit" (4:14), and that the prophecy of Isa 61:1–2 was fulfilled in his mission (Luke 4:15–21). If these introductory episodes are meant to indicate the Spirit was active throughout Jesus's mission in the rest of the Gospel stories, then presumably the Spirit was active in his prophetic proclamation and teaching as well as in his healing and exorcism. That the healings and exorcisms do not belong to some special ontological realm different from the social-cultural world in which Jesus was teaching is indicated clearly in the formation of the summary passages, as is evidently assumed in the modern concept of miracles. In summary after summary, not only do healing of sicknesses and exorcism of spirits go together,[8] but they are linked with the teaching and proclamation of the kingdom. Mark has Jesus "proclaiming the message and casting out demons" (1:39; 3:14–15). Jesus's speech parallel in Matthew and Luke (from Q) that explains to the disciples of John what is happening in his mission links the healings of the blind, the lame, lepers, and the deaf closely with the delivery of good news to the poor (Luke 7:22 and parallels). In an ostensible healing-summary immediately following the healing of the man with the withered hand on the Sabbath, Matthew's narrative states that Jesus's healing was in fulfilment of "what was spoken by the prophet Isaiah

---

8. Exorcism and healing episodes twice occur in sequence with (framed by) storms at sea and feedings in the wilderness in Mark (4:35—8:26). But they are linked as Jesus's actions reminiscent of the actions of Moses and Elijah in the deliverance and renewal of Israel. The link between Jesus on the one hand and Moses and Elijah on the other is indicated more explicitly by the appearance of those great prophets with Jesus shortly after these two sequences. The link is not indicated by a concept that distinguishes supernatural or divine acts from natural occurrences.

(Matt 12:9-14, 15-21; Isa 42:1-4). The effect of this citation in narrative sequence is to incorporate the healings into the broader program of the servant of the Lord, upon whom God has put the Spirit, of proclaiming and bringing justice to the peoples.

In the Beelzebul controversy that follows in the narrative (12:22-32), the Gospel of Matthew has Jesus state, "But if it is by the Spirit of God that I cast out demons, then the kingdom of God has come to you." Again, however, this is not an isolated statement that points to some supernatural agency beyond the social-cultural world of the people. It is rather the decisive statement in Jesus's refutation of the Pharisees' charge that he is casting out demons by Beelzebul, the ruler of demons. The point of the statement, moreover, moves through the "Spirit of God" to the declaration that "the kingdom of God has come to you." Jesus's further statements in the speech in Matthew then move to a broader historical perspective. The time in which the Spirit of God or Holy Spirit is more decisively active is after the time of the mission of "the son of man" (Jesus).

With regard to the exorcisms (in anticipation of further discussion in ch. 10, below), Luke's version of Jesus's response to the accusation in the Beelzebul controversy has "If/since by the finger of God I cast out demons...," which serves mainly to draw an analogy with the exodus: that is, the exorcisms are manifestations of a new exodus underway in the coming of the direct rule of God. This wording that keeps the focus on the action of Jesus (in interaction) may be significant in the Lukan narrative. Having laid considerable emphasis on how Jesus was "full of the Holy Spirit" and "filled with the power of the Spirit" as he entered into his mission, the narrative then focuses on the action and interaction of Jesus with those who respond and with his opponents.

This is the way Jesus's exorcisms and healings are presented in the Gospel episodes and summaries: as interactional. Given the way that they are represented as "(acts of) power(s)," the healings are portrayed in the Gospels as *relational*. The relational nature of the healings is obscured by the modern concept of miracle, which focuses attention on only the actions of Jesus that can be explained by divine or supernatural agency. Rather, as will be repeatedly evident in closer analysis of Gospel episodes in chapter 9 (below), the healings happen not only in the interaction between Jesus and the one healed, but also in the interactive part played by the family, the community, and Jesus's disciples (note especially the lame man brought to Jesus by friends). In many episodes, the person suffering the illness already has a support network of family and/or neighbors (e.g., Mark 2:1–12; 5:21–43). In many, moreover, the healing involves or results from the trust (inadequately translated "faith") that the suffering person and the support network have in (the powers working through) Jesus (e.g., Matt 8:5–13; Mark 1:40–42; 2:1–12; 3:7–8; 5:21–43; 7:24–30; 8:22–26; 10:46–52; and in two exorcism episodes: Mark 9:14–29; Luke 17:11–19). This suggests an even wider network of relationships in which people yearning for healing have heard reports of previous healings and the power that has flowed from or through Jesus.

Modernizing Jesus

In summary of this survey, the Gospels have no concept that corresponds to the modern concept of miracle. The modern concept of miracle does not appear to be applicable to the Gospel accounts of Jesus's healings and is of highly questionable application to the accounts of his exorcisms. Nor is the modern concept suggested by the summaries and discussion of the healings and exorcisms in the Gospels. Application of the modern concept of miracle to the healing stories of Jesus in fact distorts them, makes them into something they are not in themselves. There appears to be no basis in the healing and exorcism stories themselves for categorizing them as miracles stories or for referring to the healings and exorcisms of Jesus as miracles.

Ironically, the projection of the concept of miracle onto antiquity is one of the principal ways that scholars have been modernizing Jesus. As Henry Cadbury warned over seventy years ago, we forget how many of our thought categories are distinctively modern and fail to consider that ancient people had a different *Weltanschauung*. To both modern scientifically minded unbelievers and to modern conservative believers, he suggested, "miracle has a meaning which it could never have to pre-scientific minds . . . The rise of the scientific viewpoint changed the meaning of a miraculous event even for those who believe in it . . . To the modern theist the miracles are . . . a special direct intervention in an otherwise largely automatic universe."[9] Jesus-scholars who cannot themselves believe in miracles but continue to work with the modern understanding of miracle continue to project onto the so-called miracle stories in the Gospels something that these stories do not portray. Neither ordinary people nor the cultural elites in antiquity thought of the world as divided between the natural and the

---

9. Cadbury, *Peril of Modernizing Jesus*, 72, 81–82.

supernatural. It is evident in the Gospels, although not as prominent there as in near-contemporary texts produced by Judean scribes and the historian Josephus, that God and other heavenly forces were actively engaged in earthly life.[10] And in any case, the healing and exorcism stories and summaries in the Gospels present the healings and exorcisms as relational in the interaction of Jesus with the people in the course of their social-cultural life that included a range of sicknesses, disabilities, and spirit possession (further explored in chs. 9–10).

Addendum 1: Influence from Book of Acts?

In the standard Christian scheme of Christian origins, Jesus was primarily a teacher-revealer who was crucified, while the movement that became the Christian church began only after the resurrection with the outpouring of the Spirit and the disciples' formation of the earliest community in Jerusalem. But this scheme is not attested by the Gospels; it is rather projected onto them by modern scholars. The Gospels fairly clearly portray a movement of the renewal of Israel gathering around Jesus, primarily in response to his healings and exorcisms, expanding across village communities in the mission of the disciples, and reinforced by his renewal of covenantal community. The Christian scheme of Christian origins, on the other hand, may have been influenced by the narrative at the beginning of the book of Acts.

It is possible, perhaps even likely, that the same schematic narrative and speeches at the beginning of the book of Acts that influenced the standard Christian scheme of Christian origins also influenced modern biblical scholars' and other theologians' interpretation of Jesus's healings and exorcisms as miracles. The narrative early in Acts and particularly the earliest speech attributed to Peter portray God as the agent who had performed "deeds of power" and "wonders and signs" through Jesus (2:22). The narrative, moreover, sets up those "deeds of power" and "signs and wonders" as extraordinary events that are contrary to ordinary experience, inexplicable in time and space, hence explainable only as acts of God. In response to the outpouring of the Holy Spirit at Pentecost, Peter explains that this is the fulfillment of the prophecy of Joel about "portents in the heaven above and signs on earth below," the darkening of the sun, and the moon turning

---

10. Although Keener, *Miracle*, retains the concept of miracle, there are thus significant points of contact between his discussion and the discussion here.

to blood (Acts 2:1–13, 14–21). Early modern interpreters, like some still today, tended to take such prophetic language somewhat literally. This language, of course, can now be recognized as standard hyperbole in prophetic portrayals of theophany, of God's coming in judgment and deliverance that will be awesome, "earthshaking."[11]

In the book of Acts, the hyperbole, the extraordinary (divine) character of the portents and signs in heaven and on earth, carries over to the "deeds of power" and "signs and wonders" that God did through Jesus (2:22). After Peter and John are released from arrest, the people pray to the Lord to "stretch out your hand to heal," to perform "signs and wonders through the name of your holy servant Jesus" (4:23–31). And indeed, "signs and wonders" are repeatedly done by the apostles (2:43; 5:12; 6:8) as the Holy Spirit continues to be powerfully active in the early years of the movement. The phrase "signs and wonders" in Acts picks up on what was almost a cliché in Israelite tradition, mainly a reference to the "signs and wonders" that God (through/or) Moses had worked in Egypt, the exodus, and the wilderness, as mentioned explicitly in Stephen's speech (7:36). These were references to the acts that collectively meant deliverance of the people in the hoary past. Judging from appositional phrases and context in the narratives of Acts, it is clear that "signs and wonders" and "(acts of) power (*dynameis*)" refer mainly to healings and sometimes to exorcisms (2:22; 6:8; 8:13; 19:11), which constitute the corresponding deliverance of people in the mission of Jesus and the mission of the apostles in his name. But none of these terms can be appropriately translated with the modern concept of miracle. It is particularly misleading that the RSV, NRSV, and New Jerusalem Bible translate *dynameis* with "miracles." These "(acts of) power(s)" do appear as extraordinary, and God is their ultimate agent, as in the modern definition of *miracle* (as cited from Meier above). But they do not fit the modern concept of miracle, as Cadbury explained some time ago. It would appear, nevertheless, that the portrayals of Jesus's and the apostles' actions would appear to have influenced or at least attested the interpretation of Jesus's healings and exorcisms as miracles.

---

11. Horsley, *Revolt of the Scribes*, 52, 78.

Addendum 2:
The Recent Mistranslation
of Sickness and Healing as Disease and Cure

A mark of the narrowness of New Testament studies and of the modern scientific mentality that generated and reinforces the concept of miracle is the NRSV translation of the key Greek terms for sickness and healing (esp. *nosos* and *therapeuein*) as "disease" and "cure" (e.g., in Mark 1:34; 3:2, 10; 6:5, 13). The RSV (1946) still translated *therapeuein* with "heal." But the same translation committee that, with more critical awareness of the social-political history of Roman Palestine, changed the "robbers" or "thieves" crucified with Jesus to "(social) bandits" narrowed Jesus's healing to curing. Presumably they were influenced by what had happened in the ethos of health care in North America and elsewhere in the course of the twentieth century. Scientific biomedicine, having won the struggle against other forms of healing, had come to dominate health care and the health-care industry.

Language usage in reference to sickness and healing came to correspond to the dominance of biomedicine. Under the influence of scientific medicine *disease* became a or the standard term for a bodily disorder or dysfunction in a human (or animal or plant) that produces specific symptoms or signs or effects at a specific location of the body (usually not a result of injury). One of the great reasons for the success of scientific medicine was its growing ability to diagnose a specific cause for a specific disease, such as a bacterium or a virus. Perhaps the most common corresponding term became *cure*, as medical doctors and scientists discovered drugs and treatments for all manner of diseases. Meanwhile, the concepts of sickness and healing retained some of their traditional broader meaning. Sickness could still include feelings, emotional response, and social extension (as in the phrase "I am feeling sick/ill"). And healing retained the broader sense of making healthy, sound, or whole (again).

Ironically, the NRSV translation committee shifted from the word *heal* to the word *cure* at just about the same time that many in the medical profession, along with medical anthropologists increasingly aware of different modes of healing, became concerned that sickness involved more than disease (bodily or organ disorder or dysfunction) and that healing involved more than biomedical diagnosis and medical intervention. In fact, medical anthropologists and some medical practitioners began using just these sets of terms in attempts to gain leverage on the narrowness of the very biomedicine they practiced. They began using "sickness" or "illness" to include or refer to personal and social dimensions that often accompanied "disease" (biological dysfunction), and "healing" for the therapy addressed to the personal and social dimensions as distinguished from or inclusive of the cure of the disease.

In contrast to the NRSV translation, the discussions of Jesus's response to the lame, blind, deaf, or hemorrhaging people who came to him will translate *nosos* with "sickness" and *therapeuein* with "heal." Insofar as "disease" and "cure" are so closely associated with biomedicine, which did not come to prominence until the last century, those terms seem singularly inappropriate for Jesus, who could not have know about them. Some of the sicknesses he healed may have involved what today might be diagnosed as a disease. As indicated in the brief survey of the Gospel episodes, above, and in the more extensive survey in chapter 9, below, however, what Jesus did was healing that had broader personal and social dimensions than the curing practiced by contemporary physicians.

PART 2

Magic

Introduction to Part 2

JESUS WAS ACCUSED BY both ancient and modern intellectuals of practicing magic. Discussion of whether Jesus's healing and exorcism (stories) involved magic was stimulated by the early twentieth-century scholarly (re)discovery of magic in the Greco-Roman world, especially by the literal discovery in Egypt of papyri from late antiquity that were labeled as "magical." Influential scholars in the early twentieth century suggested that certain elements in the "miracle stories" resembled those in sources that had been used to reconstruct Greco-Roman magic. Like ancient Christian theologians such as Justin Martyr and Origen, twentieth-century Christian interpreters have generally defended Jesus against the charge. To do this they often argued that magic was something distinctively different from the miracles Jesus performed. Influenced by the resurgence of interest in ancient magic in the 1970s and 1980s, however, some well-known scholars made the bold claim that Jesus was a magician, primarily on the basis of the "magical papyri" and of sociological studies of (religious) movements mainly among African peoples.

Insofar as the Gospels are the primary sources for the historical Jesus, it would seem difficult to mount an argument that he practiced magic. The Gospels contain no suggestion that he was performing magic. Jesus is accused of casting out demons by Beelzebul and is crucified as a rebel leader against the Roman imperial order, but he is not accused of practicing magic in the Gospel sources. Such accusations do not come until the mid-second century. Recent discussion of whether Jesus was a magician, however, has little to do with the Gospel accounts and much to do with the concepts of modern scholarship. Both those who denied and those who claimed that Jesus was practicing magic were assuming the same modern construction of ancient magic, without critically reexamining the sources that supposedly attest it. And, closely related, both sides simply assumed the modern Western concept of magic, evidently without much critical reflection.

In order to expose the problems of interpreting Jesus as practicing magic, it may help to critically review several steps in the scholarly construction of ancient magic and the application of the concept to the Gospel stories and Jesus.

First, after the rise of interest in ancient "magic," the further scholarly construction of ancient magic in the twentieth century drew mainly on polemical and satirical sources and especially on the eclectic "magical papyri," predominantly from late antiquity (ch. 3). Meanwhile, elements in Jewish texts, mainly of late antiquity, that seemed less sober and rational than biblical and rabbinic texts were construed as "magical" (ch. 4).

Second, scholars of Jesus and the Gospels, drawing on the scholarly construction of ancient magic, shifted the focus to healing and exorcism, beyond what the sources warranted. The revival of interest in "magic" in New Testament studies in the 1970s and 1980s did not include a critical assessment of the concept and the sources. A bold and wide-ranging argument that Jesus was a magician was based on uncritical readings of both Gospel narratives and passages in the "magical papyri" (ch. 5).

Third, another argument that Jesus was a magician further broadened the concept of ancient magic on the basis of an abstract sociological typology rooted in the modern Western rationalist understanding of magic (ch. 6). All these steps suggest that the scholarly concept of ancient magic and the discussion of Jesus as a magician are based on the modern Western understanding of magic, recent criticism of which in turn suggests that it is not applicable to Jesus's practice of healing and exorcism in the ancient world.

Finally, recent scholarly investigation that is far more critical of the sources and artifacts previously classified as evidence of "magic" is showing the way past the highly problematic previous construction of ancient magic. Not only are polemical sources finally being recognized as a "discourse of magic," but particular ritual practices previously included under the synthetic scholarly construct of magic are being recognized for what they were: particular ritual practices (ch. 7). This could show the way toward consideration of the healings stories and the exorcisms stories of Jesus for what they were: stories of healing and exorcism.

3

Modern Construction of Ancient Magic

THE TWENTIETH-CENTURY CONSTRUCTION OF "ancient magic" was a quagmire of conceptual confusion. Scholars applied the concept to a wide range of material and in diverse ways, and engaged in heated debates about how it related to miracle or religion or philosophy. Most declined to define it, evidently trusting that they "knew it when they saw it." Interpreters simply assumed that there was such a reality as "magic" in the Greco-Roman world and that they knew many of its features and what it included. The concept became prominent in study of the Hellenistic-Roman context of Christian origins, and was the source of some of the principal comparative material used in study of Jesus and the Gospels. The revival of interest in magic later in the century, including the republication and translation of key sources, did not entail a critical review of the composite concept itself.[1] It did not seem to matter that most of the sources, particularly the "magical papyri," come from late antiquity. Because the composite scholarly concept of ancient magic depends so heavily on these sources from late antiquity, however, it is utterly unclear what *mageia/magos* might have meant in the first century CE. It is important, therefore, to examine the modern scholarly construct of "magic" critically in order to discern whether it is

---

1. Among the significant works that simply accept the earlier composite concept are Hull, *Hellenistic Magic*; Aune, "Magic"; and H. D. Betz, *Greek Magical Papyri*. Coming closest to a critical review are the dissertations that focused on the polemical character of texts from late antiquity: Remus, *Pagan-Christian Conflict*; and Gallagher, *Divine Man or Magician?*.

appropriate to the historical context in which Jesus and the Gospels must be understood.

The Ambiguity of *Mageia/Magos*

Part of the conceptual confusion is rooted in the very different usage of the term *mageia/magos* and terms for practices it included from as early as the fifth century BCE through late antiquity. As clearly laid out (with extensive references) many decades ago by the eminent scholar Arthur Darby Nock, the Persian *Magoi* and their arts were highly regarded in antiquity. But many references to and discussions of *mageia/magoi* were polemical attacks on "quacks" and "deceivers," in a sense that had become virtually synonymous with *goeteia/goetes*.[2]

Magos/magoi in Greek was a loanword from the Persian title for the Median priestly clan that performed the daily worship of fire (Strabo, *Geogr.*, 15.3.15; Herodotus, *Hist.* 1.101), a title that continued in use from the sixth century BCE into Sassanid times (third century CE). One of the Magi supposedly had to be present at every sacrifice to chant a hymn narrating the origin of the sacred powers of the cosmos—the "gods" (Herodotus 1.132, 140; 7.43, 113–14, where the offering is called *pharmakeusantes*). In addition to their ritual responsibilities in their services at the Persian court, the Magi were experts in dream interpretation, like many other high-ranking priestly or scribal groups in ancient Near Eastern kingdoms (Herodotus 1.107–8, 120, 128; 7.19, 39; cf. Joseph in Genesis 41; Daniel and his fellow Judeans in Daniel 1). The Greeks also believed the Magi could influence the weather, specifically that they stopped a storm on the Strymon River by their hymns or chants, or by throwing chains into it (Herodotus 7.191).

The legend in the Gospel of Matthew (2:1–12) of the Magi following the star to find the place where Jesus was born presupposed their reputation for astronomical (cosmological) wisdom. Plutarch mentions their association with apotropaic (preventative/protective) rites (*De Iside et Osiride* 46). In the limited references to the Magi there is nothing to suggest that they were "magicians" engaged in practicing "magic." The Jewish

---

2. The following discussion is dependent on the unrivaled knowledge of the ancient sources in Nock, "Paul and the Magus." (Some translated terms and phrases from ancient sources in the following discussion are taken from or depend on Nock's discussion.) Also useful for sources, despite its broad composite uncritical understanding of ancient magic, is M. Smith, *Jesus the Magician*, 69–74 and the corresponding notes on 184–85; and the recent summary in Becker, "*Magoi*," 89–101.

philosopher Philo indicates that the Magi were still held in high esteem by the Hellenistic cultural elite in the first century CE. As illustrations of the few people in the world who are truly wise and just as well as virtuous, Philo mentions "the order of the Magi" among the Persians, along with the seven "wise" men of Greece and the Gymnosophists of India. These "elders/envoys in teaching and practice (words and works) ... search out (research) the works of nature (*ta physeos erga*; i.e., the workings of the universe) to gain knowledge of the truth and, through visions clearer than speech, give and receive the revelations of the divine virtues/excellencies" (*Prob liber Sit* 73-74). Indeed "'the true wisdom' (*ten alethe magiken*), the scientific vision by which the workings of the universe are presented in a clearer light, is studied ... by the greatest kings, particularly those of the Persians," none of whom is promoted to king unless he has been made a partner with the order/ caste (*genos*) of the Magi" (*Spec. Leg.* 3.100). In the references to the Magi through the first century and on into late antiquity, they are held in high regard as model philosophers.

By the fifth century BCE, however, the terms *magos* and *mageia* had also taken on pejorative connotations of the English word *quack* and of deceptive practices in accusations and polemics. Oedipus angrily labels the diviner Tiresias as a quack (Sophocles, *Oedipus Tyrannos* 387), and Euripides (*Orestes* 1497) has Helen's disappearance explained as the result either of "medicines/poisons" or the "arts of quacks (*magon*)." The Hippocratic treatise *On the Sacred Disease* (ch. 2) argues that "those who first sanctified this disease [epilepsy] must have been of the sort of our present-day quacks (*magoi*) and purifiers and mendicants and humbugs, who pretend to be very pious and to have special knowledge." *Mageia* is associated with, almost a synonym for, *goeteia*, and *magos* is used in association with *goes* (Gorgias, *Helen*. 10). *Magoi* are "clever deceivers" in Plato (*Rep.* 572E). So-called magicians are associated with cheats, sacrificers, doctors, astrologers, and members of other kindred trades (Vettius Valens, *Anthologiae* 74). Those labeled quacks or charlatans were criticized or blamed for using *epoidai*, making a *philtron*, mixing and administering *pharmaka*, and possessing all sorts of specialized knowledge about and influence over heavenly bodies and the weather.[3]

Most such knowledge and ritual actions, however, were no different from what was practiced in accepted ancient religion and medicine. Greek as well as ancient Near Eastern myth and ritual included relations with the

---

3. See further the references in Nock, "Paul and the Magus," 310.

chthonic powers of the underworld (Hecate) as well as with the heavenly and earthly forces, the complicated relations among which determined human life and agricultural productivity. Official religion of the Greek *poleis* and Rome had specialists in knowing and predicting the behavior of these forces, handy for purposes such as formation of the calendar and determination of propitious times to make war. Specialists at Rome knew how to read the entrails of sacrificed birds and animals. The professional scribes, priests, and prophets at the imperial courts of Egypt or Babylon had extensive knowledge of omens, such as interpreting flights of birds, eclipses, sheeps livers, etc. Scribes and priests in these ancient regimes recited hymns and studied the movement of heavenly bodies for such purposes as protecting the well-being and enhancing the success of the rulers (i.e., the advantage of some over others in society). Knowledge of herbs and other plants was cultivated by healers, including respected physicians, and various heavenly and earthly forces were looked to for healing in specially dedicated hymns and prayers.

To appreciate that there were evidently little or no differences in the particular practices of legitimate religion and of the "magic" of which some were accused, we need look no further than the standard meaning of several terms that were closely associated with *magos/mageia* in Greek polemics. *Epoidai* were hymns used by doctors treating patients and by priests in religious rites, but also "charms" or "spells." A *philtron* was often highly valued for attractiveness, but might be criticized as a "love charm." *Pharmaka* were medicines or drugs used by physicians and healers, but could be attacked as "potions" or even "poisons" in accusations. Recognized religious officials as well as disapproved "deceivers" derived their power from "sacrifices" (*thusiai*) and "hymns/chants" (*epoidai*). The only difference between a prayer/hymn and an incantation was the valuation placed upon it by the observer.[4] Some (sympathetic or empathetic) ritual actions taken to influence the weather or to ensure the growth of crops, which modern scholars might classify as "magic," were regular practices of some ancient communities. Thus *magoi/mageia* and several closely associated terms, such as *pharmakon/eia*, *philtron*, and *epoidai*, were regularly used in a neutral or positive sense, on the one hand, and in a polemical sense, on the other hand. The tone and meaning must always be determined by context. The same or similar ritual practices were part of the regular official religion in one instance but labeled as *mageia* in another. There is thus no

---

4. See further the references in Nock, "Paul and the Magus," 310.

difference, other than the viewpoint of the observer, between the practices of religion and medicine and those labeled *mageia* or *goeteia*.

In his incisive survey of occurrences of *magos/mageia* and related terms, Nock concluded that the polemical usage arose against three principal targets: the possession or use by private individuals of rites, recipes, or skills to aid their clients and damage their clients' enemies; their clients' use of such rites and recipes to damage others; and the religious practices of foreigners or others of whom the speaker or writer disapproved.[5] The accusations of elite intellectuals against popular and/or foreign practices as *mageia*, in distinction from the proper, established practices of official religion, played an important role in the response to new movements such as early Christianity. This is well known from the accusations of the respectable philosopher Celsus against Jesus and his followers, to which Origen responded in his *Contra Celsum*.

In connection with healing, the rational medicine of the Hippocratic tradition provides an interesting window onto the ambiguity that *magos* and related terms had among ancient intellectuals. What may be the earliest Hippocratic treatise, *On the Sacred Disease*, criticizes the understanding, then standard in Greek society, that certain illnesses in particular were caused by certain gods or daimons (who did not so much "possess" as "arrive upon" or "attack" persons, polluting their bodies).[6] Nighttime delirium, for example, was an attack by Hecate, and acting like a horse was an affliction by Poseidon (*Sacred Disease* 1.4). Since the Hippocratics have been taken as the pioneers of scientific medicine, however, it is important to note that they never separated nature from the divine or the supernatural, but rather viewed the divine (since nature was basically good or divine) as involved in all illnesses. The treatise criticizes the standard healing practices of purification rituals and ritual chants and sacrifices. The appearance of terms such as *magos* or *epoidai* or *pharmaka* in this criticism of rituals, chants, prayers, and other acts, however, can hardly be taken as references to the practice of magic by magicians, since the targets of criticism were standard religious practices.

---

5. Ibid., 315; cf. 313, where he further specifies self-protection from harmful forces, which fits under the first two categories. The much more extensive discussion of Hopfner, *Griechisch-aegyptischer Offerbarungszauber*, 1:41–45, classifies ancient Greco-Roman magic into the four categories of protective and apotropaic, malevolent and harmful, manipulative for love and power, and divinatory.

6. Recent critical treatment in Martin, *Inventing Superstition*, ch. 4.

Although intellectuals disapproved of them, many of the practices that were viewed by some as illicit came to be sanctioned by Roman law. The early law of the Twelve Tables addressed attempts to tamper with or appropriate others' crops. Later, as concern for public order intensified, nocturnal sacrifices were prohibited. Early in the Empire, magistrates still had considerable discretion in determining what was punishable when charges were brought. Under Constantine and then under Maximian in late antiquity, more and more actions were prohibited. But in all these prohibitions there was no well-defined, coherent underlying concept of what constituted "magic"; certainly there was no sphere of "magic" as compared with "religion" or "knowledge." What gets labeled and later prohibited as *mageia/magia* is "a varied complex of ritual or revelatory practices, mainly *qua* professional or *qua* criminal in intent or *qua* alien."[7]

The "Magical Papyri"

Thus, as Nock had laid out early in the twentieth-century discussion, not only was the concept of "magic/magician" vague as well as polemical, but what was labeled, prohibited, and punished as "magic" in the Greco-Roman world was indeterminate. This polemical and indeterminate character of most references to *mageia/magoi*, however, was not sufficiently recognized in scholarly discussions of ancient texts and of those accused of being practitioners—indeed was often not recognized at all.

In fact, far from taking this adequately into account, the scholarly construction of ancient magic became based primarily on the extensive "magical papyri" (mostly in Greek but also in Demotic) discovered in Egypt in the late nineteenth century.[8] While most of these texts date from late antiquity, much of the material they contain was thought to be earlier. On the basis of these papyri, scholars projected into the first century certain language and practices they believed to be magical. Most of the references that scholars have cited to attest particular terms, language, formulas, and practices as "magical" are from the magical papyri. To understand the sources for and the supposed practice of magic in late antiquity, therefore, it is necessary to reexamine these papyri. Because interpreters of Jesus as a magician tend to cite terms or phrases from these papyri as evidence of

---

7. Nock, "Paul and the Magus," 318.

8. Preisendanz edited two volumes of *Papyri Graecae Magicae: Die Griechischen Zauberpapyri* (1928, 1931); revised by Heinrichs (1973–1974).

magic, moreover, it is necessary to examine larger sections of text, such as hymns, spells, and ritual instructions.

What have become known as the "magical papyri" appear to have been working copies of particular practitioners, perhaps evidence of their ritual practices. These manuals were evidently written to be passed on, copied, and used by other practitioners. Every so often, the collection includes a juxtaposition of two variant procedures for a rite (*PGM* III.420–423), variant versions of a "charm" (III.483, 484), or alternative versions of a recipe or "spell" ("write the following: . . ."; or "as the names are found in the authentic [text]" V.363–66; "take 28 leaves from a pithy laurel tree . . . But I have heard from a certain man of Herakleopolis that he takes 28 new sprouts from an olive tree . . ." V.370–75; cf. IV.2427). Different recensions of the spells that accompany the recipe for an offering in an extended love charm are included (IV.2441ff and 2622ff). Variant versions of the same prayers or hymns to important gods such as Hermes or Aion-Helios appear more than once at different points.[9] The collector or a copier at one point comments, "Many times I have used this spell, and been amazed. But the god said to me: 'Use the ointment no longer, but, cast it into the river . . . and consult once a month, at the full moon, instead of three times a year'" (IV.790–93).

The present form of these recipes, hymns, spells, and prayers is from late antiquity, as just noted. The style exhibits a lack of literary training and sensitivity, with insertions into hymns that destroy the metric forms that supposedly would have made them efficacious. But the hymns in the collection draw on what were well-formed metrical hymns. The Greek is a colorless koine that lacks literary artifice. The vocative address of God, *thee* (as in the Septuagint and early Christian texts), runs contrary to Greek linguistic sense. Yet often the spells or invocations resemble the formal, elevated style of hymns of the Roman Empire, as regularized in imperial-period rhetoric. The multiplication of divine epithets resembles Orphic hymns and the glorification of Isis in Oxyrhynchus papyri (e.g., POxy 1380) and a recounting of a god's previous demonstrations of power, as in the praises of Isis and Osiris in earlier inscriptions.

The collection of material in the "magical" papyri is diverse in cultural background and provenance. It can be characterized in the main as Greco-Egyptian.[10] As indicated particularly in the mix of Greek and Demotic (or

---

9. See further Nock, "Greek Magical Papyri," 179.
10. For the following see H. D. Betz, "Introduction," xlv; and Betz, "Formation of

Coptic) languages, much of the material is derived from traditional Egyptian religion, but as transformed by generations of use in Hellenistic culture. Greek gods are well represented, often juxtaposed with Egyptian gods, and elements from Greek culture appear mixed with Egyptian elements. The Greek gods, however, seldom appear in lofty poses, but as capricious, demonic, and dangerous. Hecate, Selene, and the divine powers of the underworld, in a mixture of features of Greek and Egyptian provenance, play a particularly prominent role. The cultural mix also includes material of Jewish derivation, particularly the names and epithets of god(s), and even a seemingly Christian element: "Jesus the god of the Hebrews."

On the basis of these papyri from late antiquity it has been claimed or simply assumed, not only that ancient magic was a coherent set of vocabulary, rituals, and practices, but that many terms, phrases, formulas, prayers, and hymnic elements were distinctively "magical" vocabulary and technique. It was then further assumed that when such terms, phrases, and formulas are found in earlier texts, they are evidence of a magical worldview and the practice of magic.

The eclectic mix of cultural forms and elements of different provenance, however, makes these assumptions quite unwarranted. Some of the same forms and cultural elements are found also in contemporary or somewhat earlier Hermetic, gnostic, or Neoplatonic texts. It is unclear what would justify their identification as "magical" or the corresponding implication that certain gnostics or Neoplatonic philosophers had borrowed language and cultural material from "magic." The more obvious conclusion would be that both had picked up earlier cultural material and used it in various ways. Similarly, it is quite unwarranted to label language, cultural forms, and cultural elements from earlier texts that is also found in the late "magical papyri" as (distinctively) "magical" as or evidence of "magic." Rather, the earlier Egyptian, Jewish, or Greek text attests the earlier use of those terms, forms, and cultural elements in the cultural traditions from which they came into the "magical" papyri.

There are numerous examples of the mix of forms and elements from the interaction of cultures in the Hellenistic era and early Roman times. The tales that compose Daniel 1–6 give us a legendary representation of Judean intellectuals continuing their native traditions while serving in a foreign imperial court. Best known because of surviving papyri is what happened in Egypt under the Seleucids. There indigenous scribes continued to serve

---

Authoritative Tradition."

in various capacities, cultivating their native culture and language (in Demotic), while becoming increasingly Hellenized, using Greek and learning Greek culture. But the Greeks assimilated some Egyptian culture as well, even under official sponsorship of the imperial regime. The general situation under the Hellenistic empires, which continued under the Romans, was contact between cultures, elements cut loose from their previous institutional contexts and moorings, and the mixture and new combinations of those elements.

As an illustration of how cultural materials from the Persian Magi were available for use by the later *magoi* who produced the "magical" papyri, Pliny the Elder, in his *Natural History* (especially bks. 26, 29, 30, and 37), included thousands of lines supposedly from Zoroaster in his extensive references to ancient traditions. These include a method of determining the time to sow seed (28.200), the beneficial features of puppies' brains and dog's gall (29.117 and 30.82 respectively; in Persian culture dogs were beneficent creatures), and a good deal of apotropaic and medicinal material. Fragments of cultural traditions, particularly those ostensibly of Egyptian provenance, as well as Persian or Jewish or other Eastern wisdom, can be found in sources such as Philo of Alexandria, Plutarch (e.g., *Is. Os.*), the Hermetic corpus, and the Neoplatonists Porphyry and Plotinus. The scope and tone of these collections (books, in papyri and scrolls) is broader than the later "magical papyri." But they illustrate the availability and previous mixing of cultural elements of Greek, Egyptian, Judean, and other ancient Near Eastern provenance.

In addition to borrowing cultural materials of different provenance, the magical papyri took over cultural materials from earlier traditions of knowledge and practice common to various Mediterranean and ancient Near Eastern civilizations. Along with traditions of omen interpretation, dream interpretation, and divination, the ancestral wisdom long since contained in revered books included knowledge of plants and herbs, metals and stones, animals and birds—and knowledge for their use in *pharmakeia* and healing rituals. Most important perhaps was astronomy or astrology, which in addition to being written on scrolls, had its own set of symbols that extended into more popular culture. The signs of the zodiac and other constellations were used widely in a number of connections. Moreover, during the same period of late antiquity when fragments of such knowledge were being taken into the "magical" papyri, the traditions of those (interrelated) branches of knowledge and practice were undergoing development and interaction as well as adaptation into the Hermetic, gnostic, and Neoplatonist literature of late antiquity. It seems highly questionable whether the language, symbols, and practices cultivated in these traditions of knowledge can be included in the composite scholarly concept of "magic."

The second-century-CE "astrobotanist" Thessalos provides a telling illustration of how Greek intellectuals aspired to the powerful higher wisdom they might gain from the culture of the Egyptian priests and other "Magi" (in the highly positive sense). Scholars constructed as "magicians" such intellectuals as Thessalos. Jonathan Z. Smith's influential essay on "The Temple and the Magician"[11] has lent considerable credence to the concept of "magic" among scholars of Christian origins. He presents Thessalos as an example of the entrepreneurial "creativity of magic" through which the "magician" gradually replaced the traditional sacrifices in a temple by transforming archaic practices of sacrifice into salvific events of divination.[12] Having traveled to Alexandria from his home in Asia Minor to study "dialectical medicine," Thessalos discovered in a library an astrological treatise "by [the legendary] Nechepso, which described a way of treating the whole body and every illness according to each sign of the Zodiac, along with stones and plants."[13] Having failed in his attempts to heal by following the book, he moved further into the interior of Egypt in quest of higher wisdom. Smith simply assumes that what the aged "priests, philosophers, and sages" of Thebes or *Diospolis* in upper Egypt are engaged in is "magic." And at a key point he translates Thessalos's question to them (*ti tes magikes energeias*) as whether the "energizing power of magic still exists."[14]

According to the text, comparative materials, and older scholarly studies that Smith himself cites, however, it is not appropriate to label Thessalos a "magician." The book of Thessalos, to which he provides a brief autobiography as a preface, is an astrobotanical treatise. One of the two extant versions of the book names the author as "Thessalos the Astrologer."[15] Judging from Philo's reference to "the true wisdom (*he alethe magike*) of Magi, cited above, the Greek text of Thessalos's question would be more appropriately

11. J. Z. Smith, "Temple and the Magician."
12. Ibid., 186–89.
13. Ibid., 175 (Smith translation).
14. Ibid., 179. Similarly, on 182 Smith calls the priest who is assisting Thessalos in having a vision of Asclepios a "magician."
15. Ibid., 173–74. Earlier modern scholars published it in the *Catalogue codicum astrologorum graecorum*.

translated as, "what about the power of wisdom"—that is, the really *powerful* wisdom of the Egyptian priests? Thessalos prevailed upon a priest in Thebes to initiate him into a vision of Asclepius, "alone, face-to-face." In his vision with the great healer-god, he obtained the yet higher knowledge of "the times and places" to gather the herbs, that is of the effective affinities of plants and stones with the stars for purposes of healing. His mystical quest for a revelatory vision has similarities to quests of other mystics from late antiquity. But his knowledge and practice do not constitute magic. They are rather a mystical combination of astrology and herbal medicine, the effective application of which he attributed to a visionary experience.

It is thus simply not warranted to identify certain traditions of knowledge or particular vocabulary, formulas, hymns, and prayers of diverse cultural provenance as inherently or distinctively "magical." This is true even of the long sequences of seemingly nonsense syllables, names of (strange or foreign) gods and daimons (in other or foreign languages), the signs or symbolic representations of certain transcendent powers, and the chanting of the sounds of the (seven Greek) vowels that have been such striking features of many of the incantations in the papyri. These represent the special language(s) necessary in communication with the superhuman powers.[16]

The Christian philosopher Clement of Alexandria spoke for others involved in the spiritual culture of late antiquity in explaining the necessity of transcending normal human language in addressing gods and other higher powers (*Stromata* 1.143.1). He appealed to Plato as the authority that the gods communicated in a special discourse (*dialektos*), a conclusion based on the experience of oracles, dreams, and the language of those possessed by daimons. The Neoplatonist Iamblichus (ca. 300 CE) argued that recitation of their foreign names and symbols opened access to the power of the gods, which would be lost by translating them into Greek. The Christian theologian Origen, who defended Jesus against charges of magic, observed that "a man who pronounces a spell in its native language can bring about the effect that the spell is claimed to do. But if the same spell is translated into any other language whatever, it can be seen to be weak and ineffective" (Chadwick, trans., *Contra Celsum* 1.25). Nor was the chanting of the vowel sounds distinctive to the "magical" papyri and the practitioners who produced and used them. The first-century-CE rhetorician Demetrius (*On Style*, 71) mentions that "in Egypt the priests, when singing hymns in praise

---

16. Gager, "Introduction," 9–10; Wallis, "Spiritual Importance"; Miller, "In Praise of Nonsense."

of the gods, employ the seven vowels, which they utter in due succession; and the sound of these letters is so euphonious that men listen to it in place of flute and lyre." Similarly, Irenaeus reports that the Valentinian Christian (gnostic) Marcos, had his followers recite the vowels to praise and evoke the Father of all (*Adversus Haereses* 1.14.1ff.).

Distinctive to the "magical papyri" are the practical purposes for which language, formulas, recipes, prayers, and (fragments of) hymns are used. These are often indicated at the outset of particular units of text. Included in the collection of papyri are more than seventy (misnamed) love spells, usually to get a woman to submit to a man; prayers and phylacteries for protection from daimons and fate; spells for invisibility; pleas to gods or daimons for divination, revelation, dreams and dream interpretation, or foreknowledge for private purposes; spells to induce insomnia; spells to interfere with rival charioteers and for other ways of causing harm to enemies; charms to attract business; and spells or charms for a variety of other private purposes.

Of particular importance are the rites and incantations for obtaining a god, daimon, or spirit as an assistant, companion, or "familiar," who performs particular tasks or empowers the practitioner to do so. These often lengthy texts include recipes for offerings, instructions for rituals, instructions for making incantations and conjurations, hymn and prayers to gods, many secret sacred names that may or may not have meanings in a given language, instructions for sacred writing and amulets, and indications of what the god or daimon will do or empower the practitioner to do.

"The spell of Pnouthis, the sacred scribe, for acquiring an assistant" (*PGM* I.42-195) presents an unusually comprehensive list of what the assistant will do, along with the ritual for summoning the assistant (quoted here at some length, with abridgements, to provide a fuller sense of the contents of the papyri). It is significant that Pnouthis is identified, as to his profession, as a "sacred scribe" (not a "magician").[17]

> Pnouthios to Keryx, a god[-fearing man], greetings . . . After detaching all the prescriptions [bequeathed to us in] countless writings, . . . I have dispatched this writing so that you may learn thoroughly. For the spell of Pnouthis [has the power] to persuade the gods and all [the goddesses]. *[The] traditional rite* . . . : After preliminary purification, [abstain from animal food] and from all uncleanliness and, on whatever [night] you want to, go [up] onto

17. This translation is by E. N. O'Neil, from H. D. Betz, *Greek Magical Papyri*.

a lofty roof after you have clothed yourself in a pure garment . . . [and say] the first spell of encounter as the sun's orb is disappearing . . . with a [wholly] black Isis band on [your eyes], and in your right hand grasp a falcon's head [and . . .] when the sun rises, hail it as you shake its head [and] . . . recite this sacred spell as you burn [uncut] frankincense and pour rose oil, making the sacrifice . . . a falcon will [fly down and . . . drop] an oblong stone . . . Once it has been engraved, . . . wear it around your neck. But in the evening go up to [your] housetop [again] and facing the light of the (moon) goddess, address to her this [hymnic spell] as you again sacrifice . . . [A blazing star] will descend and come to . . . the housetop . . . and before your eyes, you will behold the messenger (angel), whom you have summoned . . . Taking his right hand, kiss him and . . . adjure him . . . that he remain inseparable and that he not . . . disobey in any way . . . He is an aerial spirit . . . If you give him a command, straightway he performs the task: he sends dreams, he brings women, men without the use of magical material, he kills, he destroys, he stirs up winds from the earth, he carries gold, silver, bronze, and he gives them to you whenever the need arises. And he frees from bonds a person chained in prison, he opens doors, he causes invincibility . . . He brings water, wine, bread . . . foods . . . Conjure up in your mind any suitable room and order him to prepare it for a banquet . . . Golden ceilings . . . walls covered with marble—and you consider these things partly real and partly just illusionary—and costly wine . . . He will quickly bring daimons, and . . . adorn these servants with sashes . . . He stops ships and [again] releases them, he stops very many evil [*daimons*?], he checks wild beasts and will quickly break the teeth of fierce reptiles, he puts dogs to sleep and renders them voiceless. He changes into whatever form [of beast] you want . . . He will carry you [into] the air . . . And the gods will agree to everything, for without him nothing happens. Share this great mystery with no one [else] . . . [the spell spoken to Helios seven times seven] And engraved on the stone is Helioros as a lion-faced figure, holding in its left hand a celestial globe and a whip, and around him in a circle is a serpent biting its tail . . . [Spell to Selene . . . Further instructions on communication with the god(s) and what the assistant will do . . .] When you are dead, he will wrap [up] your body as befits a god, but he will take your spirit and carry it into the air with him . . . Whenever you wish to do something, speak his name alone into the air [and] say, ["Come!"] and you will see him actually standing near you, And say to him, "Perform this task," and he does it at once . . . And he will tell you about the illness of a man, whether he will live or die, even on what day and at what hour of night. And he will also give [you both] wild herbs and the power to cure, and you will be [worshiped] as a god since you have a god as a friend.

Revival of Interest in Ancient "Magic"

The revival of interest in ancient magic by scholars of Christian origins in the 1970s and 1980s appears to have involved little critical review of the sources. Scholars simply assumed that there was a "system of magical belief" and that the "magic" expressed in the "magical" papyri was a coherent worldview.[18] Betz even argued that the syncretism in the "magical papyri" was more than a hodgepodge of heterogeneous items, in effect, "a new religion altogether, displaying unified religious attitudes and beliefs."[19]

But it is difficult to discern what that unity may have been. The various rites, incantations, spells, and recipes seem to express rather an ad hoc approach to an utterly unpredictable array of largely hostile superhuman powers. The rites and spells outlined in the papyri appear to be private measures of individual protection and advantage taken in the face of an opaque, arbitrary world. As has often been observed about life in the Roman Empire, and especially in late antiquity, previously established worldviews connected with the broader political-economic-religious order of ancient civilizations and empires had broken down. The powers or gods of order, heaven, life, or light no longer held in check the powers or gods of disorder, darkness, and death. Those at the mercy of a myriad of arbitrary forces and searching for love, health, wealth, fame, assurance about the future, or control over or harm to another person, for instance, appealed to whatever forces they might gain influence with. Gaining influence with forces that transcended the powers of the dominant order or that came from outside it was especially appealing.

Nock was struck, not only by the drive exhibited in the papyri to obtain intimate association with a god, to have power from and over a god as an assistant or consort (*paredros,* e.g., I.179–80), but also by the ritual and vocative manipulation and compulsion of the gods or daimons that the practitioners purported to command, even to the point of threatening them

---

18. Hull, *Hellenistic Magic,* 37.
19. H. D. Betz, "Introduction," xlvi–xlvii.

(by exposing them or revealing their secrets).[20] Instructions for practitioners include threats, for example, to compel the superhuman power at their command by appeal to a superior power, a greater god (e.g., IV.197–200; 2065–66; 2093–99; 2310–42; 2343ff; "Jesus, god of the Hebrews" is one of those superior gods, IV.3020). Typical is the appeal to Helios (Sun):[21]

> Come to me from the four winds of the world, . . . grant all the [petitions] of my prayers completely, because I know your signs [symbols and] forms, who you are each hour and what your name is . . . (long list thereof).[22] I have spoken your signs and symbols. Therefore, lord, do the NN deed by necessity, lest I shake the heaven . . . Come to me with a happy face to a bed of your choice, giving to me, NN, sustenance, health, safety, wealth, the blessing of children, knowledge, a ready hearing, goodwill, sound judgment, honor, memory, grace, shapeliness, beauty to all who see me, . . . persuasiveness with words. (III.494–611, esp 495–500, 537–38, 575–81; cf. IV.684; 2171ff)

In some of these instructions, incantations, and appeals to gods or daimons one senses a kind of individual mystical piety, an intimate relationship with a divine consort, almost as a by-product of the quest to obtain and command an assistant or "familiar." These passages in the papyri include cultural materials that appear also in Christian gnostic texts (such as *Pistis Sophia*) and in Neo-Pythagorean texts that focus on individual spiritual salvation or transcendence, or in Hermetic texts that focus on achieving individual immortality in a mystical transcendence invulnerable to Fate and all demonic powers. As Nock put it some time ago, however, whereas "the readers of the *Pistis Sophia* (like the Neoplatonic students of theurgy) were passionately eager to know how the wheels went round, the readers of the magic papyri desired simply to be able to make them turn."[23] The gnostics desired gnosis for the personal transcendence it would afford them; those who used the papyri sought mystical intimacy with a divine power for the more mundane purposes of personal security and advantage.

This brief examination of the collection of "magical papyri" from late antiquity—a collection that has provided the principal basis for the composite scholarly construct of "magic" in the ancient Mediterranean

---

20. Nock, "Greek Magical Papyri," 184–86.
21. This translation is by W. C. Grese, in H. D. Betz, *Greek Magical Papyri*.
22. The additions of NN and (long list thereof) are mine.
23. Nock, "Greek Magical Papyri," 193.

world—indicates that several standard generalizations are unwarranted. It is unclear on what basis one could argue that there was a coherent magical worldview or a distinctive kind of religious practice, as is often assumed. The spells, incantations, formulas, and recipes in the papyri are a varied mix of cultural forms and elements of different provenance, taken over from earlier Greek, Egyptian, Jewish, Persian, and other cultural traditions. Many of these cultural contents of varying background had also been taken into gnostic texts, Hermetic literature, and Neoplatonic philosophy. Therefore, particular vocabulary and practices cannot be identified as distinctively magical, but had long been current in the eclectic Hellenistic mix of cultural traditions. It would be difficult in the extreme to discern what language, formulas, or techniques might have been used by the hypothetical first-century predecessors of the people who later produced the papyri that modern scholars labeled "magical."

Insofar as the composite scholarly construct of ancient magic is based heavily on the magical papyri, therefore, it does not seem applicable to stories of Jesus's exorcisms and healings or to any other texts of earlier centuries. Moreover, most of the practices labeled as *mageia* and the people labeled as *magoi* in earlier centuries appear in polemical or satirical attacks on the popular or foreign practices, or on enemies suspected of maleficence, and it would hardly be defensible method to place credence in those sources. We simply do not have sufficient sources on the basis of which to construct a picture of what the practice of "magic" might have looked like in the Hellenistic world and early Roman Empire.

4

Construction of Jewish Magic

INCREASING ATTENTION HAS RECENTLY been given to what is labeled "Jewish magic" as the background and comparative material for interpretation particularly of Jesus's exorcisms. Jewish "magical texts" and "magical bowls" from late antiquity (like the Greek "magical papyri") offered many examples of adjuration of spirits and demons. More strikingly, the heretofore unanticipated texts found among the Dead Sea Scrolls dealing with strange spirits were taken as evidence for the practice of exorcism by Judeans more closely contemporary with Jesus.

Orientalist Stereotypes in Biblical Translations

Moving into even a cursory investigation of what has become the scholarly composite of "Jewish magic," however, brings us up against the confusing and multilayered influence of Orientalism, ancient as well as modern, in Western scholarship of ancient Near Eastern culture in general and of Judaism in that cultural matrix.[1] The English terms *magic* and *magician* are of course derived from the Latin *magus/magia* and the Greek *magos/mageia* and all the negative connotations of practices that are devious, suspicious, dangerous, illegal, and even punishable by death. Well before modern

---

1. The groundbreaking history and criticism of modern Western Orientalism, in which the origins of biblical studies in its ancient Near Eastern context is heavily implicated, is Said, *Orientalism*. One of the classics of ancient Greek Orientalism is the *History* of Herodotus. For the link between ancient and modern Orientalism, see Toner, *Homer's Turk*.

scholars developed their composite construct of magic, however, not only the threatened Roman elite but intellectuals of the newly established Christian church denigrated a wide range of practices as magic. And, as mentioned in the previous chapter, these practices and the esoteric knowledge that accompanied them were identified with the East, mainly with Egypt and Mesopotamia, as well as Persia (where the Magi came from). In early modern times, well before Sir James Frazer and early anthropologists labeled the beliefs and practices of conquered and colonized "primitive" peoples as "magic," Protestant intellectuals polemicized against Catholic rituals as "magic."

Christian and Jewish biblical scholars, by their training deeply rooted in this intellectual heritage, are working on the basis of the Orientalism resulting from all of these layers of influence. In fact, Orientalist stereotypes are deeply inscribed in the standard modern translations of the Bible as well as in the fields of biblical studies and Jewish history. Numerous biblical texts are concerned to differentiate Israel or Judah from hostile neighboring peoples or imperial regimes. The two most obvious examples, perhaps, are the narrative of the contest between the wise men at the court of Pharaoh and Moses and Aaron, and the portrayal of Daniel and the other Judean scribes in conflict with the wise men at the Persian imperial court. Moses and Aaron are performing unusual feats that are then mostly matched by Pharaoh's wise men. Daniel and his friends are trained in all the same forms of courtly wisdom that would qualify them to serve in the Persian court (Dan 1:4). In distinction from the Israelite heroes of the narratives, however, the Egyptian and the Persian wise men are labeled "magicians" and "sorcerers" and "enchanters" in nearly all of the standard English translations, including the RSV and the NRSV (Exod 7:11, 22; 8:7; 9:11; Dan 2:2, 4:7; etc.). At least the translators of the NRSV are consistent; when they come to the description of the collapse of the monarchy and its officers in Jerusalem (in Isa 3:1–3), their list of the royal officers that Yahweh will take away, in addition to the warrior and soldier, judge and counselor, includes "diviner and elder, skillful magician and expert enchanter." The staff of the Jerusalem monarchy was simply a smaller-scale version of the Egyptian and Assyrian imperial regimes. The officers at the court were indeed skillful and expert wise men; *magician* and *enchanter* are seriously misleading terms.

These wise men at the imperial courts were the highly educated staff of the regimes, trained and functioning in various specialties, such as interpretation of omens, astronomy/astrology, and forms of divination, which were all helpful to the regime. These are the intellectuals who produced the multiple forms of high knowledge, such as the astronomy from which the ancient Greeks borrowed. As the legendary figure of Daniel illustrates, and as biblical scholars are now beginning to recognize, learned Judean scribes also cultivated this higher learning—various forms of wisdom, such as meteorology, cosmology, botany, and interpretation of omens and signs—and adapted it for the needs of the temple-state. The "Book of the Luminaries," included in the book of 1 *Enoch* (chs. 72–82), is an example of cosmological wisdom inherited from the Assyrians and Babylonians.[2] Perhaps because of its association with the magi, but also certainly because it was threatening and suspect to the Roman imperial elite and the Christian church, this wisdom of the East became labeled generally as magic. And despite the negative connotations the label has stuck in Western academics.[3]

Rabbinic Discussions

Scholars of Jewish magic, in contrast with those of Greco-Roman magic, always knew that the principal texts on which they based their concept were polemical. The touchstone of all subsequent discussion of "magic" in Jewish tradition was the ban, in Deut 18:9–14, on certain ancient Near Eastern wisdom and ritual practices, particularly those that had become standard in royal regimes, such as divination, soothsaying, augury, and "sorcery." Centuries later, as the rabbis became the intellectual leaders in (rabbinic) Judaism, the Mishnah (*m. Sanh.* 7:11) included a definition of a deviant so threatening that he merited punishment: "The *mechashef* (usually translated "magician") if he actually performs an action is liable to punishment, while the one who merely creates illusions is not liable." The *mechashef* was included in a list of dangerous deviants such as sexual perverts, idolaters, and those who misled people. Women were more likely than men to be suspect. Rabbinic discourse becomes much more elaborate in the Babylonian Talmud, at *b. Sanhedrin* 65a–67b. Rabbinic scholars who have studied the discussion, however, admit that they are not sure exactly what deviant practices the rabbis were concerned about.

In any case, like some of the ancient Greek accusations, the rabbinic discussions proscribe unauthorized knowledge and ritual practices as

2. VanderKam, *Enoch*, chs. 3–4; Horsley, *Scribes, Visionaries*, 156–57.

3. One of the principal scholarly journals in which biblical scholars as well as Assyriologists and others publish is the *Bulletin of the American Society of Oriental Research*.

dangerous to the community and offensive to the divine. In scholarly discussions of these biblical and rabbinic references, *magic* became the standard term and concept for ritual practices that were disapproved, viewed as suspicious or dangerous, or simply forbidden. This was understood as part and parcel of the official attempt to define Israelite culture and its practices in opposition to or distinction from those of the peoples round about—and from whomever on the inside of the society might be tempted to dabble in or resort to those ritual practices. Modern scholarly presentation (not just the classic surveys by Ludwig Blau and Joshua Trachtenberg,[4] but more recent studies and review essays) accept the rabbinic sources' viewpoint, and assume that there were indeed ancient Jewish magicians practicing Jewish magic.[5] Pertinent to the context of Jesus's mission, a review essay in a standard handbook concluded that most Judeans in the late second-temple period believed to some extent in the power of magic.[6]

Mystical Texts and Protective Inscriptions

When scholars began to delve into esoteric and mystical Jewish texts from late antiquity and medieval times (some of them only recently discovered), the engagement of the texts with spirits and demons and heavenly powers led scholars to classify them as magical.[7] Indeed, the *Book of Mysteries* (*Sepher ha-Razim*) and other such texts are even discussed as "magical manuals of spells and incantations," the "stock-in-trade of working magicians."[8] Similarly, when amulets and bowls with esoteric Hebrew inscriptions were discovered, mainly in Syria, they too were classified as magic.[9] That these texts and inscriptions had much in common with biblical and rabbinic texts, however, led to their recognition as genuinely Jewish expressions. Thus the tendency among scholars of such material was to relax the

---

4. Blau, *Aljüdische Zauberwesen*; Trachtenberg, *Jewish Magic*. Criticism in Schiffman and Swartz, *Incantation Texts*.

5. For example, Veltri, *Magie und Halakha*; and the overview of research in Becker, *Wunder und Wundertaeter*.

6. Alexander, "Incantations."

7. Schiffman and Swartz, *Incantation Texts*; Margalioth, *Sepher Ha-Razim*; the latter book, which is a reconstruction of modern scholarship, is often referred to as a "magical handbook."

8. Alexander, "*Sepher Ha-Razim*," 170.

9. Naveh and Shaked, *Amulets and Magic Bowls*.

distinction between genuine religion and deviant magic and to make magic a subdivision of religion. After all, even the rabbis themselves evidently had knowledge of mysteries and delved into certain esoteric practices.[10]

The complex way in which the composite construct of Jewish magic has developed, however, leads to questions about whether the concept magic is appropriate—or necessary—for understanding these texts and amulets and bowls. Whether or not knowledge and rituals designated as magic are contrasted with or viewed as a subset of knowledge and rituals designated as religion, what differentiates the one from the other? What is gained in clarity or illumination to classify Jewish texts from late antiquity as "magical" that share so much of the content and concerns of rabbinic texts or of those previously understood as mystical? When does Merkavah mysticism and the Hekhalot literature somehow become magic? If the adjurations in the *Book of Mysteries* are similar to those known from rabbinic texts, what makes them magical rather than rabbinic? Invoking pagan gods and offering incense to the host of heaven had been practiced for centuries in Israelite/Judean society, as we know from the attempts of the Deuteronomic and rabbinic authorities to suppress such practices. What makes them magic in texts of late antiquity?

A recent argument for the distinctive reality of Jewish magical piety expressed in magical texts is their combination of an emphasis on the power of the name of God, appeals to the intermediacy of (benign) heavenly forces (angels) in mediating divine attention to human needs, and the use of divine names and ritual practices for the needs of particular individuals.[11] Each of these components, however, and often the combination, are found in other Jewish expressions (e.g., texts, ritual practices) that are considered religious or mystical but not magical. Interpretation would be more intelligible and appropriate by simply dropping the modern concept of magic and focusing on just such questions as the power of the *name* of God (and the *names* of superhuman powers), the need for and appeal to intermediary heavenly forces, and people's needs (for protection, special knowledge, reassurance, and the like).

The inscriptions on bowls and amulets are mostly appeals for or means of reassurance about protection: in general, from demons, from named persons, and for babies, for healing. They often include words, phrases, or

---

10. Discussed in the early research of Jacob Neusner. See Neusner, *History of the Jews*, vols 4 and 5; several chapters collected in Neusner, *Wonder Working Lawyers*.

11. Swartz, "Magical Piety," 171.

longer passages from Scripture, most of which also were included in weekly prayers and liturgies (which, given the largely oral communication and paucity of written scrolls, the scribes who inscribed the messages would have been more familiar with). This leads to the obvious question: how the "magical" bowl or amulet differed from (personal) prayer and scriptural or liturgical piety. How are appeals to God for protection on bowls somehow "magical" while the same or similar language in weekly prayers is genuinely "religious"?[12] How does the citation of a prophetic line from Zech 3:2 ("may the LORD rebuke you, O Satan/Accuser") somehow become a "magical formula" when inscribed on a bowl? How do phrases from the Song of the Sea (Exod 15:3), used in the New Year service, followed by a doxology that was also used in daily prayers, become elements of magic when inscribed on bowls? How can scriptural or liturgical appeals to Almighty God become spells or incantations when inscribed on bowls but expressions of piety when used to describe how a youth is protected by reciting Torah (*m. Qiddushin* 4:14)?

It is a commonplace that words have power. In prayers and rabbinic piety, the recitation of words in prayers, liturgies, and learning of Torah had power to protect. What is less familiar to scholars embedded in modern print culture, however, is that written words had a special power for people in cultures where communication was largely oral, and where writing was unusual. Scripture had a special authority that was a function of it standing "written"; it had the numinous power of writing (in societies where this was rare). The quotation formula "it is written" was an appeal to that higher authority. Similarly, inscriptions on bowls or amulets had protective power in the face of a field of powers, some of which might be hostile or maleficent.

What has become classified and discussed at length as Jewish magic is thus largely Jewish and ancient Near Eastern ritual practice of divination and the related knowledge of heavenly bodies/powers/gods, their interrelations, and their relations to human affairs. The Jewish texts from late antiquity that have been (inappropriately) classified as Jewish magic, however, portray a relation to superhuman powers strikingly different from that represented in Greek "magical papyri," also from late antiquity. Whereas the hymns and prayers in the papyri are used to gain control of a daimon or

---

12. Naveh and Shaked, *Amulets and Magic Bowls*, are evidently aware that scholars are imposing a modern construct onto Jews of late antiquity, with "fanciful interpretations and unreasonable speculations" (23), that the ancient Judeans would say that they were practicing healing and protection, in reliance "not on magical powers, but on the power of God and his angels" (36)—but Naveh and Shaked continue to use the construct.

superhuman power (an assistant to do the practitioner's bidding), the Jewish prayers and inscriptions seek protection against demons or superhuman powers that threaten to do one harm. With regard to the healings and exorcisms of Jesus, the Jewish texts misleadingly labeled magical, like the "magical papyri," offer little illumination or material for comparison, with one possible exception. The Jewish texts from late antiquity do indicate that people were seriously concerned about the hostility of superhuman forces or spirits.

Prayers for Protection among the Dead Sea Scrolls

Given the centrality of intimate knowledge of and/or protection against the heavenly bodies and superhuman powers in the Jewish texts that were classified as magical, it is not surprising that some of the texts that came to light in the discovery of the Dead Sea Scrolls were taken as magical. Qumran texts interpreted as examples of magic include particularly psalms or prayers of defense against spirits, such as the *Psalms of the Maskil* (4Q510 and 4Q511), the *Apocryphal Psalms* (11Q11), and the adjuration *Against Demons* (4Q560), along with texts of divination (4Q318 and 4Q186).[13] Interpreters paid particular attention to the passage in the *Genesis Apocryphon* (20:16–32) that they interpreted as exorcism, and some took the psalms of protection as texts of exorcism, making them potentially significant for interpretation of the exorcisms of Jesus.

For this investigation of whether Jesus's healings and exorcisms can be understood as magic, the two key—and interrelated—questions are whether these Qumran texts are examples of magic, and whether they are appropriately understood as evidence of or interest in exorcism. The *Songs of the Maskil* (4Q510, 4Q511, and perhaps similarly 4Q444 and 6Q18) are apotropaic psalms or prayers for protection.[14] The teacher-leader "proclaims the majesty of (God's) beauty to frighten and ter[rify] all the spirits of the angels of destruction and the spirits of the bastards, demons, Lilith, 'howlers and yelpers,'" who might lead

---

13. Alexander, "'Wrestling,'" 319, calls these "magical texts" that indicate the Qumran sect "had a deeply magical outlook on life." Lange, "Essene Position on Magic," holds that magic was an integral part of Jewish belief in the second-temple period. Schiffman, *Reclaiming*, 351, understands magic in Qumran texts and Judaism generally very broadly as "eliciting God's help in warding off the forces of evil." For a more circumspect critical review, see Brooke, "Deuteronomy 18:9–14 in the Qumran Scrolls."

14. Eshel, "Genres of Magical Texts."

astray "the sons of light," to which the community responds by blessing (God's) name (4Q510 1:4–8). One of the very specialists in Jewish "magical" texts who claims these psalms as an expression of a deeply "magical worldview," however, admits that they are "conspicuous for the absence of *materia magica,* of technical magical rituals and formulae and of divine names" (and of *nomina barbara*).[15] There is nothing magical about these psalmic prayers for protection, which simply presuppose the same worldview of a struggle between the two Spirits (the Prince of Light and Belial) most familiar from the opening covenant renewal ceremony in the *Community Rule* (1QS 3–4).

The *Apocryphal Psalms* (11Q11; and 4Q560) are incantations or adjurations addressed directly to the hostile spiritual force, that "YHWH will strike you . . . to destroy you . . . and [will send] against you a powerful angel . . . [And] the chief of the army of YHWH [will bring] you down . . ." (11Q11 4–5). "The absence of technical magical praxis is once again striking."[16] These psalms are hardly magical. And although they do presuppose a worldview in which exorcism could function, they stop short of exorcism. Recitation of these adjurations/incantations, speaking the very name of Yahweh, declare directly to the hostile superhuman spirit(s) that God will surely strike/defeat (and again, contain/control) them. If, as has been suggested, these psalmic adjurations were pronounced over or in defense of a person who had fallen ill, then they are also ritual acts of protection, warning off the hostile spirit(s) in anticipation of God's action, but are not (yet) a casting out or defeat of a spirit that had taken possession of the person.

The supposed exorcism of Pharaoh by Abram in the Genesis Apocryphon (20:17–32), which some have also classified as magic, occurs in a very different, narrative genre, and assumes a somewhat different worldview, in which God still has control of spirits. Indeed, God has sent the spirit to protect Sarai and Abram, and the spirit afflicts, but does not possess, Pharaoh and his household. Abram is the agent in alleviating the affliction. But he cannot act until Pharaoh ceases the behavior for which he is being afflicted. Then Abram prays for and lays hands on Pharaoh's head, and the spirit departs. Given these standard religious practices by Abram himself, this is

---

15. Alexander, "Incantations," 323–24.

16. Ibid., 326. Cf. the rather uncritical discussion of Penney and Wise, "'By the Power of Beelzebul.'"

hardly an act of magic. And, like the psalms from Qumran, it is not (yet) an exorcism of a spirit that has taken possession of a person.[17]

Eleazar's Exorcism and Solomon's Wisdom

Perhaps the case of "Jewish magic" most widely cited in relation to the exorcisms of Jesus is Josephus's claim to have witnessed how a Judean named Eleazar, before the soon-to-be emperor Vespasian and his officers, drew a demon out of a man through his nostrils by placing a ring to his nose that had under its seal a root prescribed by King Solomon (*Ant.* 8.45–49).[18] This is an exorcism, drawing out a spirit that had possessed a person. But there is no evident basis for believing that Josephus and his readers understood it as magic. This is clearest from the literary and cultural-historical context of Eleazar's exorcism as an illustration of Solomon's great wisdom. As noted in ch. 3, above, the Greek and Roman cultural and political elite sometimes accused foreigners as well as people of lower rank of performing harmful rituals (some of which were considered threatening to the established political order). Augustus had ordered two thousand of what were thought to be "magical" scrolls burned in 13 BCE. During and after the great revolt of 66–70, in the aftermath of which Josephus composed the *Antiquities*, there was great suspicion of and hostility to "the Judeans," not a context in which to boast of great acts of *mageia* by Solomon, the renowned king of the Judeans.

Far from presenting Eleazar's feat as a case of *mageia*, Josephus touts it as an impressive illustration of the great wisdom (*sophia*) that God had granted to the philosopher-king Solomon (*Ant.* 8.21–49). Solomon had not only composed many books of odes and songs, parables and similitudes, that displayed his wide general knowledge of trees, birds, animals, and fish, all of which he had studied "philosophically," but Solomon had gained knowledge of the art (*techne*) used against demons/spirits (*daimonon*) for the benefit and healing (*therapeia*) of people. He also composed songs (*epoidas*) by which illnesses could be relieved, and left behind forms of exorcisms with which those possessed by spirits (*daimonia*) could drive them out, never to return. There thus does appear to have been a Judean tradition

---

17. Sorenson, *Possession and Exorcism*, 64–74, discusses most of these Qumran texts with an overly broad understanding of possession and exorcism.

18. Critical analysis of Josephus's account of Eleazar's exorcism in Duling, "Eleazar Miracle."

of exorcism. Strange as its cases may seem to modern readers, however, exorcism was evidently not understood as *mageia* among the Judean cultural elite any more than it was among the Hellenistic-Roman elite in the first century. Josephus certainly does not seem to be worried that his boast of Solomon's great wisdom and its efficacy in exorcism would result in Roman accusations that Jews were practicing magic.

There is thus more among the texts that have been classified as Jewish magic than there is in what was claimed as Greco-Roman magic that may provide background and comparative material for the healings and particularly the exorcisms of Jesus. The psalmic appeals for protection and the adjurations of hostile spirits, along with sections of the *Community Rule* and the *War Rule*, offer a window onto the scribal elite's understanding of the contending heavenly spiritual forces in the historical context in which Jesus worked. And Josephus's report of Eleazar's exorcism before Vespasian suggests at least some practice of exorcism was known in Judea at the time. There is no justification, however, for taking any of these texts or practices as magic, or for projecting the concept of "Jewish magic" onto the context and mission of Jesus.

5

Construction of Jesus as Magician

AFTER A CRITICAL REVIEW of the sources from which modern scholars constructed their composite picture of magic in the Greco-Roman world, it must seem odd that New Testament scholars find "magical" elements in the miracle stories, much less entertain the notion Jesus was a magician. As discussed in the previous chapter, the sources for ancient "magic" either are polemical or, in the case of the "magical papyri," are very late and focused largely on divination, obtaining a divine assistant, protective rituals, bringing a woman under a man's control, harming an enemy, or enhancing one's business. The "miracle stories" in the Gospels, by contrast, have Jesus doing none of those things, but rather mainly healings and exorcisms.

Biblical interpreters, however, are dependent to a considerable extent on the work of scholars of the ancient Near East and the Greco-Roman world for their knowledge of the context of biblical texts and figures. New Testament scholars, moreover, whose training was heavily philological, tended to focus narrowly on discerning the meaning of particular words and phrases in New Testament text fragments on the basis of their occurrence in other text fragments, in Greek or Latin or Hebrew. Hence they did not focus on longer or more complete texts of Hellenistic hymns and prayers or natural history or the various "spells" and other rituals in the "magical papyri."

A Shift in the Focus to Healings and Exorcisms

Most striking, however, when we move from the sources from which scholars constructed their understanding of ancient magic to interpretation of Jesus, is that New Testament scholars shifted the focus of ancient "magic" to healing and exorcism, evidently without critical investigation.[1] This is understandable insofar as they were attempting to understand healing and exorcism stories that included extraordinary elements, and insofar as they were narrowly focused on parallels to unusual words, phrases, and other elements.

The threads by which New Testament scholars connected the stories of Jesus's exorcisms and healings to "magic" were thin indeed, consisting of a few terms and phrases that occur in a few late "magical" texts. In the early twentieth century, for example, Deissmann, whose main interest was philological, called attention to the "binding" in "magic" texts in connection with the healing of the deaf-mute in Mark 7:32–37, and to the importance in "magic" of knowing a daimon's name in connection with Jesus's question to the exorcized demon in Mark 5:9.[2] In the 1920s form critics such as Rudolf Bultmann pointed to certain terms in healing and exorcism stories paralleled in ancient "magical" texts as traces of magic.[3]

More recently it has been claimed that the command "come out" (*exelthe*) in some of the exorcism stories of Jesus is the standard form of address to demons in the magical papyri.[4] It is also claimed that the purpose of the formula "I adjure you (by . . .)" (*horkizo se [kata . . .]*) is "to harness supernatural powers in order to effect the exorcism."[5] None of the three passages cited, however, concerns exorcism. The one (III.1–164, esp. lines 11, 36, 70–80), in the lengthy summoning of Helios/the (cat-faced) Chthonic One/the daimon of the place, which follows the ritual of drowning

---

1. E.g., see Aune, "Magic." When Aune moves his discussion of ancient magic to Jesus (1523–24), he suddenly shifts to a list of the "miracles." More telling may be his insertion of "healing" into his paraphrase of Hopfner's inventory of the goals of Greco-Roman magical activities. Other discussions of Jesus and magic similarly focus on healing and exorcism.

2. Deissmann, *Light from the Ancient East*.

3. Bultmann, *History of the Synoptic Tradition*, 232–33, 236–37. However, he focuses far more on parallels in other texts.

4. Hull, *Hellenistic Magic*, 68; Aune, "Magic," 1531, points out that it occurs only four times in the papyri, but does not note that one of those does not have to do with exorcism at all.

5. Aune, "Magic," 1531–32.

a cat, adjures (a/the) god/daimon to impair rival chariots, charioteers, and racehorses. The second (IV.286-95) is an adjuration of a plant to work for the practitioner for an unnamed purpose. The third (VII.222-49) adjures the daimon to "rise up" in order to give the practitioner revelation "concerning the NN matter, without deceit, . . . immediately." Adjuration of daimons does indeed appear in the papyri, but not necessarily for purposes of exorcism. As with other terms, phrases, forms, and names that appear in the papyri, moreover, it is unwarranted to conclude that adjuration was distinctively "magical."[6] Indeed, it seems likely that the magical papyri took over adjuration from its wider use in earlier syncretistic Hellenistic culture.

With regard to healing, it is often claimed that Jesus's touching and his use of spittle are magical techniques. But neither touch nor spittle is mentioned much in the magical papyri or in any other sources for ancient "magic." Again the use of touch in healing was common and hardly distinctively "magical." And spittle, like other bodily fluids, was commonly believed to carry certain powers (helpful and/or harmful).

Far more problematic for Jesus scholars' assumption that healing and exorcism were included in the practice of "magic," however, is the lack of sources that might suggest this. Not even the elite intellectuals' accusations of "magic" in the first century and before seem concerned about healing or exorcism. Although terms and phrases in the "magical papyri" have been used as sources to argue that the language and techniques in the stories of Jesus's exorcisms and healings are magical, few of the ritual texts have anything to do with either exorcism or healing.

While texts in the "magical papyri" often have to do with daimons and gods, the aim is almost always to bring a daimon or other superhuman power into the control of the practitioner as a familiar or assistant, to do his bidding (e.g., as in *PGM* V.96-172, esp. 165-70), not to expel the daimon or superhuman power from someone. Morton Smith's statement that "spells and amulets for exorcism are frequent in the papyri and in literary collections of magical materials,"[7] is simply wrong with regard to the papyri, as well as misleading on literature in late antiquity, such as apologetic biography (Philostratus), satire (Lucian), and polemic (Celsus).

---

6. As Aune notes in his survey ("Magic," 1532), "Jesus' use of the imperative mood in exorcisms is in fact a widely known and used form of adjuration in the ancient world" (citing Philostratus, *Vit. Apoll.* 4.20; Acts 16:18). It is thus puzzling how he can conclude that Jesus's authoritative commands to demons are "formulas of *magical* adjuration" in particular.

7. M. Smith, *Jesus the Magician*, 107.

Only four or five among the hundreds of ritual texts in the magical papyri appear to be concerned with protection against or driving out of demons. That New Testament scholars have claimed so much on the basis of these few references invites a review of these texts.

Protection against demons is mentioned only in a brief phylactery and as the effect of speaking a certain divine name in two brief "charms" (IV.86–87; XIII.242–44; XXXVI.275). Exorcism appears only in three long conjurations with phylacteries in which the language is clearly derived from earlier Jewish and/or Christian tradition. (1) An "excellent rite for driving out demons" (that uses an olive branch as a whip) has a formula in Coptic appealing to "God of Abraham . . . Jesus Chrestos, the Holy Spirit," and the command to "come out (*exelthe*), daimon . . . ," in Greek (IV.1227–64). The background in Hebrew tradition and adjuration of the Jewish and/or Christian God to gain power over demons is even more extensive in the other two (IV.3007–86; V.96–172). (2) "A tested charm of Pibechis for those possessed by *daimons*" includes the command to "come out (*exelthe*) from NN," a phylactery of secret names of superhuman powers, and the adjuration to "the god of the Hebrews, Jesus (followed by more secret names) . . . , by the God who appeared to Israel [sic] in a shining pillar," and other extraordinary actions of God in Israel's history. Toward the end the text adjures whoever receives this conjuration "not to eat pork, and every spirit and daimon . . . will be subject to you, . . . and to keep yourself pure, for this charm is Hebraic" (IV.3007–86). Finally, in (3) "the stele of Jeu the hieroglyphist," the practitioner identifying himself as "Moses your prophet" summons the "Headless one, who created earth and heaven" to "deliver NN from the daimon which restrains him," with accompanying secret names addressed to "the Holy Headless One" (V.96–172). The preparation for the ritual is to write the formulaic names on a new sheet of papyrus attached to the forehead, "while declaring 'Subject to me all daimons, so that every daimon, whether heavenly or aerial or earthly or subterranean or terrestrial or aquatic, might be subject to me and every enchantment and scourge which is from God.'"

These texts are obviously dependent on earlier Jewish and/or Christian tradition. They can thus hardly be used as evidence that exorcism was included in the practice of "magic" in the first century CE. That exorcism appears in only these few out of the hundreds of ritual texts in these extensive papyri, moreover, suggests that even in late antiquity it was a rare practice in the repertoire of the practitioners who may have used them.

The suspicion that exorcism was not standard in the supposed practice of "magic," either in the magical papyri of late antiquity or earlier in Greco-Roman culture, is confirmed by the paucity of references to it until later antiquity. It is not found in Greek healing traditions, whether in the rationalist Hippocratic corpus or the widespread temples and inscriptions of Asclepios or among healing practitioners such as Galen (late second century CE). Pliny the Elder does not include it in his catalogue of healing techniques (*Natural History* chs. 20–32). Exorcism begins to make an appearance in literature of the late second and early third centuries. The philosopher and emperor Marcus Aurelius disdains exorcists (*ad se ipsum* 1.6). The satirist Lucian portrays them as fraudulent entrepreneurs (*Philops.* 16–17). The jurist Ulpian distinguishes exorcism from acceptable medical practice (*de omnibus tribunalibus* bk. 8). Philostratus portrays Apollonios of Tyana performing exorcisms, but under suspicion and subject to repression by the Roman authorities. In most of these references, exorcism is associated with Egypt or Syria or elsewhere in the East, one among many expressions of ancient Greco-Roman (negative) Orientalism.[8] By contrast, Josephus's earlier account of the exorcism by the Judean Eleazar is a highly positive, if sensationalist, example of the great wisdom of the legendary King Solomon. And that account along with the Gospel accounts of Jesus's exorcism suggest that exorcism may well have entered the mix of cultures in late antiquity from Jewish tradition and from that of other subject peoples of the East.

As for healing, several very short passages in the "magical papyri" have to do with "cure" of relatively simple "diseases" (which, incidentally, seem comparable to problems dealt with by modern doctors). Some brief remedies or phylacteries, for scorpion sting, discharge of the eyes, migraine headache, coughs, hardening of the breasts, swollen testicles, and various fevers, appear in a sequence (from VII.193–96 through VII.218–21). Among the myriad tasks an angel assistant will perform, including killing and destroying, are finding wild herbs and empowerment to cure (I.42–195). Beyond those brief items and a one-line prayer, a brief charm, and a geometrically arranged set of secret names for various fevers (XVIIIa.1–4; XVIIIb.1–7; XX.13–19), it is difficult to find any (other) healing rites among the hundreds of ritual texts. Healing, like exorcism, is simply not a major concern of the "magical papyri."[9] The papyri are concerned far more with

---

8. See further Sorenson, *Possession and Exorcism*, 6–8.
9. Again, Smith overstates the case: "cures are a major concern of magic . . . [and

causing bodily suffering and incapacitating illness and other forms of harm than with curing fevers and headaches and sexual dysfunction.

Quite apart from the magical papyri of late antiquity, some ancient intellectuals charged that herbalists and others were causing harm with their *pharmakeia*, i.e. their mixing and application of medicines. But such accusations are hardly good sources for something that was supposedly a common practice of magic. In any case, neither the few phylacteries and amulets mentioned in the magical papyri nor the accusations of mixing potions remotely resemble (the stories of) Jesus's healings. Neither provides evidence that healing was understood as magic in the first century, much less provides a basis for classifying Jesus's healings as magic.

That exorcism and healing figure so little in the magical papyri that have been the principal basis of the composite scholarly construct of ancient magic, and that the few incantations for exorcism are derived from earlier Jewish tradition (not vice versa) leave us with no basis for believing that exorcism and healing were considered part of the supposed practice of magic in the first century. There would thus appear to be *no basis in ancient sources for applying the scholarly construct of ancient magic to the healings and exorcisms of Jesus.*

A Broad Argument That Jesus Was a Magician

The most provocative initiative in the revival of interest in ancient magic in the 1970s and 1980s was Morton Smith's presentation of Jesus as a magician in the broadest terms, with extensive references to ancient sources, particularly the "magical papyri."[10] He built on the composite concept of magic and magician constructed earlier in the century, and expanded it dramatically to include not only healing and exorcisms but even prophecy, revelation, and divination as well. He argued that much of what Jesus is presented as (or charged with) doing was familiar from the (expanded) sources for ancient "magic."

A critical examination of his presentation, however, shows that many of his claims do not rest on convincing parallels and are simply not credible. Even the center of his argument, that in his healings and exorcisms Jesus

---

amount to] prescriptions or stories of cures for most afflictions cured by Jesus" such that "the miracles with which Mark represents Jesus at the beginning of his career in Galilee are drawn entirely from the magician's repertoire" (M. Smith, *Jesus the Magician*, 107).

10. M. Smith, *Jesus the Magician*.

was a magician, still depends on thin philological threads connecting the stories about Jesus's "miracles" with phrases mainly in the magical papyri.

Smith acknowledged that still two centuries after Jesus, despite elite suspicions of certain foreign and lower-class practitioners, only a narrow range of supposedly harmful rituals with which certain people were charged were prosecuted under Roman law. According to the Roman jurist Paulus, the offenses for which people would be crucified or thrown to the beasts in the arena were limited to the performance of "impious or nocturnal sacrifices to enchant, curse, or bind anyone with a spell" or to human sacrifice or to pollution of a temple or to possession of "books of the magical art."[11] Even a century later, Constantine was still concerned only narrowly about threats to people's safety or about perversion of modest persons to libidinous practices ("love magic"), and explicitly excluded from prosecution medicines/drugs and rites to influence the weather.

Smith was distinctive among scholars in how frank he was about projecting the modern view of magic onto antiquity, scouring ancient sources to document everything "we now regard as 'magic,'" "actions we commonly think magical," whether or not they were regarded as *mageia* (or related rituals and knowledge) in antiquity.[12] In Smith's view, "private dealings with supernatural beings make up most of what we call 'magic' as well as what we call 'private religion.' There is no clear line between the two."[13]

In contrast with more cautious previous construction, Smith significantly broadened the scope of "magic/magician" to include "some of the sorts of magicians that circulated in Jesus' world," those of a certain "social type" (hence hardly strictly "private").[14] These included deified philosophers and wonder-workers, such as Apollonios of Tyana, whom Smith himself had labeled "divine men."[15] He included also "prophets who pretended that they are filled with the god" and "those who introduce new sects or religious observances unknown to reasonable men" proscribed by the second-century jurist Paulus (but not for *magia*!). He added also "madmen" who had been divinely possessed[16] and the prophets who led popu-

11. Ibid., 75–76.
12. Ibid., 76.
13. Ibid., 69. Smith rejects the argument that "the religious man petitions the gods while the magician tries to compel," a view restated by Kee, *Miracle*.
14. M. Smith, *Jesus the Magician*, 69.
15. Hadas and Smith, *Heroes and Gods*.
16. M. Smith, *Jesus the Magician*, 77; on the analogy of the synthetic construction of

lar movements mentioned by Josephus, claiming that "false prophet" and "magician" were often used almost as synonyms.[17] On the basis of legends repeated in Josephus and late rabbinic texts, he also included Solomon as a "prestigious magical figure" famous for his control of demons. Finally, he asserted that miracles of exorcisms, cures, and predictions were fundamental among common magicians, along with the claim of divinity[18]—although these "marks of a magician" did not appear in the references that he adduced in the previous chapter for the practices of *goetes* and *magoi*. Smith's magicians were thus hardly a certain "social type," but a mishmash of what appear in the sources as several distinctive social types.

With this greatly expanded composite picture of an ancient magician in mind, Smith argued that many of "the traits in Jesus' life" were those of a magician.[19] He based his argument on what he saw as parallels between portrayals of Jesus in the Gospels and phrases and motifs mainly in the magical papyri. In discussion of each trait he comes to in the Gospel sequence, he starts from phrases in rituals, "incantations" (songs), and "spells" (prayers) in the "magical papyri" or other "magical" texts and then looks for potential parallels in Gospel episodes. He cites page after page of extensive quotation from and summary of accounts in the "magical papyri" (for example, of how practitioners obtained daimons as servants who would perform what they commanded) but then offers supposed "gospel parallels to magical terms and phrases" in the text "only when they are isolated and can be cited briefly; so he relegates "large groups of them" to the endnotes.[20] In two of his more far-fetched arguments he even finds Jesus's "conversion" of the disciples to be magical (comparable to "love charms" such as *PGM* IV.327–28; 2708–84)[21] and finds the Eucharist to be "a magical rite."[22]

---

shamanism, primarily on the basis of Siberian materials, see Eliade, *Shamanism*.

17. M. Smith, *Jesus the Magician*, 79, with no discussion. Sanders, *Jesus*, 170–72, who takes Smith and his use of sources very seriously, demurs on this connection.

18. M. Smith, *Jesus the Magician*, 91.

19. Sanders, *Jesus and Judaism*, 169–70, finds much of Smith's argument credible: "[Jesus's] miracles exemplify some of the traits of magic," so that he "may be said to have practiced 'magic'"; yet Sanders stops short of concluding that Jesus *was* a magician. In a telling commentary on the positive impression of Smith's presentation on well-known scholars, Sanders declares (167) that "I have appreciably more confidence in Smith's reading of the *PGM* than in Billerbeck's interpretation of Rabbinic religion."

20. M. Smith, *Jesus the Magician*, 97–100.

21. Ibid., 106–7.

22. Ibid., 152, cf. 124, 146.

CONSTRUCTION OF JESUS AS MAGICIAN

Smith interprets Jesus's "conversion" of the disciples who left their homes and families to follow him (which Smith sees as one of Jesus's miracles) in terms of "love charms" (such as *PGM* IV.327–28; 2708–84) that aimed to get women to forget father and mother, brothers, husband, friend, "all of these except me."[23] His presentation of such "parallels," however, ignores the social contexts, social relationships, and stated purposes involved, respectively, in the Gospel accounts and the papyri. The Gospel accounts state explicitly that Jesus "calls" the disciples as "twelve" representatives of the people of Israel in their twelve tribes and then as his envoys to extend his mission in village communities. His statement that his followers must "hate father and mother" (Luke 14:26–27) is clearly hyperbole indicating the seriousness of their commitment. By contrast, one of Smith's examples of "conversion by love spells" (*PGM* IV.327–28) is part of a "wondrous spell for bringing a lover" (by, among other things, sticking thirteen copper needles in key parts of the anatomy of a wax figure, such as the brain and the pudenda, saying each time "I am piercing such and such a member of her, NN, so that she may remember no one but me"). Another "love charm" (*PGM* IV.2708–84), after an offering of Ethiopian cumin and fat of a dappled virgin goat, is a long incantation mainly to Hecate to bring the designated woman "to my bed of love," by inflaming her with passion so that she forgets even her children and holds fast to him alone.

Also on the basis of such spells Smith finds that "the clearest evidence of Jesus' knowledge and use of magic is the eucharist, a magical rite of a familiar sort."[24] Even though the Gospel of John does not include a Last Supper scene, Smith focuses on the mutual indwelling symbolism of the Johannine Farewell Discourse (John 13–17), which he takes semiliterally. That leads him to references to "enchanted food to cause love" (in the "magical papyri"), spells accompanying love potions and love cups. Further in this connection he cites references in the rites and incantations for obtaining a god or a daimon as an assistant to the god coming to the practitioner's house, sharing his table and even his bed.[25] Again such arguments seem oblivious to the social relations and social contexts indicated in the respective texts.

In accord with his assertion (without documentation from ancient sources for *mageia*) that the most fundamental marks of a magician were

---

23. Ibid., 106–7.
24. Ibid., 152; cf. 146.
25. Ibid., 124; references on ibid., 201.

"miracles" such as exorcism and cures, Smith devotes most discussion to these "traits in Jesus's life." Unlike New Testament scholars who assert only that there were elements of magic in Jesus healings and exorcisms, however, Smith also argues that Jesus was empowered to perform healings and exorcisms by the intimacy he had gained with a divine spirit, just as other ancient magicians obtained gods or daimons as constantly available servants to perform their every command. Smith makes extensive comparison of the story of the Spirit's coming upon Jesus at his baptism with "magical" papyri (e.g., *PGM* I.54–195; IV.1930–2005; 2006–2125) that contain lengthy descriptions of the ritual procedures of purification, sacrifices, hymns, and spells by which a practitioner could obtain the desired god or daimon.[26] Smith claims that Jesus had obtained "the spirit of a murdered man," that of John the Baptist, as his servant/assistant. This hardly helps illuminate Jesus's healings and exorcisms, however, since, as he explained early in his discussion of demon-assistants, Smith admitted that the spirits of dead men were most often employed for single assignments, usually to harm enemies or to bring women to would-be lovers, whereas Jesus was mainly a healer.[27] He even claims that the Spirit's descent on Jesus, making him a "son of god," resembles "an account of a magical rite of deification," and that the Spirit's driving Jesus into the wilderness also "fits the pattern of a magician's life."[28]

Smith's claim, however, is hardly a convincing interpretation of the accounts of Jesus's baptism, which so clearly build on Israelite tradition of the commissioning of a prophet. In the incantations and other rituals by which practitioners in late antiquity supposedly obtained gods or daimons as servants, any intimacy with a divine spirit/daimon is incidental and is instrumental to particular tasks of self-aggrandizement or of harm to others—tasks that do not include exorcism or healing, at least healing comparable to that of Jesus. As an example of a dead man's spirit being conjured, "one of whose many powers will be to drive out demons," Smith summarizes the "spell of attraction" in *PGM* IV.2006–2125.[29] This text lists the powers of attracting, of causing illness, of sending dreams, of restraining, and of obtaining revelations through dreams, but not of expelling demons. Smith quotes at great length "the spell of Pnouthis, the sacred scribe, for

26. Ibid., 96–104.
27. Ibid., 97–98.
28. Ibid., 104, again appealing to Eliade's synthetic sketch of shamanism.
29. Ibid., 98.

acquiring an assistant" (*PGM* I.42–195; see the abridgement quoted in ch. 3).[30] It has a long list of the tasks that the servant-god will perform upon command: sending dreams; bringing women or men; killing; raising up winds; bringing gold, silver, or the like; making invisible; bringing food; stopping ships; calming wild beasts; and breaking the teeth of savage serpents. Smith himself, however, has supplied the suggestion that exorcism is included by conjecturing "demons" to fill the lacuna in the phrase, "stops many evil [. . .]." Toward the end of the lengthy spell comes another list of ways the god will empower the practitioner. It includes information about the illness of a man, whether he will live or die, even on what day and hour, and "he will also give [you] wild herbs and the power to cure"—powers that are not to be shared. Smith claims that "the miracles this magician is enabled to perform include most of those with which Jesus is credited."[31] That is clearly more than an exaggeration. The lists do not include exorcism, and the power of divination (when someone will die) and herbal medicine hardly need be labeled as "magic." Most of these are hardly comparable to the healings and exorcisms of Jesus.

At points in his discussion, Smith seems aware that the traits of Jesus are more complicated than his simplistic, synthetic construct of magic/magician would allow. He evidently believes that most of Jesus's "cures," like the "cures" in the magical papyri, can be explained in a much more naturalistic way. References to the raising of dead bodies he explains as necromancy, i.e., getting in touch with the spirits of the dead. What are often called the nature miracles involving control of purely physical objects, such as the multiplication of food and the calming of a storm, he sees adjustments to "Old Testament" tradition.[32] He knows enough about visionary experiences in Judean apocalyptic texts to be cautious about attributing the transfiguration episode to "magic." But for the transfiguration as well as most other traits of Jesus he cannot resist coming back around to magic as

---

30. Ibid., 98–99. He used this rite as his prime example of how a "magician" acquires a spirit-assistant (listing parallels mainly from Paul's letters and John) and claimed that it resembles the gospel story (Mark) in five points. Smith's comparison of such a ritual with a story of a figure such as Jesus is problematic. Further, his points of comparison are off base: the purifications are not comparable; the birds have different functions; the relation between the Spirit that descends upon Jesus at baptism and his acts of power is not clear and is hardly direct; the Spirit does not lead to Jesus's being worshiped as a god; and the rite in the papyrus is not an attempt to explain the origin of a social figure, but a ritual by which to obtain power.

31. Ibid., 100.

32. Ibid., 118–20.

the ultimate explanation: the event interpreted in the Gospels with reference to "Old Testament" lore was "the familiar story of a magical séance that ends abruptly when the spell [is] broken."[33]

Smith's wide-ranging argument that Jesus was a magician is thus a mix of supposedly parallel motifs taken out of context, gross exaggerations of questionably similar motifs, and idiosyncratic interpretations. Most striking in what Smith and others failed to notice is the contrast between the private goals of the ritual texts in the "magical papyri" (to do harm or to fetch food or wealth or otherwise advance their individual desires) and the public healings, exorcisms, and debates in which both the followers and opponents of Jesus are involved in the Gospel stories.

33. Ibid., 120–22.

6

Magician—and Jesus— as a Sociological Type

LITTLE MORE THAN A decade after Morton Smith—and following his presentation in certain regards—John Dominic Crossan mounted an even broader argument that Jesus was a magician. He sharply opposed, not only the distinction between miracle and magic, but that between religion and magic; Crossan insisted that magic was merely deviant, individualistic religion. While presupposing the composite scholarly concept of ancient magic,[1] he did not base his argument primarily on similarities of terms and techniques attested in ancient sources for *mageia/magoi*. Rather he dramatically broadened the concept of magic on the basis of an abstract typology from the sociology of religion.[2]

Attacking the distinction between miracle and magic and that between religion and magic as Christian apologetic, Crossan followed Aune's argument that magic was simply deviant individual religion.[3] This returned to the classic statement over a century ago (1902) by Marcel Mauss (following Durkheim), that magic was private, secret, mysterious rites outside of official organized religion.[4] Like Smith, Crossan understands magic as individual or private religion. Unlike Smith, however, he seems to discern that in the ancient Greco-Roman world, as in other societies, magic was a

---

1. As reviewed by Aune, "Magic."
2. Crossan, *Historical Jesus*, 137–38; 303–4.
3. Aune, "Magic," 1511–16.
4. Again picked up from ibid., 1514.

pejorative concept of accusation and polemic, that the rites labeled as magic are similar to or the same as those of legitimate religion. Yet he continues to assume that there were magicians that practiced magic.

Crossan is thus simply presupposing and following the scholarly construction of ancient magic, again following mainly Aune and Smith. He cites both, for example, in his discussion of Jesus's use of spittle in healing a man's blindness (Mark 8:22–26; cf. John 9:1–7) as "magical technique."[5] But Smith relied for parallels on older secondary works and on sources from late antiquity whose references to spittle do not necessarily have to do with techniques thought to have been "magical."[6] Aune based his assertion that saliva and foreign words are "magical techniques," not on texts typically cited to attest magic, but on his own definition of what constitutes "magic," that is, "the deviant context" in which the rites were performed, and on Jesus's having made health available to an individual "by means which were thought guaranteed of success."[7] While presupposing the scholarly construct of ancient magic, Crossan gives little attention to the texts on which it is based.[8]

Crossan rather bases his argument that Jesus was a magician on his own adaptation of an abstract typology from the sociology of religion, that of Bryan Wilson. Toward the end of his career, Wilson applied his typology of religious sects in modern Western societies to "deviant religious responses to the world (or evil)" among "less developed" peoples, in a study that became familiar to some New Testament scholars.[9] Among the many types of deviant religious response he delineated, he saw as the most frequent the *millennial* or *revolutionist*, and the *thaumaturgical* or *magical*, which he saw also as the pristine religious orientation. (We may wonder how the pristine religious response to the world can be classified as deviant.) Impressed that Wilson's typology of religious responses to evil was "most profound," Crossan makes it the controlling "strand" in his construction of Jesus.[10] In part 2 of his magisterial book on Jesus, he had delineated four types of leaders, following the *historical, social forms* of (leaders of) renewal-and-resistance

    5. Crossan, *Historical Jesus*, 325–26.
    6. M. Smith, *Jesus the Magician*, 204.
    7. Aune, "Magic," 1537–38.
    8. Crossan's sole reference to the "magical papyri" is to a recipe-ritual-incantation in III.410-23, which has nothing to do with healing.
    9. Wilson, *Magic and the Millennium*.
    10. Crossan, *Historical Jesus*, 303–4.

movements that I had discerned through the accounts of Josephus.[11] Having adopted Wilson's *thaumaturgical/magical* response as determinative for his interpretation of Jesus, however, he has to add "magician" as a fifth (sociological) type.[12]

While Wilson used the term *thaumaturgical* to avoid the controversial term *magical*, Crossan writes boldly of magic and the magician, with emphasis on two interrelated aspects. He repeatedly emphasizes that magic focuses on "the private, personal, and individual" in contrast to the communal.[13] First, the *magician* attempts "to change the sorry state of the individual rather than that of the group" (the prophet's role).[14] In this respect, Crossan's fifth type of figure, the magician, is significantly different from the historical forms of leadership—particularly from the popular prophets and kings known through Josephus; in Josephus, leaders of religious-political movements were trying to renew the society in resistance to society's rulers. Second, for Crossan magic is also unofficial, unapproved, and often lower-class religion, in opposition to the official, established rituals and institutions.[15] The *magician* can make divine power present *directly through personal miracle* rather than *indirectly through communal ritual*.[16]

With this broad yet individualistic definition of *magic* in mind, controlled by Wilson's *thaumaturgical* type of response to evil, Crossan "presumes" (his term) that Jewish "magicians" were "widespread" on the popular level around the time of Jesus.[17] But he needs some examples. And as evident from the review of Jewish magic in ch. 4, except for Eleazar, there is a paucity of references to historical figures who are reported to have performed exorcism or healing. Nearly two decades before Crossan, however, Geza Vermes had claimed that Honi the Circle-Drawer and Hanina ben Dosa were Galilean "charismatics" or "holy men" who did rainmaking and

11. Ibid., part 2 and 137–58, with numerous references to my earlier works, for example: R. A. Horsley, "Popular Messianic Movements"; and the more accessible R. A. Horsley and J. S. Hanson, *Bandits, Prophets, and Messiahs*.

12. Ibid., 421, where he admits that this is "a type barely discernible behind and despite later rabbinical prophylaxis."

13. Ibid., 140–41.

14. Ibid., 137.

15. Evidently following Aune, "Magic," 1515; except that by Aune's account, "magic" included either individual or social goals sought by means alternative to the dominant religious institutions.

16. Crossan, *Historical Jesus*, 138.

17. Ibid., 157.

healing miracles and hence who were supposedly figures comparable to Jesus as healer and exorcist.[18] Crossan simply reclassified them as "magicians." Drawing on studies of how the later rabbis had "rabbinized" these figures by attributing their deeds to prayer and proper piety,[19] he found "magical" rainmaking and healing in the earliest layer of their legends, individual magic underneath the communal concerns of the rabbis.[20] Crossan concludes, rather grandly: "in all of this the point is . . . the fundamental dichotomy of magician as personal and individual power against priest or rabbi as communal and ritual power. Before the second temple's destruction it was magician against Temple, thereafter magician against rabbi."

A Historically Problematic Sociological Typology

Crossan's construction of Jesus as magician, however, is problematic in nearly every major respect, from its uncritical acceptance of the standard scholarly construct of ancient magic to his creation of ancient magicians from rabbinized legends and his adaptation of Wilson's thaumaturgical type of response to evil.

Allowing Polemic and Accusation to Define Reality

In collapsing the distinction between magic and miracle and defining "magic" as unofficial, unapproved individual religion as opposed to the official, approved, established religion, Crossan accepts the earlier scholarly construction of ancient magic without subjecting it to critical examination. This means, in effect, taking many of the Greco-Roman sources at face value, without critical assessment. Crossan had, by contrast, made critical use of Josephus's hostile accounts of popular prophetic leaders as "charlatans, impostors, and deceivers" in the same chapter, "Magician and Prophet." Studies of "magic" and/or "miracle" in the early 1980s had highlighted the problem of categorization in dealing with the many ancient sources that use the concept of magic in accusations against the religious practices of ordinary people, foreigners, or opponents.[21] As I outlined in

---

18. Vermes, *Jesus the Jew*, had suggested that these were the figures most comparable to Jesus as healer and exorcist.
19. Green, "Palestinian Holy Men"; Bokser, "Wonder-Working."
20. Crossan, *Historical Jesus*, 142–56.
21. See Gallagher, *Divine Man or Magician?*; and Remus, *Pagan-Christian Conflict*.

ch. 3, Arthur Darby Nock some time ago pointed out how the suspicious views of prominent intellectuals and the accusations by the elite gradually became the dominant understanding of "magic" in elite Hellenistic-Roman culture. Those practicing astrology, divination, rituals for influencing the weather, herbal medicine, the mixing of medicines ("potions"), or reciting certain prayers and hymns ("incantations," "spells") were accused of practicing *mageia* or *pharmakeia*, for which they might be brought to trial or even executed. To persist in referring to such practices as "magic" performed by magicians is thus to make polemics and accusations in the elite's view of reality into *the* definition of historical reality. In effect Crossan (like Smith) is saying that Celsus had it right: Jesus had been a magician.

In allowing polemical and accusatory sources to become the definition of reality, classics scholars and New Testament scholars have paralleled historians of the European witch hunts of the sixteenth and seventeenth centuries. Sophisticated demonologists, including some of the most distinguished intellectuals of the day, defined *witchcraft* to include a wide range of popular and alternative religious and medical practices. They also claimed that witches gained their power through intimacy with demonic forces or with Satan himself. Once the Protestant and Catholic machinery of witch hunting was set in motion, tens of thousands of (mainly) women were burned at the stake: midwives accused of killing babies, women involved in rainmaking rituals, local wise women consulted as diviners and herbalists, and poor elderly widows who had cursed their neighbors for not giving them a crust of bread. Except for rationalist scholars, who dismissed the whole enterprise as an utterly irrational craze, established historians continued to take the elite and official sources at face value, that these women were witches. Not until the 1970s did some historians seriously criticize the sources, and even then continued to refer to these women as witches (without quote marks), rather than as the midwives, herbalists, wise women, and diviners that they had been before being accused.[22]

Aune had noted but not stressed that accusation of magic was used as a means of social control.

22. Critical discussion in Horsley, "Who Were the Witches?"; and Horsley, "Further Reflections on Witchcraft."

Creating Magicians from Legends of Prayers for Rain and Healing

Crossan's creation of supposedly historical magicians out of legends of holy men lacks historical credibility. His claim that a "magician" was a type of popular figure in first-century Palestine on the basis of Honi and Hanina is no more credible historically than Vermes's claim of a "holy man" tradition within what he posited as "charismatic Judaism" in Galilee. Yet Crossan deemed Vermes's view "profoundly correct" as a framework for discussion of Jesus.[23] From the criticism of Vermes's construction prior to the emergence of more critical analysis of the late rabbinic sources Crossan knew he needed to "prune" the "correct framework" back a little. He finds the evidence for the specifically Galilean provenance of the traditions, for example, "very doubtful." Nevertheless he presumes that magic was widespread on the popular level.

Following Vermes's wide-ranging presentation, Crossan argues that the tradition of magical miracle working goes back to Elijah and Elisha. Anticipating Honi's supposed rainmaking and Hanina's supposed healing, he focuses selectively on the legends concerning rain and the "private and individual miracles" (instead of the "public and communal miracles") included in 1 Kings 17 through 2 Kings 9. He claims that Elijah and Elisha "combine magic and prophecy." To project the concept of magic onto the Elijah–Elisha legends, however, is unwarranted and only distracts attention from the prophetic tradition of liberation in which they appear as the last effective examples—at least prior to the leaders of popular prophetic movements in the decades immediately after Jesus of Nazareth. Crossan points to allusions such as to God's communication to Moses in the exodus tradition (Exod 19:16–19) in God's commissioning Elijah as the prophetic agent of the overthrow of the oppressive Omride dynasty (1 Kgs 19:11–12). Unmentioned is that Elijah and Elisha follow in the tradition of liberators-prophets such as Deborah, Gideon, Samuel, and Ahijah, all of whom catalyzed and led movements of liberation among the people. These prophets are called by God; their divine authority corresponds to their leadership of the people, which generates an esprit de corps flowing from the *ruach Yahweh*. The stories of Elijah's and Elisha's healings and other acts of power are framed by their acts as catalysts or leaders of popular resistance and renewal. Such acts include the ceremony involving Elijah on Mount Carmel

---

23. Crossan, *Historical Jesus*, 157. Among the retrospective criticisms of Vermes's construction of the Palestinian "holy men," in addition to the critical analysis of the sources by Green and Bokser, see especially Meier, *Mentor*, 581–88.

around the altar of twelve stones that symbolize the people in their twelve tribes. Both Elijah and the very different prophets of Baʻal (Lord Storm) perform (very different) complex public rituals. Elijah's include imitative or sympathetic ritual acts: pouring water (imitating the needed rain) and filling a trench with grain (imitating the productivity resulting from the needed rain). And, in the story, Yahweh's sending fire onto the altar, symbolic of the people, leads directly to popular insurrection as well as to the desired rain. Elijah and Elisha, moreover, are the most prominent among the many spirit-filled *bene-nabi'im* who are leading resistance. The legends begin with Elijah's, under divine inspiration, delivering the prophecy that Yahweh rather than the Canaanite Baʻal (Lord Storm) is ultimately in control of the rain that will end the drought and famine. And central in the collection of legends is the commissioning of Elijah and Elisha to foment active resistance by the anointing of a popular king to lead it, as had Samuel and Ahijah before them. Healings and other acts of power are included in the prophets' leadership of the people in time of political-economic-ecological crisis. To project the modern construct of magic/magician onto Elijah and Elisha only diverts attention from the broader political role they play as prophets interacting with the people—roles within which the healings and multiplication of food (amid famine) they perform for particular people. The figures from the time of Jesus who fit in this tradition of prophets are the prophets who led movements of renewal and resistance—whom Crossan discusses at the end of the same chapter—not Honi and Hanina.[24]

In his argument that magicians lie underneath the legends in later rabbinic texts, Crossan follows and himself practices the sophisticated analysis developed by rabbinic scholars in the 1970s and 1980s. Contrary to his claims, however, the critical analyses of Josephus's account of Honi and the legends of Honi and Hanina in rabbinic texts from later centuries find it impossible to establish anything about them other than their rough dating, to a century before and a few decades after Jesus, respectively.[25] The legends have Honi praying successfully to God to send rain (but not actually

---

24. Crossan, *Historical Jesus*, 159–66.

25. Green, "Palestinian Holy Men," esp. 627; and Bokser, "Wonder-Working." At one point Crossan, *Historical Jesus*, 147, seems to misuse a statement by Green (641) about the function of a "rabbinized" legend of Honi in order to insinuate that the historical Honi had practiced rainmaking and hence was a "magician." Bokser, "Wonder-Working," 69–70, did find a concern about "a community in danger" (not an individual religion) in the earliest layer of the legend about Hanina's protective action against the dangerous lizard's bite (cf. Crossan, *Historical Jesus*, 153).

making rain) and Hanina knowing whether his prayers for healing will be answered (but not actually doing acts of healing). The argument from the later rabbinization of Honi and Hanina—the rabbis' representation of them as piously devoted to and knowledgeable in Torah—to the conclusion that they were magicians requires the *interpreter* to supply the interpretation of prayer for rain or healing as magic. Again as Nock explained decades ago, suspicious intellectuals in ancient Greece viewed some strange or lower-class prayers as *mageia*, even though they differed little from approved or official prayers. And, as I discussed in ch. 3, the "magical papyri" include prayers and hymns evidently simply taken over from earlier public and official prayers and hymns. Prayers and other ritual acts to influence the weather were common in the ancient world, in the Persian magi, in Greek city cults, in the villages of agrarian societies, and in the prophetic legend of Elijah's contest with the prophets of Ba'al (Lord Storm, 1 Kings 18). It is interpreters who label them "magic"—official and/or intellectual interpreters. Rabbinic representations of Honi and Hanina are not among them; they offer no basis for modern interpreters to do so. What we are left with in their case is merely prayer that was not official or officially approved, a point in Crossan's presentation that is well taken.`

A Poorly Attested Abstract Scheme That Does Not Fit the Historical Situation

As his concluding point about Vermes's "profoundly correct" framework for interpretation of Jesus's healings and exorcism, Crossan declares that "before the Second Temple's destruction it was magician against Temple, thereafter magician against rabbi." The image of "magician against Temple" surely derives from Jonathan Z. Smith's influential essay, "The Temple and the Magician."[26] Smith, however, made his grand generalization about how the sophisticated and well-educated (not peasant) "holy man" or "magician" had come to rival the traditional temple in late antiquity in the Roman empire as a whole, which was a significant change from the situation in earlier centuries in areas such as Judea. But this is not just another case of projecting (a scholarly generalization about) the situation in late antiquity back into the time of Jesus, as often happened in the construction of the

---

26. Discussed in ch. 3; Smith in turn owes a great deal to Peter Brown's well-known essays, such as "Sorcery, Demons" and "Rise and Function of the Holy Man," which in turn apply schemes borrowed from social anthropologists such as Evans-Pritchard.

composite scholarly concept of magic as supposedly attested in the magical papyri. As I explained in ch. 3, Smith's grand generalization about late antiquity was based narrowly on one source: the preface to the astrobotanical treatise of Thessalos, which told of his quest for higher wisdom from the lector-priests of the temples in upper Egypt. If Thessalos is to be called a *magos*, then it is in the sense of the highly revered Magi. He was not the magician imagined by Smith and not a magician by Crossan's definition.

The situation in Palestine in late antiquity might be said to match the demise of temples in Smith's grand scheme. The Temple in Jerusalem had been destroyed by Roman armies in 70 CE. But there is no evidence of "magicians" in opposition to the small rabbinic circles that emerged in Galilee during the second century CE. Prior to the Roman destruction, there was extensive opposition to the Jerusalem temple-state, which had become even more closely subjected to (and the local representative of) the imperial regime than it had been in its original foundation by the Persians. At the popular level, opposition took the form of movements led by prophets or by popularly acclaimed kings—that is, religious-political movements—and of bands of brigands, which sometimes became politically disruptive, as Crossan discusses at length in part 2 of *The Historical Jesus*.

Making a Concept More Incoherent

By subsuming "magic/magician" under the "thaumaturgical" response to evil in Wilson's sevenfold typology of movements among undeveloped peoples, Crossan has made the concept of magic even more incoherent. The focus of Wilson's "thaumaturgical" type on "the individual's . . . relief from specific ills by special dispensation"[27] is attractive to Crossan's own individualistic orientation. But Wilson understands thaumaturgy (magic) very broadly as including basic religious rituals that were central to traditional tribal culture and persisted in most religions (including what he calls the great "founded" religions) and even a magical worldview or way of thinking. And while he sees the particular working of wonders as happening to individuals, it is usually not private but public. Wilson's "thaumaturgical response" is far broader than the scholarly construct of ancient magic based on the "magical papyri," in which magicians obtained superhuman spirits as assistants through certain rites and then used them for private advantage.

27. See Wilson, *Magic and the Millennium*, 243–45.

The resulting conceptual incoherence is evident in the tension between Crossan's quotations from Wilson and his own editing and application of them. What Wilson was discussing was very different from what Crossan is after. Wilson was discussing numerous movements among underdeveloped peoples that exhibited somewhat the same "response" to evil or the world (abstractly conceived). Crossan is trying to create a type for Jesus as an unapproved individual worker of miracles for individuals, in opposition to the official rituals of "Judaism" in the Temple. In the discussion from which Crossan takes the epigraph to his chapter 8, Wilson was discussing "new thaumaturgical *movements*" that were "deviant" because of their "*organizational forms*" that constitute protest against traditional religious practice ("itself highly *thaumaturgical*") because of their new conceptions of "*social nexus*."[28] Crossan immediately, in the first sentence of ch. 8, shifts Wilson's typology of *movements* (e.g., "magical or millennial") to one of *individual figures*, in a discussion that drives toward establishing "the magician as type" of individual figure over against the Temple.[29] The same tension is evident in Crossan's first quotation from Wilson, taken from the chapter on how thaumaturgy becomes "denominationalized" by borrowing organizational forms from the colonizers' churches.[30] Wilson explains that individuals' charisma must be validated in their communities and, to a degree, manifested for corporate benefit, and that thaumaturgical movements become agencies of rationalization and socialization, enabling "underdeveloped peoples" to assimilate into the dominant order. This is strikingly different from what Crossan has in mind for Jesus as an individual performer of magic for individuals.

In one of the key statements he makes in *The Historical Jesus*, Crossan asserts that Jesus's individual practice of magic was pointed directly against the "patronage and clientage" at the heart of (urban) Mediterranean society.[31] Ironically he takes the quotation used to set up this declaration from Wilson's discussion of "Thaumaturgy and Organization."[32] Wilson had just explained that at an early stage in the development of some movements,

---

28. Ibid., 192 (italics added).

29. Again in his next quotation from Wilson, Crossan is aware that Wilson's typology is about movements, in many of which the thaumaturgical response is dominant (Crossan, *Historical Jesus*, 303, quoting Wilson, *Magic and the Millennium*, 131), but immediately shifts to individual "magicians," Jesus in particular (Crossan, *Historical Jesus*, 304).

30. Crossan, *Historical Jesus*, 137, quoting Wilson, *Magic and the Millennium*, 170.

31. Crossan, *Historical Jesus*, 303–4.

32. Ibid., 303, quoting Wilson, *Magic and the Millennium*, 131.

"the thaumaturge may train acolytes," who establish themselves as operators of shrines, setting up the "need to claim superior powers in order to sustain patronage and to satisfy their clientele."[33] In the movements they headed, Wilson's thaumaturges created networks of patronage in rural areas. Having made Wilson's typology the controlling strand in his construction of Jesus, Crossan supports his argument that Jesus's practice of magic was directed against patronage in the Roman world from Wilson's discussion of thaumaturges who set up patronage networks. One of Wilson's examples is particularly ironic for Crossan's argument. Crossan cites possession by *bindele* spirits among the Lunda-Luvale in what was Northern Rhodesia as a telling analogy for the spirit named Legion in Roman Palestine (Mark 5:1–20).[34] Almost certainly he found this illustration in Wilson's summary of how the "theurgist" Rice Kamanga founded a church with the first twelve patients he healed of their possession by *bindele* spirits as an example of "the Organization of Thaumaturgical Movements."[35] Rice Kamanga, of course, was influenced by the role of the twelve disciples in the Gospel story, about which Crossan is skeptical because of his critical assessment of the sayings of Jesus.[36] The controlling theumaturgical type on which Crossan bases his construction of Jesus's individualistic practice of magic as opposed to patron-client relations includes acolytes and patronage networks in its organization of movements.

This incoherence of the sociological type of magician only compounds the incoherence resulting from Crossan's evident acceptance of the modern scholarly construction of ancient magic (from Aune and others). The scholarly construction of ancient magic was based heavily on the magical papyri from late antiquity, as I noted in ch. 3. And the literate practitioners who used the "magical papyri" in late antiquity were clearly brokers of individualized access to superhuman powers for people seeking self-aggrandizement. They were indeed individualistic, and their practice was "deviant," not approved by (and an alternative to) official religion. The sociological type of magician makes the concept magic/magician increasingly vague, imprecise, and incoherent.

33. Wilson, *Magic and the Millennium*, 129.

34. Crossan, *Historical Jesus*, 315.

35. Wilson, *Magic and the Millennium*, 92–93, working from the 1963 study by Barrie Reynolds cited in Crossan, *Historical Jesus*.

36. It is hardly a sound approach to construct a type of an individual figure with which to interpret Jesus based on a type of movement influenced by the larger Gospel story of Jesus.

JESUS AND MAGIC | PART 2: MAGIC

Sacrificing History to Types in the Sociology of Religion

Finally, it is problematic to take from the modern Western *sociology of religion* the highly abstract sociological type of "magic/magician" as the controlling concept for a *historical* inquiry into a historical figure in an ancient historical context.[37] In the revival of interest in magic in the 1970s and 1980s, New Testament scholars did not critically review the scholarly concept of ancient magic or the sources from which it had been constructed. Similarly, they often did not critically examine the orientation, conceptual apparatus, and agenda of the social scientists whose schemes they applied to Jesus and his contemporaries.

Wilson presents *Magic and Millennium* explicitly as a sociology of religion, and a highly comparative one.[38] Insofar as possible in dealing with peoples who were living under colonial domination, he focuses on religion to the exclusion of political-economic relations, referring instead in abstract terms to "the world" and "evil." Wilson states at the outset precisely how he is proceeding. He begins with "an earlier taxonomy" that he had developed in dealing with "sects" primarily in Britain and America.[39] Claiming to have weeded out the specific Christian connotations, he "looked for continuities between sectarianism in western countries and the new sectarianism of the third world."[40] Most of his questions and concepts thus unavoidably come from studies of Western religious movements in their reaction to the "founded" religions, as in the focus of the whole study and its typology on "the search for salvation." Echoing the orientation of much Western social science, his orientation is also toward individual behavior, not social and political-economic relations. Ironically, while he criticizes some of the problematic theories and concepts of "structural-functional" sociology, Wilson exemplifies them by subsuming particular movements into his general types by virtue of their similarities of "structure, function,

37. Wilson's typology is not anthropological, despite what Crossan suggests (*Historical Jesus*, 303), although he draws on numerous anthropological studies of particular peoples from the 1950s and 1960s.

38. In a sharply critical review of *Magic and the Millennium*, Burridge calls Wilson's sociological framework "outmoded," resembling "the functionalism of the 1920s and 1930s"—with its merely "epiphenomenal" analysis, fuzzy categories, and with "little or no sense of history." Less severe but also still critical is the more extensive retrospective review by an Africanist thoroughly knowledgeable in the studies Wilson had used: Peel, "Africanist Revisits."

39. Wilson, *Sects and Society*; Wilson, *Religious Sects*.

40. Wilson, *Magic and the Millennium*, 2.

and process." Wilson is remarkably candid that his approach means, not just inattention to, but the sacrifice of history and historical context. "What the sociologist hopes to gain must be reluctantly paid for in the coin of the historian and the anthropologist."[41] By making Wilson's abstract sociological type of "thaumaturgy" the controlling "strand" of his construction of Jesus and making it even more individualistic, Crossan deflects attention to the historical interactions of Jesus with others in the circumstances of the historical crisis of his society under Roman rule.

The other key concepts that Wilson applied to the development of movements that he used to illustrate one or more of his types are organization, rationalization, and institutionalization. Those specific sociological terms suggest that the ghost of Max Weber is lurking behind the principal questions Wilson poses and the discussion he offers. And this, finally, may explain why magic or thaumaturgy is such a broad, vague concept *and* so fundamental for the search for salvation and the development of the various movements as he presents them. Wilson has, in effect, substituted "magic/thaumaturgy" for Weber's concept of *charisma* as the energizing force in the development of religions, which then move through a process of development of organization and rationalization—the "routinization" of charisma.[42] Unfortunately Wilson's concept of thaumaturgy/magic lacks the *relational* meaning of Weber's *charisma* and the historical depth of Weber's own scholarship on India, China, and ancient Israel, as well as on modern European society.[43] The concept of "charisma," while vague and abstract, at least invites us to pursue historical inquiry into the three-way relations between leader, followers, and historical situation in particular cases. Crossan's incoherently vague Wilsonian concept of magic, however, leads us to nothing other than some mysterious ad hoc individual works of wonder. It is quite unclear how such individual acts could constitute or even point the way toward a "social program" or a "corporate plan."[44] Such a broad, vague concept of individualistic magic offers little help for a

---

41. Wilson, *Magic and the Millennium*, 18, cf. 133–34.

42. Wilson says as much, *Magic and the Millennium*, 133–34, as he discusses how "thaumaturgy/magic" gets organized and rationalized.

43. Worsley, *Trumpet Shall Sound*, tried to restore the relational meaning of Weber's concept of *charisma* in his treatment of some of the same movements that Wilson discusses.

44. What Crossan, *Historical Jesus*, 304, suggests his discussion of "Magic and Meal" in chapter 13 will explain.

historical investigation into what the Gospel sources portray as relational acts of power in difficult historical circumstances.

Magic: A Modern Western Concept That Distorts Historical Life

Crossan's adaptation of Wilson's *type* of thaumaturgy leads directly to the principal reason for simply dropping the term *magic* in consideration of Jesus's exorcism and healing: the baggage that the concept carries in Western culture of (scientific) reason and imperial power-relations. And Wilson's typology in *Magic and Millennium* provides a prime illustration of this baggage.

Under the influence of the Reformation (and Counter-Reformation) and the humanists' emphasis on reason, religion came to be understood in elite Western culture increasingly in terms of true belief. In defining and defending official, established religion, intellectuals and Church authorities defined other, often popular, "beliefs" and practices as "magic." What was identified as magic was often closely associated with the practice of witchcraft, with tragic implications for midwives, herbalists and other folk healers, and local diviners. While the dawning Enlightenment may have contributed to the demise of the officially sponsored witch burnings, the rise of Reason further crystalized the differentiation of (true) religion as rational belief, and magic as the dark realm of popular superstition, irrationality, and coercive manipulation. Reason was understood in terms of Nature; what was natural was rational. With the rise of science, particularly empirical science, the rational came increasingly to be defined in terms of what was empirically valid, as judged by the senses.

Closely interrelated with the consolidation of the Enlightenment rational-natural worldview in elite Western culture was European intellectuals' emergent understanding of the so-called primitive or savage peoples of the world whom Europeans were encountering and subjugating, from the so-called voyages of discovery to the intensifying colonization of the late nineteenth century. It is impossible to separate the colonial encounter from European intellectuals' delineation of the evolutionary scheme of development, of the increasing triumph of reason: a development from magic to religion to science.

Particularly influential in making this evolutionary scheme universal by applying it to what was known of earlier cultures or so-called primitive peoples were the works of E. B. Tylor and Sir James Frazer.⁴⁵ The scheme is an abstract one of the stages of thought as it perfects itself, without correlation with social structure or historical context. Frazer's highly influential formulation came to dominate elite cultural views both of evolution in Western civilization and of more (so-called) primitive peoples to whom the Europeans had only recently brought the enlightenment of rational thought: "magic" was an early expression of science based on a deluded sense of cause and effect; religion advanced manipulation and coercion of forces to supplication and veneration of the gods; science returned to principles of cause and effect but now on the basis of true correlation known from observation of nature. An alternative, but far less influential, view was that "magic" was the decay of "religion."

At least three full generations of anthropologists focused on magic as one of their principal concerns.⁴⁶ The superiority of reason and science in Western society over the so-called backward peoples of the world had become an integral component of the West's "grand narrative." By the 1950s and 1960s the difference between "magic" and "religion" was no longer so clear, but "magico-religious thought" was still understood as an earlier or more primitive stage that had yielded or would yield to the spread of reason and science.⁴⁷ The social sciences were clearly backing away from this abstract, synthetic construct. As a significant review (in 1968) concluded, somewhat tentatively, "Magic is not a uniform class of practices and beliefs which can be immediately discerned in every society."⁴⁸

Wilson's typological definition of *thaumaturgy*, however, which Crossan makes the controlling "type" for Jesus the magician, perpetuates the

---

45. Tylor, *Primitive Culture*, 1871; Frazer, esp. the one-volume edition of *The Golden Bough* from 1922.

46. From the evolutionists of the 1870s and after to the structural-functionalists in the first half of the twentieth century. As a mark of how important the concept was, the *Encyclopedia of Religion and Ethics*, published in 1917, devoted seventy-six double-column, small-print pages to magic. The history-of-religions school's construction of magic in the ancient world was a parallel in German classical and New Testament scholarship. Malinowski, *Magic, Science, and Religion*, widely read in liberal-arts programs in the 1950s, exhibits an interesting mix of an evolutionary view of societies and (based on Malinowski's fieldwork in the Trobriand Islands) an appreciation of the positive *social-cultural* function of magic as ritual acts that bridged dangerous gaps of knowledge in every important pursuit.

47. See earlier review articles such as Wax and Wax, "Notion of Magic"; and Aberle, "Religio-Magical Phenomena."

48. Yalman, "Magic," 521. The article is only seven pages of large print.

evolutionary scheme of magic, religion, and science/reason that had become part of the West's "grand narrative."[49] This can be seen both in Wilson's understanding of "magic" and in his assumption of the evolutionary perspective on magic among "less developed peoples" and in religion in general. Magic is by definition contrary to natural reason and science. "The thaumaturgical [= magical] response is a refusal to accept the testimony of the senses and natural causation as definitive."[50] Throughout his discussion, thaumaturgy "is belief in empirically unjustified practices and procedures which affect personal well-being."[51] Indeed, the evolutionary view of "magic-religion-(empirical-scientific) rationality" determines much of his agenda in the book, including how thaumaturgy gives way to rationalization: "Such belief in thaumaturgy has greatly declined in the nineteenth and twentieth centuries, as empirico-rational explanation has expanded, and has declined perhaps even more sharply than specifically religious belief and practice have declined."[52]

Moreover, Wilson understands "magic" in religious movements among less developed peoples as the beginning stage in "wide, evolutionary processes."[53] "Thaumaturgical practice is usually part of the tradition of primitive religion itself."[54] "Thaumaturgy is the primal stuff of primitive religion. Curing ceremonies, protective devices, and miracle-making are found very widely . . . in almost all preliterate societies."[55] The very starting point of his presentation, therefore, is that "thaumaturgical (or more simply, if not quite synonymously, magical) preoccupations are the fundamental orientation of new religious movements among simpler peoples—just as they were of their indigenous religion. Movements arising among indigenous peoples soon after cultural contact with white men are, understandably, fundamentally magical."[56] As the movements develop, accordingly, "magical explanations give place to better-tested hypotheses

---

49. Wilson, moreover, was relying on studies (largely by anthropologists) of African and American peoples carried out from the 1940s to the 1960s (some much earlier), many of which also still shared the evolutionary scheme.

50. Wilson, *Magic and the Millennium*, 70.

51. Ibid., 484.

52. Ibid., 71.

53. Ibid., 4.

54. Ibid., 54.

55. Ibid., 70.

56. Ibid., 5.

... Thaumaturgical movements themselves embrace more rational procedures, and more systematic patterns of organization ... Sometimes they come to accept the insights of science ... and increased education and medical facilities."[57]

In his "Conclusions," Wilson complains that the problem with "broad categories—such as *anomie, charisma, relative deprivation, nativism,* and *culture-shock*—is their tendency to become catch-all phrases, ... summary solutions to intellectual problems, ... [adding] to the problems of comparative sociology by reducing the rigour and the exact specification of abstract propositions."[58] Ironically the same can be said of "broad categories" such as "less-developed people," "thaumaturgical," and "rational." From the vantage point of critical retrospect, such categories appear to be "summary solutions" to intellectual problems generated among modern Western academics. As some historians of religion are now saying, however, "magic does not exist; it is the product of scholars' minds."[59] An even more important reason for not perpetuating the concept, however, is its Western rationalist and imperial baggage that seems singularly inappropriate to antiquity in general and to Jesus's exorcism and healing in particular.

---

57. Ibid., 8.

58. Ibid., 498.

59. Penner, "Rationality, Ritual, and Science," applying to magic what Levi-Strauss had said about totemism. That magic, like miracle, is an issue in modern scholars' minds (that does not correspond to historical literary references and ritual practices) seems to be illustrated in successive efforts by a theologians, biblical scholars, or sociologists to review and reconceptualize it. For example, sociologist Stark, "Reconceptualizing," recognizes that "the term *magic* has been a conceptual mess" but remains imprisoned by the modernist "scientific" mentality and discourse in which science deals with the natural, and religion and magic with the supernatural. Stark's own "reconceptualization," partly a "throwback" to Malinowski, is heavily indebted to Christian theological understanding of magic (and miracle).

7

Discourse, Ritual Practices, and Healing

THE RESURGENCE OF SCHOLARLY interest in ancient "magic" had barely begun at the time of Smith's and Crossan's presentations of Jesus as a "magician." Investigations during the 1990s, like that of Nock eighty years ago, recognized not only that what ancients thought of as "magic" was different from the modern concept but also that polemical references and accusations are not good sources for historical practice. Investigators have also considered whether the modern concept may hinder understanding.[1] The more candid scholars, aware of earlier critical reflection by social anthropologists in the 1960s, sensed that there is no longer much point in "reification of transcultural categories at the expense of history, culture and social context."[2]

Yet even the most critical scholars, after issuing caveats about how problematic the concept is, continued to write as if, historically, there were *magicians* engaged in the *practice* of *magic* in the ancient world, not only in late antiquity, but also earlier in the Greek and Hellenistic-Roman world.[3]

---

1. Not only is the term *magic* "one of the most persistent problems in the study of magic in the ancient Mediterranean," as noted by Rives, "*Magus*," 53; but also "there has been a loss of faith in the traditional underpinnings of the category magic itself," as noted by Gordon, "Reporting the Marvelous," 65.

2. Gordon, "Reporting the Marvelous," 65, citing Tambiah, *Magic, Science*, 29.

3. In the recent surge of interest in magic in antiquity, leading scholars see themselves as creating a new (sub)field of study (with academic conferences and expanding publication of papers, dissertations, and books): see, for example, Faraone and Obbink, "Preface," vii; and Gordon and Simon, "Introduction," 1. Perhaps it would be academically impolitic for a scholar such as Gordon to state frankly that the modern concept of

The continuing critical investigations and discussions have nevertheless resulted in important recognitions that should enable New Testament scholars finally to move beyond the problematic twentieth-century construction of ancient magic and to focus on discussion of Jesus's healings and exorcisms not as magic or miracle but as healings and exorcisms.

The Ancient Discourse of Magic

Increasing recognition that references to *magoi/mageia* and *magi/magia* and related terms were polemical and accusatory has led to critical discussion of such references as a *discourse of magic*, not evidence of the historical practice of magic. Well-known scholars produced major books that restated the modern scholarly construction of magic from Greek and Latin sources, insisting that "the practice of magic was omnipresent in classical antiquity."[4] Knowing that such sweeping statements were simply untrue, however, repeatedly issued caveats that the sources in fact do not attest the practice of magic and that the concept is problematic. One even admitted, "the truth of the matter is that we are in no position to assert that belief in magic was the norm at any period in Classical Antiquity, let alone in the first centuries of our era."[5] The recent shift in the focus of discussion to the *discourse* of magic avoids the previous naïve use of literary references as if they were straightforward evidence of historical ritual practice. They are rather evidence of what some people (the elite, who produced literature) believed or feared about secret rituals, particularly divination and the social and political function of such beliefs or fears. The principal function of the beliefs was to discourage and control marginal ritual practices through belittlement, scary exaggeration (e.g., of necromancy), silencing, and even trials, executions, and lynchings.[6]

Nock had long since concisely laid out the evidence of the discourse of magic in Greek sources. Recent studies now supply the corresponding

---

magic is hopelessly problematic and that the modern scholarly construct of magic in the ancient world limits critical analysis of ritual practices in antiquity—that is, to suggest that the nascent (sub)field of study bears an inappropriate title.

4. Graf, *Magic*, 1; Dickie, *Magic and Magicians*.

5. Dickie, "Magic in the Roman Historians," 85, although in the next sentence he writes as if somehow behind Tacitus's accounts of political accusations of dangerous divination were actual *magicians*.

6. Gordon and Simon, "Introduction," 6, referring to other studies such as Ogden, *Greek and Roman Necromancy*; and Rives, "Magic in Roman Law."

evidence for the discourse from Latin literature, with warning about how remote the concept of magic in the modern scientific world is from the ancient discourse[7]—to which we should add how different the twentieth-century scholarly construction of ancient magic still presupposed in many studies is from the ancient discourse. References to *magi/magia/magicus* from roughly 50 BCE to the mid-second century CE are relatively limited, with dramatic differences between prose and poetry. A minimally coherent discourse of "magic," including the first occurrence of the noun *magia* (in Apuleius's self-defense), did not develop until the second century CE, and even then was not particularly prominent. The discourse, moreover, made reference only to a few ritual practices about which some elites were anxious, such as divination, as well as to fearsome mythic figures, such as Circe and Medea. The discourse consisted, variously, of poetic references to those mythic witches and their chants and spells, prose traditions of the venerable Persian Magi, with their divination and other rituals, and accounts in Tacitus (and other historians) of a handful of high-level trials, mainly of women, for unauthorized divination threatening to prominent imperial figures. Clearly there is no evidence in this discourse for assertions about practice of magic in the Roman Empire at the time of Jesus.[8]

The Transformation of Egyptian Religion That Led to the "Magical Papyri"

Egyptologists have recently explained the transformation of traditional Egyptian religion under Roman imperial rule that led to its Western misunderstanding as magic and to the background from which the "magical papyri" emerged.[9] In archaic Egyptian culture the divine figure Heka ("One Who Consecrates Imagery") was the creative Word-Force that transformed performative speech-acts into tangible earthly form, becoming a real presence in every temple ritual. The scribal lector-priests, as extensions of Pharaoh, were responsible for composing, collecting, learning, and performing this ritual repertoire, and maintaining it in written collections (of hymns, prayers, ritual techniques, curses, healing rites, and so forth) in the "houses

---

7. See especially Rives, "*Magus*," on which the following discussion is based.

8. Critical studies of the ancient discourse of magic continue; see, for example, Janowicz, *Magic in the Roman World*; and Stratton, *Naming the Witch*.

9. On the following, see e.g., Ritner, *Mechanics*; and Ritner, "Religious, Social, and Legal Parameters."

of life" (temples). People could petition a god publicly during regular processions of statues, or privately under priestly instruction (via lamps, bowls, and images). Such rituals led by lector-priests staffing local temples became the standard arbiters of justice.[10]

Under Ptolemaic rule, Greek became, to a considerable extent, the language of the temples and of lector-priests as well as elite culture generally, although Egyptian culture continued in Demotic as well. Insofar as the divination, oracles, and other wisdom of the lector-priests were analogous to those of the Persian *magoi*, outsiders understood them as practicing *mageia*. In the modern Western (Orientalist) construction that persisted in academic circles, it became standard to refer to Egyptian divination, wisdom, and culture generally as "magic," and to the priests as "magicians." But there were evidently no itinerant ritual experts in chanting or drugs or cursing or divination in Egypt that corresponded to the "charlatans" accused of harmful rituals in Greece. Rather the lector-priests of the local temples, keepers of all the traditional ritual texts, also served the needs and desires of the local population, private as well as public.[11] Second-century sources such as Plutarch and Clement of Alexandria suggest that Egyptian priests and the traditions they cultivated and rituals they practiced were still alive (Plutarch, *De Iside et Osiride*; Clement, *Stromateis* 6.4.35, 37; *Paedogogus* 3.2.4; *Protrepticus* 2.39).

The Romans, long suspicious of foreign religious practices, especially of Egyptian and other Near Eastern religions, cut off state subsidy of the temples, leaving the lector-priests all the more dependent on the local population whose religious needs they had traditionally served. Eventually suspicious Roman officials moved to suppress the practices of the lector-priests that they saw as a threat to Roman morals, social control, and financial domination.[12] Q. Aemilius Saturninus, prefect of Egypt under the Emperor Septimius Severus, in 199 CE, for example, decreed that "no one, through oracles, that is, by means of written documents supposedly granted in the presence of the deity, nor by means of the procession of cult images or suchlike charlatanry, pretend to have knowledge of the supernatural, or profess to know the obscurity of future events"—under threat of capital

---

10. Ritner, "Religious, Social, and Legal Parameters," 51–55.

11. Ibid., 55–56; Frankfurter, "Ritual Expertise," 120; and Frankfurter, *Religion in Roman Egypt*, ch. 5.

12. Ritner, "Religious, Social, and Legal Parameters," 57; Frankfurter, "Ritual Expertise," 125; see further Gordon, "Religion in the Roman Empire," 241–42.

punishment.¹³ "Much of what had constituted public religion was driven underground, becoming secretive and 'private' practice"¹⁴—performed in household shines rather than in the temples—thus coming to match the discourse of magic.

For the way in which Roman Egyptophobia may have led to the emergence of "magical" papyri, the parallel phenomenon of Egyptomania must also be taken into account, as exemplified by the Greek "astrobotanist" Thessalos, particularly in his collaboration with the priest in Diospolis (Thebes) who arranged his face-to-face encounter with Asclepius. While Roman officials were suspicious of the Egyptian lector-priests' divinations, and Greek and Roman intellectuals were eager to obtain their higher wisdom, like what Philo had referred to as "the true wisdom" (*ten alethen magiken*) of the Magi. A recent study of Thessalos's self-serving preface argues that in publishing what he claimed surpassed even the knowledge of the legendary Egyptian astrologer Nechepso, he was creating a commodity to be consumed in the elite intellectual circles of the Roman Empire, pandering to the burgeoning fascination with the "magical powers" of "the East."¹⁵ As for the priest in Upper Egypt who had set up the vision of Asclepius for Thessalos, who had come to Egypt "with a large amount of money," his collaboration with Thessalos may have become his ticket to prestige and fortune, say, in the more cosmopolitan cultural milieu of Alexandria.¹⁶ In the Egypt of late antiquity those who knew the ritual texts were literally hungry, and Western (Greek and Roman) intellectuals hungry for the wisdom of the East provided an eager market.

Not Magic but Particular Types of Ritual Practice

A critical review of recent scholarship shows that the phenomena labeled "magic" and the supposed evidence for them from texts and artifacts were in fact a number of different kinds of ritual practices that became lumped together under the synthetic scholarly construct. The late collections of texts in the "magical papyri," moreover, are texts of various types of rituals. It is surely significant, further, that the ancient Greek and Latin discourses

---

13. Papyrus Yale Inv 299, translation adapted from Rea, "A New Version," in G. H. R. Horsley, *New Documents*, 1:47–51.
14. Ritner, "Religious, Social, and Legal Parameters," 57.
15. Moyer, "Thessalos of Tralles," 52–56.
16. See also Frankfurter, *Religion in Roman Egypt*, 225–33.

of magic included anxiety and accusation about only a few of these different kinds of (secret/unofficial) rituals. Recent studies are focusing on some of these particular kinds of ritual practices/artifacts, sometimes without application of the concept "magic." These more focused studies are suggestive for how the problematic concept of magic could simply be dropped and focus shifted to the actual (attested) particular ritual practices in the ancient world. It is appropriate for historical investigation to consider such ritual practices according to type and according to the way they functioned, with appropriate attention also to their common features, their overlap, and the relation between them.

The best-attested, hence probably most common, type of private (unofficial) ritual practice in antiquity, was *protective* in the broadest sense (*apotropaic* or *eudaemonic*). Most familiar are the (inscribed) amulets or phylacteries of small pieces of papyrus or metal or precious stones.[17] Recitation and inscription of a text invoking a superhuman force or god invested these amulets with special protective power. These are closely related to the extensive Greek and Roman Lapidaries, or "Books of Stones" that describe the marvelous powers (properties) of precious stones (most familiar through bk. 37 of Pliny the Elder's *Natural History*). In the lapidary tradition, the properties (powers) of stones were correlated with those of plants and animals, drawing on the earlier Babylonian lapidaries that were translated into Greek in the Seleucid period.[18] Even studies that still assumed that amulets were "magic" found that the chants and prayers inscribed on amulets were not appreciably different from chants and prayers not usually labeled "magical" by scholars.[19] There would appear to be no good reason why amulets inscribed with Homeric verses or standard angelic and divine

---

17. For a list of the published catalogs of these, see Gordon and Simon, "Introduction," 31nn91-93.

18. It has commonly been supposed that protective ritual practices were derived from and remained rooted in the nonliterate indigenous wise folk, herbalists, and diviners. This supposition may be rooted in the Western elite attitude toward peasants (*pagani*). The role of writing in the evolution of the lapidaries and of the herbalist tradition of classical Greece and of the lapidary tradition from the so-called high culture of the Near East, however, all suggest rather an elite cultural basis of such practice. Cf. Gordon and Simon, "Introduction," 40-42.

19. Kotansky, "Incantations and Prayers," 107-8: "the use of magic for protection." The conceptual muddle becomes impossible to maintain when Kotansky (121-22) writes of "prayers for salvation that seem embedded in an indisputably magical context" (labeled *Charm of Hekate Ereschigal against fear of punishment*, PGM 70:4-25).

names or well-known lines from Jewish (or Christian) Scripture should continue to be classified as "magic."

Katadesmoi and *defixiones* were another distinctive type of ritual practice. Because they were so aggressive, coercive, and self-serving – and appeared to rational, scientific moderns to be based in superstition, they attracted a great deal of attention and were labeled as "malign and aggressive magic" or "sorcery." But again there is no good reason to classify them as "magic." Brief, formulaic messages inscribed (or scratched) mainly on thin sheets of lead (or on ostraca, papyrus, gems, or bowls), pierced by a nail, and deposited in graves, springs, or other bodies of water, were surreptitiously deployed by individuals against some private or public rival or enemy such as a lawyer or orator, or a chariot driver, or to coerce a desired woman. These so-called binding spells have now been analyzed, grouped into subtypes, and suggestively interpreted without recourse to the modern construct of magic. That problematic concept would only obscure their interpersonal functions as the spells became articulated with the wider social and political dynamics of a given city.[20]

Other widespread ritual practices included *hymns/chants* and *prayers* and the *mixing and administering of medicines*. These practices were very widespread, and only a fraction of them were attacked as harmful acts (*veneficia*) by those anxious, for example, that their crops were being "charmed away" or that they were being "poisoned."[21]

One of the most widespread and prominent kinds of ritual practice, especially in political circles, was *divination* by various means. Closely related or interrelated were astronomy/astrology, necromancy, soothsaying, dream interpretation, and interpretation of omens. Divination had been of great importance in the royal courts of the ancient Near East. Imperial regimes and subordinate temple-states maintained extensive staffs of highly trained scribes and priests who cultivated the traditional higher knowledge and rituals.[22] The official civil religion in the Greek *poleis* and in Rome had

---

20. Review of older and more recent investigations in Gordon and Simon, "Introduction," 14–30; and Gager, *Curse Tablets*.

21. Plato proposed a law against certain kinds of *pharmakeuein* (including chanting) that would be harmful, in which the perpetrator who was a skilled healer or herbalist would be punished more severely. But by no means were most chants, prayers, drugs, and other healing attacked or banned, much less attacked as magic.

22. In the Christian intensification of attacks on what had become defined as magic the learned Egyptian and Babylonian priests and scribes who cultivated divination and related practices became demonized in biblical (mis)translations that persist even in the

well-developed standard rituals for divination. As I discussed above, however, anxiety focused on dangerous private divination that might lead to subversive action. Perhaps because scholars of ancient "magic" also know about the importance of divination to ancient regimes, they have not labeled divination generally as "magic."

These results of studies of ancient ritual practices in the last two decades further confirm the conclusions reached in the review of the discussion of Jesus as engaged in "magic." The shift of focus to the discourse of magic is the confirmation as well as the result of the recognition that Greco-Roman references to "magic/magician" were polemical and accusatory and hence were not evidence of historical ritual practice. The explanation of the transformation of Egyptian religion under Roman rule confirms that the "magical papyri" of late antiquity were hardly good sources for the general practice of "magic" by "magicians" at the time of Jesus. Recent analyses of particular kinds of ritual practice without reference to the scholarly construct of ancient magic, not only illuminate these practices and their functions, but suggest that the synthetic concept only obscures social and political functions and contexts. Since the scholarly construct of ancient magic is without evidentiary basis and is problematic in various ways because of its roots in and continuing connotations of the Western concept of magic, it should simply be abandoned.[23] That construct never did pertain much to healing and exorcism, except in adaptation by scholars of Christian origins and of ancient Jewish religious practice.

Just as at least some classical scholars now feel free to discuss protective rituals and divination without the baggage of the concept of magic, so New Testament scholars may now be free to discuss the healings and

---

(N)RSV. In the book of Exodus (7:11; 8:7), Moses is engaged in competition with "sorcerers and magicians" with "their secret arts" (and ironically Moses is portrayed as performing the same magic tricks, only better). The key term translated "magician" (*hartom*) is borrowed from the Egyptian *hr tp*, "lector-priest" (that was not earlier associated with the *magoi*, as noted by Ricks, "Magician as Outsider," 135–36. In the book of Daniel, the Judean youth are trained, like all the other learned court functionaries, "in all the branches of wisdom, endowed with knowledge and insight," so as to be able to serve in the king's court (1:4). But the other court functionaries are then labeled "magicians and enchanters" and "sorcerers and Chaldeans" and diviners (Dan 1:20; 2:4; 5:7, 11). At least the translations leave intact the information that their sophisticated training in various forms of wisdom, knowledge, and understanding is so that they can interpret dreams, explain riddles, and solve problems.

23. See also the critical reflections on the term/concept of magic in J. Z. Smith, "Trading Places," and his suggestion that there is no reason to continue using it in scholarly discourse.

exorcisms of Jesus as healings and exorcisms—without the distortions of the modern concept of miracles and the modern scholarly construct of ancient magic, with its modern Western baggage.

PART 3

Jesus's Healings and Exorcisms

Introduction to Part 3

THE CRITICAL REVIEW OF modern scholarly constructs and ancient sources in the preceding chapters should clear the way for focusing on the stories of Jesus's healing and exorcism as stories of healing and exorcism. Once it is recognized that the concept of "miracle" is a construct of modern Western culture that is absent in the Gospels, there seems to be no justification for lumping healings and exorcisms together with other acts of power into such a category. Once it is recognized that the concept of "magic" is also a modern Western construct, then there seems little warrant for mistaking the rhetoric of "magic" as reference to the practice of "magic" or for categorizing a variety of different ancient ritual practices as "magic." The modern construct of ancient magic, especially as broadened by New Testament scholars, does not fit the healing and exorcism (stories) of Jesus.

How might the healing and exorcism stories of the Gospels appear if, instead of classifying them as "miracle" or "magic," we take them as stories of healing and exorcism? And how might the healings and exorcisms of Jesus appear if, instead of looking narrowly for hints of historicity, we attend broadly to the key interrelated features of the healing and exorcism episodes?

As I noted above, in the introduction to the book, the stories (separated by scholars) and isolated from the Gospels (which were assumed to have been mere containers) reinforced the narrow focus on the extraordinary (and supposedly supernatural) elements that led to the scholarly classification of healings and exorcisms as miracles. Jesus-interpreters have thus abstracted the healing and exorcism stories from the main (or only) sources that might offer indication of their social and meaning context. The increasing recognition by interpreters of the Gospels that they are sustained stories in an often carefully arranged sequence of episodes now offers a route to an alternative approach to the healing and exorcism stories, with two main features. (1) By gaining a sense of the overall portrayal of Jesus in interaction with followers and opponents in each Gospel story, it is possible to appreciate the importance and function of the healing and exorcism episodes. (2) Appreciation of the function of episodes in an overall story of Jesus's mission forces open a wider focus of investigation of the key features in the particular episodes, some of which figure again in other episodes.

In order to prepare the way for an alternative investigation of the episodes of healing and exorcism, it is thus necessary first to reconsider critically the Gospel sources and the appropriate approach to them, which will be the agenda of chapter 8. That will set up a provisional alternative exploration of the Gospel episodes of healing and exorcism in chapters 9 and 10, respectfully.

Admittedly this very limited procedure is a compromise, an attempt to work halfway between what has evidently been standard procedure, judging from solid and influential scholarly treatments, and the much farther-reaching rethinking called for by new researches in the field, which have serious implications for the context of and approach to the Gospels and the historical Jesus. More wide-ranging and precise studies of the historical situation of Roman Palestine, and more critical studies of contemporary Judean texts, have opened up a far more complex and precise sense of the political and cultural context in which Jesus operated and the Gospel stories emerged. New studies of the limited literacy, of scribal practice, and of the unstable (even chaotic) history of written texts have brought about grudging recognition that the Gospel sources were probably orally composed and orally performed, and that there was no change in the (in)stability of texts when they were written onto scrolls.[24]

The implications of all of these new researches will make it necessary to move ever more completely into a relational and contextual approach to historical figures in interaction and historical social-cultural context.[25] In order to remain in at least some viable conversation with what seems to have become the standard approach and interpretation of Jesus's healing and exorcism, however, the following investigation will examine each

24. On the political situation, see now Horsley, *Jesus and the Politics*; for cultural situation, see now Horsley, "Oral Communication"; and Horsley, *Text and Tradition*; Kelber, *Imprints, Voiceprints*; and Wire, *Case for Mark Composed*.

25. In another project I hope to develop the approach outlined in Horsley, *Jesus and the Politics*, taking into account recent work on Jesus's healing and exorcism such as Pilch, *Healing*, and Craffert, *Life*.

episode, only in the context or sequence of the Gospel story, rather than in categories and forms determined by modern scholarship. While focusing on particular episodes, what follows gives some passing attention to how certain features do not fit the modern concept of miracle or the scholarly construction of magic. The principal concern in examination of particular episodes, however, will be to discern their significant features as Jesus interacts with the sick and the spirit-possessed in the context of village communities.

8

The Gospel Stories as the Sources

Gospels, Not Gospel Fragments, as Sources

ONE OF THE FIRST and most fundamental steps in historical inquiry is to assess the character of the sources for the subject of the investigation, in this case the Gospels as the sources for the healings and exorcisms of Jesus. The standard approach in dealing with Jesus's healing and exorcism, as described briefly in the Introduction above is highly problematic. Interpreters of Jesus treat the Gospels not as the sources but as containers or collections of text-fragments that they take as the sources. They then make broad general formal classifications of those fragments into individual sayings and individual stories, lumping stories of healing and exorcism together with stories of "nature miracles" and "raisings of the dead" into the broad category of "miracle stories." Next, they ignore the advice of Rudolf Bultmann, the great pioneer of the form-critical procedure they are following, who concluded that there is "no great value in investigating more closely how much in the gospel miracle tales is historical."[1]

This procedure is problematic in two major ways. First, as I explained in part 1, they have classified the healing and exorcism stories into a modern concept that is inappropriate to stories and practices in antiquity. Indeed, the probing of each separate story for elements that go back to Jesus is a symptom of the skeptical modern worldview that categorizes reality

---

1. Bultmann, *Jesus*, 174.

into the natural and the miraculous and, having trouble believing that particular miracles could really have happened, attempts to salvage credible, reliable elements from the generally incredible stories.

Second, this procedure of focusing on individual sayings and stories separated from the supposed mere containers or collections of the Gospels is based on the assumption that such text-fragments somehow existed as isolated individual sayings and stories separate from some literary and social context in which they had meaning. That is, prior to their inclusion in (one or more of) the Gospels, they circulated separately, were transmitted or "passed down" from one individual to another in a vaguely conceived period of the "early church" following the crucifixion and resurrection. In a further refinement of form criticism now focused mainly on the form (separate from the function in a community context), interpreters of the historical Jesus attempt to discern and strip away the Gospel "writer's" touches and "fictional embellishments" and trace backwards the development of a story to establish its "original oral form" in hopes of finding "the details of a historical report."[2]

If we step back from what somehow became standard scholarly practice of classification of text fragments, however, it is difficult to imagine, as historians of a particular historical figure in human interaction and communication, how individual stories any more than individual sayings could have simply circulated or been transmitted as if in some ancient game of telephone. Neither the original form critics in the 1920s nor the interpreters of Jesus who have refined the procedure have offered evidence from the Synoptic Gospel tradition or comparative evidence that individual sayings or stories circulated or functioned separately. They have simply assumed this, and not offered justification for the assumption. As the original form critics themselves emphasized, but what was seemingly forgotten in the subsequent focus on form by itself, the synoptic tradition of Jesus's teaching and practice had contexts and functions in the life of communities of people. And it is difficult to imagine that an individual saying or story in isolation from other sayings or stories could have had any function in a community context.

---

2. Funk and the Jesus Seminar, *Acts*, 83, etc.; Meier, *Mentor*, repeatedly. In 1968 Hengel, *Charismatic Leader*, 3, expressing a commonly held view, stated that "progress in Synoptic research to a great extent depends on . . . detailed analysis of small units." See the telling criticism of detailed analysis of small units in Sanders, *Jesus and Judaism*, 133–39.

THE GOSPEL STORIES AS THE SOURCES

While interpreters of the historical Jesus have been refining the form-critical analysis of individual sayings and stories, however, colleagues who study the Gospels have long since recognized that they are not mere containers or collections of individual sayings and stories. Rather the Gospels are sustained stories of Jesus's mission, overall narratives with main plot and subplots. This means that what Jesus-scholars isolate as individual "miracle stories" were, rather, in their own proper literary context, component episodes of a sustained story.[3] In the first flush of (re)discovery that the Gospels are stories, interpreters tended to treat them like modern short fiction, applying concepts and questions developed in literary criticism of modern fiction (e.g., the concept of character development). More recently, Gospels have been analyzed as ancient stories composed and read (or heard) in the historical context in which they originated.[4]

Yet another problem with the standard procedure of isolating individual stories from their literary context is that it ignores the only possible indication of the meaning context in which the stories functioned. Insofar as the healing and exorcism stories are integral components of a developing overall Gospel story, they can only be approached as and understood in terms of the development of the story.[5] The Gospel of Mark, still by consensus understood as the earliest Gospel story, may be the most salient example. As I have argued strongly and at some length, the Gospel of Mark is a story of Jesus engaged in the renewal of the people of Israel in opposition to and opposed by the rulers of Israel. The episodes of healing and exorcism not only are integral to this story but carry the story forward for at least the first half of the narrative. The starting point (and meaning context) for use of these stories as sources for understanding Jesus's healing and exorcism is thus the overall story of Mark and the other Gospels' overall narratives and the function of the healing and exorcism stories in the Gospels' portrayals of his mission.

Contrary to the assumptions operative in much study of the historical Jesus, moreover, it is not at all clear that it is possible to move very far behind the Gospel stories to isolate some action that is somehow independent

---

3. See the pioneering analysis of Kelber, *Mark's Story*; Rhoads, Dewey, and Michie, *Mark as Story*; and the critical reflections in Moore, *Literary Criticism*.

4. See, for example, Horsley, *Hearing the Whole Story*.

5. A similar point is made by Alkier, "'For Nothing Will Be Impossible,'" 7-8—that rationalists from David Hume on, including form critics such as Theissen, fail to read particular stories with their "meaning generating relations to other parts of the macrotext," yet without attention to the overall Gospel story (of Luke).

of its portrayal in Gospel episodes. For example, it is often asserted that references to the fame of Jesus as a healer or the theme of faith as a factor in the healing are the contributions of the composers of one or more of the Gospel narratives. These are claimed to be independent of the fundamental form supposedly taken by the stories in their development before adaptation into the Gospel story. Are we to imagine that, in some form abstracted from real-life social interaction, the sick person just happens to come into the presence of the healer utterly independent of contingent social circumstances and processes (e.g., that the sick person had never heard of the healer and had no sense of what might happen)? In real-life social interaction that the form of the stories presupposes, the relation between the person seeking healing and the healer involve previous reputation and trust, even if it is not explicit in the story. The stories and the interaction they portray, moreover, include and assume a particular cultural context. Isolating so-called "miracle" stories from the sequences and broader narrative contexts that indicate the cultural patterns, however, leave them without social connections and cultural meaning.

For example, many societies have particular ways of dealing with skin lesions; the story of Jesus's declaring clean the man with skin lesions is more fully intelligible only in the context of the overall Gospel story of Jesus's conflict with the prerogatives claimed by the Jerusalem Temple. Whether the linking of the healing of the paralytic with the forgiveness of sins is attributed either to the interests of the early church or to memory of Jesus's conflict with the scribes and Pharisees and with a deeply ingrained pattern in Israelite culture, the link between healing and forgiving is unintelligible without the overall Gospel story and its rootage in Israelite culture.

Since the sustained stories of the Gospels constitute the starting point and provide the meaning context of the healings and exorcisms of Jesus, it is important to have a sense of those stories before considering the episodes of healing and exorcism that make up some of their components.

The Gospel of Mark

For much of the last century the Gospel of Mark was thought to revolve around "the messianic secret," with Jesus repeatedly ordering demons and others not to reveal who he is. It is only gradually disclosed that he is "the Messiah."[6] If there is such a secret in Mark, however, the story never gets

6. On the continuing debate, see the essays in Tuckett, *Messianic Secret*.

around to revealing it. Midway through the story, Peter does indeed declare that Jesus is "the messiah." After he then objects to Jesus's disclosure that "the son of man" must suffer and be killed, Jesus rebukes him sharply: "get behind me Satan." Jesus is at least rejecting Peter's understanding of the role, perhaps even rejecting the role altogether. In comparison with the Gospels of Matthew and John, portrayal of Jesus as an anointed king is conspicuous by its absence in the Gospel of Mark.

The Gospel has usually been understood as a story about discipleship, especially about the difficulties of being a faithful disciple of Jesus. And indeed the disciples' increasing misunderstanding of Jesus's mission and their eventual betrayal, denial, and abandonment is a prominent sub-plot in the story. But it is not the main plot.

If the main plot of the story indicates what the story is about primarily, then the Gospel of Mark focuses on Jesus's renewal of the people of Israel in opposition to and opposed by the rulers of the people.[7] Jesus proclaims the direct rule (kingdom) of God, but what that means is the renewal of the people. After being tested in the wilderness for forty days (like Elijah), Jesus calls and appoints twelve disciples (1:16-20), representatives of the people of Israel (in its traditional, symbolic twelve tribes). He then commissions them to extend his own mission of proclaiming the presence of God's rule and to cast out demons in the village communities of Galilee and beyond in manifestation of that rule (3:13-19). In the second main narrative step of the story, following the parables speech (4:1-34), Jesus performs two sequences of acts of power: sea crossings and feedings in the wilderness as had Moses, the founding prophet of Israel; and exorcisms and healings, reminiscent of the works of Elijah, the great prophet of renewal (chs. 5-8). As if the audience of the story had not already recognized that Jesus has assumed the prophetic role as the new Moses and the new Elijah, both figures appear transfigured with Jesus on the mountain (9:2-6). As he moves from Galilee up to Jerusalem, Jesus delivers new commandment-like pronouncements in a series of dialogues in which he cites most of the Ten Commandments, again appearing as a Moses-like prophet in renewal of the covenant (chs. 9-10).[8]

---

7. Fuller exploration in Horsley, *Hearing the Whole Story*.

8. The recognition that the Gospel of Mark—or as will become evident, all four Gospels—presents Jesus engaged in the renewal of the people of Israel is not to claim that this was Jesus's project. The reluctance of some scholars to entertain this possibility, however, such as the fellows of the Jesus Seminar (Funk and the Jesus Seminar, *Acts*, 86) has obvious roots in the assumptions and procedures of New Testament studies. For example, in

The episode of the Syrophoenician woman (6:24–30) and Jesus working in villages across the frontiers of Galilee under the political jurisdiction of Tyre and Caesarea Philippi indicate that the movement to which the Gospel is addressed is open to peoples other than those of Israelite heritage. But the Gospel of Mark gives no indication of any split between Israel and early Christianity. Jesus's mission is the renewal of the people of Israel, albeit a renewal open to other villagers.

It is striking in a fresh reading of the Gospel that the first half of story is composed largely of episodes of healings and exorcisms and of repeated summaries of how Jesus healed many who were sick and cast out many demons. Jesus commissions the disciples specifically to heal diseases and to cast out demons, as well as to proclaim. Jesus's renewal of the people is focused mainly on healing and exorcism, which are manifestations of God's direct rule.

Jesus's exorcism and healing in the renewal of the people, however, is threatening to the high-priestly rulers and their scribal and Pharisaic representatives, who "come down from Jerusalem" to Galilee to oppose him (3:22). Even the episodes of Jesus's conflicts with the scribes and Pharisees focus on or include healing and exorcism. Early in the story, the Pharisees conspire with the Herodians to destroy him (3:6), and the scribes charge him with "having Beelzebul," and "casting out demons by the ruler of demons" (3:22). Speaking in defense of the people's interests, Jesus condemns the scribes and Pharisees for making void the basic covenantal commandment of God in their attempt to divert to support of the Temple the resources needed for economic support of families (7:1–13). Finally Jesus marches boldly up to Jerusalem at the Passover celebration of the people's exodus liberation from bondage, where he engages in sustained confrontation with the rulers. Jesus carries out an obstructive prophetic demonstration against the Temple and tells a prophetic parable that condemns the high priests for oppression of the people (chs. 11–12). As the rulers lay a plan to arrest him, Jesus celebrates the Passover meal as a ceremony of covenant renewal

---

the standard Christian scheme of Christian origins, Jesus was a teacher-revealer to individuals who only after recognizing that he was resurrected formed a movement focused on him. Moreover, insofar as it is standard procedure in study of the historical Jesus to focus narrowly on individual sayings and individual stories, it is difficult in the extreme to imagine historically how they might have fit together. In Crossan, *Historical Jesus*, for example, the sayings come from an itinerant "Jewish Cynic sage" who addressed individuals; the "miracle stories" look back to a holy man who practiced magic on individuals; but suddenly the traditions about Jesus's eating suggest a social sharing of meals, at least with selected individuals.

(the blood of the cup being an allusion to the blood that bound God and the people in the original covenant ceremony on Sinai; ch. 14). The Roman governor crucifies him on the charge of being "the king of the Judeans": that is, leader of insurrection against the Roman imperial order. In what is known as its open ending, the Gospel suggests a continuation of the movement back up in "Galilee," where the disciples are instructed to meet Jesus (chs. 15–16).

The Gospel of Mark portrays Jesus as a prophet like Moses and Elijah, carrying out a renewal of Israel, manifested primarily in exorcisms and healings as well as in proclamation of the direct rule of God—in opposition to and opposed by the rulers of Israel.

The Gospel of Matthew

The Gospels of Matthew and Luke have most of same episodes that are in Mark and mostly in the same sequence, as has long been recognized. The scholarly consensus continues to hold that both knew and followed the Markan Gospel story. The Gospels of Matthew and Luke, however, are much longer and more complex insofar as they include large blocks of Jesus's teachings that do not appear in Mark, most of which they have in common, sometimes closely parallel or verbatim in wording.

These large blocks of prophetic teaching appear in shorter or longer speeches on particular concerns, evidently of the communities or movements to which they were addressed. It is commonly thought that in addition to following Mark's story, Matthew and Luke had a common source (Q for *Quelle*, the German term for "source"). As can be seen in how the parallel prophetic teaching on various subjects appears in Matthew and Luke, it seems clear that this source must have been not a mere collection of individual sayings but a series of prophetic speeches.[9] As is evident, for example, in the speeches on covenant renewal, in the sending of the disciples on mission into village communities, in the woes against the scribes and Pharisees, and in the prophetic condemnation of the Jerusalem ruling house, the agenda of this series of speeches appears to be the renewal of Israel in opposition to the Jerusalem rulers and their representatives. That is, in a series of prophetic speeches instead of in a narrative sequence of episodes, as in Mark, the teachings of Jesus in Matthew and Luke portray

9. Kloppenborg, *Formation of Q*; Horsley with Draper, *Whoever Hears*, 61–93; Robinson et al., *Critical Edition of Q*, lxii–lxvi.

Jesus as engaged in the renewal of the people in opposition to the rulers. Thus in the Gospels of Matthew and Luke, not only do the narratives as wholes focus on Jesus's renewal of Israel over against the rulers, but the speeches reinforce and strengthen this agenda.

The Gospel of Matthew, while following most of the Markan episodes, presents Jesus prominently as a teacher in five long speeches, beginning with the Sermon on the Mount. Seated on the mountain as the new Moses, Jesus delivers a programmatic speech of covenant renewal, a covenantal charter for the movement of renewal of Israel (Matthew 5–7). After each successive narrative step, Jesus again delivers speeches, sending the disciples out on mission, teaching in parables, instructing the movement in community discipline, and addressing future expectations (Matthew 10; 13; 18; 24–25). The prophetic speeches of Jesus in Matthew tend to make the conflict with the scribes and Pharisees more intense (esp. Matthew 23). And the prophetic renewal of covenant and instruction on community discipline make much more evident how Jesus is generating a renewal of the people of Israel in their common community life. More explicitly in Matthew than in Mark, Jesus's renewal of Israel is also the fulfillment of Israelite tradition and specifically of "what was spoken by the prophets."

The effect of the five long speeches might seem to be to lessen the importance of the healings and exorcisms, which are so prominent in the first narrative steps in Mark. Healings and exorcisms, however, compose the focus of the Gospel story in Matthew, particularly in the first narrative steps. These episodes are considerably simplified and shortened in Matthew, and some of the healing and exorcism episodes from Mark are missing in Matthew. But others are added. And the summary passages are stronger in Matthew.

Particularly striking in the Matthean narrative is the focus on healings and exorcisms at the beginning of Jesus's mission of renewal. The summary of Jesus's action that sets up the long covenant renewal speech has Jesus proclaiming the kingdom in the village assemblies but expands upon how his healing of every kind of sickness, including demon possession, leads to the spread of his reputation so that crowds of people from Galilee, the Decapolis, Jerusalem, Judea, and beyond the Jordan come to him bringing their sick (4:23–25). Then the Gospel concentrates most of the healing and exorcism episodes also found in the first two narrative steps of Mark (except the exorcism in the Capernaum assembly and the healing of the deaf-mute) and adds other episodes of healing and the exorcism of a demon that makes a man mute (chs. 8-9). This tour de force of healing and exorcism (summarized in 9:35), leads directly into Jesus's mission speech to the disciples. Significantly this begins not with instruction to preach, but with his giving the disciples "power over the unclean spirits, to cast them out, and to heal every illness and every sickness," that is, to extend what he has just been doing himself in the preceding narrative (10:1). The Gospel continues to focus on healing and exorcism following the mission speech (ch. 10), as Jesus affirms that he is indeed "the one who is to come" (11:3), as is evident in the healing of the blind, the lame, lepers, the deaf, and in the preaching of good news to the poor (11:2-6). After the Matthean narrative again follows the Markan episodes of eating on the Sabbath, healing on the Sabbath, and a summary of healing ("he healed them all": Matt 12:1-8, 9-14, 15; cf Mark 2:23-28; 3:1-6; 7-12) comes the declaration that the healings are done in fulfilment of what was spoken through the prophet Isaiah. The ensuing narrative includes the exorcism of the Canaanite woman's daughter (15:21-28), that of the possessed "epileptic" (17:14-21), and the healing of two blind people (20:29-34). In a special touch not found in the other Gospels, Matthew has Jesus continue his healing in the Temple (21:14), after he marches up into Jerusalem for his sustained confrontation with the rulers. The Matthean narrative has Jesus's renewal of the people focus as much on healings and exorcisms as on covenant renewal and community discipline.

The Gospel of Matthew, like the Markan story, gives no indication of any split or separation between Israel undergoing renewal and early Christianity. Only at the very end of the story does Jesus give the command to make disciples of all peoples (28:19). Otherwise the mission of Jesus and the disciplines throughout the story is the renewal of ("the lost sheep of the house of") Israel (10:6; 15:24), and the story is addressed to a movement of the renewal of Israel.

The Gospel of Luke

The Gospel of Luke also repeats and reinforces the same story found in Mark, of Jesus engaged in a renewal of the people of Israel in opposition to and opposed by the rulers. While Luke has much of Jesus's teaching in somewhat the same sequence as Matthew, the Gospel has Jesus deliver a few key speeches, such as the covenant renewal, in the narrative of his activity in Galilee, then presents shorter Jesus-speeches (than in Matthew) as episodes in a long journey that Jesus makes from Galilee to Jerusalem for the climactic confrontation with the rulers. As in Matthew so in Luke Jesus acts and proclaims (explicitly so) in the role of a prophet throughout his mission of renewal, while (by contrast with Mark) being identified also as the messiah, son of David, in the infancy narratives. More explicitly than Mark's story, the Gospel of Luke presents the mission of Jesus, not only as the renewal of Israel, but as the fulfilment of Israelite tradition and expectations, beginning with the infancy narratives and repeatedly in the story.

The Gospel, however, works from the perspective of a movement that has spread further into the Roman imperial world and looks back and from outside Roman Palestine. While nearly all of Jesus's action and teaching takes place in Galilee or on the long journey from Galilee to Judea, the Gospel is oriented to Judea and Jerusalem in ways that Mark and Matthew are not (although not as much as John). And while Jesus's mission is the renewal of Israel in opposition to the rulers, it seems clear, as indicated early in the narrative in Acts, that the Gospel story is being spread (and addressed) "to the ends of the earth" (Acts 1:8) Yet no less than in Mark and Matthew, in Luke Jesus carries out his renewal of Israel in dramatic opposition to and opposed by the rulers and their representatives.

As in Matthew, healings and exorcisms compose the focus of Jesus's activity in the first steps of the Gospel story in Luke. In a broad parallel of narrative sequence, moreover, Luke has Jesus's healings and exorcism lead up to his covenant speech (4:31—6:19; 6:20–49), then further healings and exorcism lead directly to the (first) mission speech (7:1—8:56; 9:1–6). In these narrative steps Luke includes all of the episodes from Mark's first two narrative steps except the second sequence of five "acts of power," and includes also two additional healings. Healing episodes (blind Bartimaeus and three distinctive to Luke) continue, though less frequent, in the long journey narrative. While healing power is not any more prominent in particular episodes in Luke than in Mark or Matthew, it seems somewhat more prominent generally. Jesus enters his mission in Galilee "in the power of the Spirit," the healing of the paralytic is prefaced by Jesus coming with "the power of the Lord to heal," and in one summary, when people were trying to touch him, "power came forth from him and healed them all" (4:14; 5:17; 6:19).

The Gospel of John

The Gospel of John has been understood as a spiritual Gospel, as heavily theological, and hence is downplayed as a source for the historical Jesus. More than the other Gospels and with tragic historical effects in Christian hostility to Judaism, John's story of Jesus has been (mis)read as a Christian text that portrays Jesus in opposition to and opposed by the Jews and Judaism. It is crucial therefore to recognize at the outset that "the Judeans" (*hoi ioudaioi*) in John, contrary to many standard translations (such as the NRSV) should not be translated as "the Jews." The Gospel of John, like the near-contemporary Judean historian Josephus, refers to the people of Israelite heritage in Roman Palestine by the region in which they live: *hoi ioudaioi* in Judea, *hoi samareitai* in Samaria, and *hoi galilaioi* in Galilee. Many Judeans in John's story come to "trust in" or become "loyal to" Jesus ("believe in" is an inadequate translation).[10] But the Gospel frequently uses "the Judeans" in reference to the high priests and Pharisees, the rulers of the Judeans in Jerusalem.

As these and other passages indicate, the dominant conflict in John's story is between Jesus (and those Galileans, Samaritans, and especially Judeans who trust in him), on the one hand, and the rulers of the Judeans based in the Temple in Jerusalem, on the other. In a conflict more sustained than in the other Gospels, John's story has Jesus repeatedly go up to Jerusalem at the time of one of "the festivals of the Judeans" where he confronts or is confronted by the high priests and Pharisees, a.k.a. "the (rulers of the) Judeans." In a sequence of these confrontations in Jerusalem, John's story portrays Jesus, who is a Galilean, working in all areas of Israelite heritage. Not only Galileans, but also Samaritans, people in the Transjordan, and especially large numbers of Judeans come to "trust in" or become "loyal to" him (4:1; 6:60–66; 8:31; 9:27–28; 15:8). Jesus is thus clearly leading a renewal movement of the people of Israel in opposition to the rulers based in Jerusalem.[11]

The Gospel of John has previously been thought to have drawn upon and elaborated a so-called signs gospel, a chain of miracle stories (often associated with the sequence(s) of "miracle stories" detected in the Mark narrative (esp. in 4:35—8:26). But John's story makes no mention of exorcism

---

10. In the context of Roman imperial rule, the Greek term *pistis*, like the Latin *fides*, meant political loyalty, as in being loyal to one's patron or to the imperial lord.

11. See the fuller explanation in Horsley and Thatcher, *John, Jesus*.

and has only three healings, only one of which is called a sign, while the other two function mainly as springboards for some of Jesus's confrontations with the rulers in Jerusalem: the recovery of the royal officer's son from a fever (4:46–54), the disabled man's becoming whole/healthy on the Sabbath (5:2–9), and Jesus's "opening the eyes" of a man blind from birth (9:1–7). Nevertheless, the Gospel story repeatedly states that Jesus did numerous signs, and it is clear that many of those involved healing the people (e.g., 6:2). Indeed, as the narrative states repeatedly, it was because of such signs that so many people trusted in Jesus and joined his movement, finally leading the Jerusalem rulers to arrest him and turn him over to the Roman governor for crucifixion.

9

Healing Episodes

THE HEALINGS OF JESUS as represented in the Gospels are healings. They are not miracles and not magic. It is inappropriate even to conclude that the healing episodes in the Gospels include elements or techniques of magic.

The examination of healing stories here will include those in all of the canonical Gospels. Insofar as the consensus is holding among Gospel scholars that Matthew and Luke both knew the Gospel of Mark and included most of his episodes, mostly in the same order; and insofar as exorcism and healing episodes make up so much of the Gospel story in Mark, most attention will go to the healing episodes in the Markan narrative context.

Healings in the First Narrative Step in the Gospel of Mark

As I summarized in the previous chapter, the Gospel of Mark portrays Jesus as generating a movement of renewal of the people of Israel in their village communities in opposition to and opposed by the rulers and their scribal and Pharisaic representatives. What often passes unnoted is that in the first half of the story, in its first two major narratives steps (1:16—3:35 and 4:35—8:26), exorcisms and healings, not only dominate, but compose the substance of the developing story.

In the first narrative step come an almost programmatic exorcism episode followed by three healings; then another healing, interwoven with several summaries of the healing and exorcism; opposition from the scribes and Pharisees, who find the implications threatening to the established order; and Jesus's appointment of the Twelve to extend his mission of exorcism and proclamation; followed by his refutation of casting out demons by the ruler of demons; and closing with his recognition of the followers as a familial, covenantal community. The healings, set up by the exorcism, compose the substance of Jesus's renewal of Israel, which is so threatening to the representatives of the high-priestly rulers. Examination of the particular episodes in sequence can help us discern how and why.

Healing Simon's Mother-in-Law (1:30–31)

The first healing in this Gospel story is simple indeed. In the house of Simon and Andrew, with James and John, the disciples tell Jesus of Simon's mother-in-law's fever. He "took her by the hand and lifted her up ... and the fever left" (1:29–31). The disciples are evidently already aware of the healing power working through Jesus. His gestures enact the healing.

Meanwhile, as indicated in the two summaries that follow (1:32–34, 39), word has spread widely about his healing and exorcism "with authority." His fame and the people's trust are implicit in the summary: "they brought him all who were sick or possessed with demons ... and he healed ... and cast out ..." But of course this is his mission of renewal: "proclaiming the message in their assemblies and casting out demons."

Healing and Declaring Clean the Man with Skin Lesions (1:40–45)

To perpetuate the terms *leprosy* and *leper* in translation and interpretation of this episode is misleading since the Greek term *lepra* did not mean what is known today as leprosy. Like its Hebrew counterpart, *sara'at*, the Greek word was a general term for various skin lesions.

According to the purity code of the Judean temple-state (Leviticus 13–14), several kinds of skin lesions made a person impure, as determined by a priest's examination, and the person was (temporarily) excluded from normal social interaction. It is assumed that some of these lesions would gradually heal, in which case a priest might declare the person clean again. The required sacrifice specified for such purification was two unblemished male lambs and an unblemished year-old ewe lamb, plus an offering of cereal and oil, from which sacrifices the priest would purify the person while retaining possession of the meat. Few families would have possessed such resources. If the (healed) leper could not afford so much, the reduced rate was one male lamb and two turtledoves or pigeons—still a serious cost for a poor family. Considering that scrolls including such law codes, like literacy itself, were limited mainly to scribes (and priests), it is difficult to know how the regulations of purification would have been applied—particularly in Galilee, which was a considerable distance from Jerusalem.

The episode in Mark assumes that the man with skin lesions has become viewed as unclean and is excluded from normal social interaction, hence his (trusting!) appeal to Jesus, "If you choose (will) to do so, you can make (declare) me clean." His appeal suggests that he has already heard of Jesus's reputation as a healer and appeals to him in the confidence that Jesus has the authority/power to declare him clean. The trust of the person seeking healing is an important factor in this and other episodes in the Gospels, whether or not it is explicitly highlighted; the healings are relational-in-context: having heard of the powers operative through him, people come to Jesus with the trust that he can heal them.

In the episode Jesus stretched out his hand, touched him, and said "I do choose, 'Be (made) clean!'" The next sentence, "Immediately the skin lesion left him and he was made clean," indicates that Jesus's declaration that he was clean was also a healing. Jesus's action in the healing/cleansing is twofold: it includes both the touch and a declaration in simple performative speech. In addition to including Jesus's touch and declaration, the episode suggests no supernatural agency (i.e., God's) in the healing and hence does not fit the modern scholarly definition of a miracle (story). Amid the general lack of evidence for the concrete practice of what modern scholars call "magic" in ancient sources, however, and the rarity of healing in the "magical papyri" (the prime source for the modern scholarly construction of "magic"), it seems quite inappropriate to label Jesus's touch as a "characteristic magical technique."[1]

Of considerable significance for understanding the Markan story and Gospel portrayal of Jesus, by contrast, is the political conflict integral to this episode.[2] Jesus's declaration that the man is clean is an alternative to (hence a challenge to) the prerogatives assumed by the temple-state to declare unclean or clean, that is, to exclude or include people in normal social interaction. (Note the repeated "cleanse/cleansing" [*katharizo/katharismos*] through the episode.) In Israelite tradition where healing is prescribed, it is done by a prophet, not a priest (2 Kings 5). Priests might diagnose, but

---

1. Crossan, *Historical Jesus*, 323, claims that "touch was a characteristic magical technique used by Jesus," which he would have used when confronted by a leper.
2. Discerned by Crossan in ibid., 323, and by many others.

prophets heal (1 Kgs 17:17–24; 2 Kgs 4:17–37; 30:7 // Isa 38:2). In healing and declaring clean of the man with skin lesions, Jesus is not only acting in the role of a prophet but also assuming the prerogatives of priests in the Temple. The opposition to and by the temple-state in this episode is not explicit, as it is in the next two healing episodes. But once interpreters are no longer attempting to construct Jesus as loyal to the Temple or as aiming at (mere) reform of the temple-state, then it is clear that his instruction to the newly cleansed man to "show himself to the priest, and offer for [his] cleansing what Moses commanded" is meant to be "a testimony to (against) them." That is, it is a demonstration against what the temple-state demands—with its law codes that guard the prerogatives of the Temple, and priests that further drain away resources from the people. The alternative reading of "snorting with anger" in place of "moved with pity" (1:41) suggests further that he was angry at the temple-state's exclusionary law code. In reaction, Jesus's healing-and-declaration that the man was clean brought him back into the society, back into normal social interaction with others, in pointed opposition to the temple-state's (attempted) control of the people.

The Healing of the Paralytic and Forgiveness of Sins (2:1–12)

The healing of the paralytic picks up just where the healing of the man with skin lesions concludes, as Jesus's declaration that he is clean reintegrates him into the community: the paralytic is being carried by a remarkably supportive network of relatives and friends. Their bold action in lowering the paralytic into the presence of Jesus in (the house of) his apparent home base in Capernaum dramatizes the deep trust they have in the healing that is working through Jesus. Far from this or other healings of Jesus being discrete (individual) acts by an individual practitioner that fit the modern construction of "magic,"[3] they are relational events that happen in interaction. In this case the interaction is not simply between the person seeking healing and Jesus, but also between the sick person, his wider circle of supporters, and Jesus, to whom they come with trust. Jesus heals in response to, enabled by, their trust. Thus the healing of the paralytic also does not fit the modern scholarly understanding of "miracle," insofar as it gives no hint of a special intervention by God.

3. Cf. ibid., 324.

While Jesus both (reached out and) touched the man with skin lesions and declared him clean, to the paralytic he simply declared, "Son, your sins are forgiven." This is an act of performative speech that enacts what it pronounces, as when a judge declares someone innocent of charges. Interpreters who are still proceeding from form criticism emphasize that this episode is a composite of a healing story and of a controversy story (that has been inserted into it). Some even conclude that the controversy about the forgiveness of sins reflects "the interests of the later Christian community."[4] Regardless of whether the controversy story and the healing story are analytically separable in the composition history of the Gospel, however, sin and sickness were not separable in the Israelite culture in which both the Gospel and Jesus were rooted. This can be seen, not just in the Gospel of Mark more widely and elsewhere in the Gospel tradition, but as the result of the use (and abuse) of the Mosaic covenant, the center of Israelite tradition.

Inherent in several key texts in the books later included in the Hebrew Bible, scholars have discerned a certain distinctive cultural pattern. In Yahweh's giving of the Mosaic covenant through Moses on Mount Sinai (Exodus 20; Deuteronomy 5), the covenant renewal ceremony led by Joshua (Joshua 24), and the overall structure of the book of Deuteronomy, are three interrelated components: a declaration of God's deliverance of the people in the exodus, God's demands of the people to keep the commandments, and (as a sanction) a declaration of blessings for compliance and curses for disobedience, which would endure for several generations. The prophets pronounced God's sentence (punishment) against kings and their officers for oppressing the people in violation of the commandments. Most prominently in the Judean texts later included in the Hebrew Bible, the Babylonian conquest was interpreted as God's just punishment for the violation of the covenant commandments (this is particularly poignant in Jeremiah). The sense of guilt was so overpowering that Jeremiah and (Second) Isaiah attempted to alleviate it in prophecies, of a new covenant "written on the heart," and of a fresh start in a new exodus (Jer 31:27–34; Isaiah 40). The scribes and priests serving in the Judean temple-state, however, made the blessings and curses that had functioned as sanctions on covenant keeping into an effective means of social control. Misfortunes such as poverty and sickness were interpreted as or taken as God's punishment for violation of the covenant commandments. In particular, sickness was

---

4. Funk and the Jesus Seminar, *Acts*, 64.

taken as punishment for sins—for one's own sins or the sins of the parents. Correspondingly, one could be healed only by repentance and appeal to Yahweh. As the learned scribe Jesus ben Sira declared,

> My child, when you are ill, . . . do not delay,
> > but pray to the Lord, and he will heal you.
> Give up your faults . . .
> > and cleanse your heart from all sin. (Sir 38:9–10)

In effect, the Mosaic covenant was interpreted such that the people blamed themselves for sickness or other misfortune. This understanding of sickness as the result of sin is what is presupposed and addressed in the healing of the paralytic. The same self-blame and social-blame for sickness and physical disability is presupposed and addressed in the account of Jesus's healing in John 9, following the disciples' question: "Who sinned, this man or his parents, that he was born blind?"

In declaring to the paralytic, "Son, your sins are forgiven," Jesus was addressing this direct relation between his paralysis and the debilitating self-blame that overlaid it and perhaps underlay it as well. In responding to the man's and his supportive friends' trust, the healer gave the man, along with the crowd, a new lease on life. No longer expending so much life-energy in self-blame and self-control amid difficult circumstances, the paralytic could be released from the (complex) paralysis and be restored to wholeness in his family and community. The dialogue with the scribes serves to drive home what is implicit in Jesus's declaration, unspoken but understood because of the cultural assumption shared by all. Jesus's response makes it explicit that saying, "Your sins are forgiven" is tantamount to saying, "Stand up, take your mat, and walk"—except of course that the first is more radical: it gets to the root of the debilitating personal and social self-blame. Moreover, the scribes' objection (their charge that Jesus is committing blasphemy because God alone can forgive sins), channeled through the Temple and priestly prerogatives, exposes their own role and program of social control through the ideology that sickness is due to sins. Like the previous episode, only now quite explicit, the healing involved the conflict between the temple-state and the people.

Jesus's concluding statement that "the son of man has authority/power to forgive sins in effect escalates this conflict. After sustained scholarly debate about the meaning of the phrase "the son of man" it has become clear that even if this is a self-reference by Jesus in the Gospel of Mark, it is also a reference to humanity or people in general. If this is somehow insufficiently explicit in the Markan episode, it is made clear in the Matthean version of this same episode. There the crowds "glorified God, who had given such authority/power to human beings/people." In stating that people have the authority to forgive sins Jesus is also rejecting the authority of the temple-state.

Healing of the Man with a Withered Hand (3:1–6)

The episode of the healing of the man with a withered hand does not fit either the modern scholarly construction of magic or the modern scholarly definition of miracle story. The healing is not an individual action, but happens in a local village assembly (which is what *synagoge* means in the Gospels), that is in the midst of a gathering of the whole community on a Sabbath (as in the first exorcism episode). Moreover, while Jesus takes the initiative, he does not do or even say anything to effect the healing: no touch or other action and no declaration or command other than "Stretch out your hand."[5]

While recent interpreters recognize that this episode exhibits marks of a broader plot in the Gospel of Mark, they presume to separate a "miracle story" from "Markan redaction." They thus find "Mark's enhancement of Jesus as 'Son of Man/Adam and Lord'" as a "Christian overlay superimposed on the material" and take the legal dispute over Sabbath observance to be a projection of the "Christian concerns of the early church."[6] While recognizing the coherence of the narrative from Mark 2:12 through 3:6 in its focus on disputes between Jesus and the scribes and Pharisees over issues of healing and food, they do not attend to the overall plot of the Gospel that represents Jesus and his movement in unrelenting conflict with the temple-state, represented by the scribes and Pharisees in the narrative of his mission in Galilee. Interpreters find nothing in this "miracle story" that would warrant the conspiracy against Jesus to which the healing leads. But that may be largely because, besides not taking the Gospel whole in its overall plot, Christian interpreters still take the dispute about Sabbath observance as reflecting Christian concerns. In the overall story of the Gospel, however, a division between Judaism and Christianity has not yet appeared. Rather, as I discussed in chapter 8, the Gospel portrays Jesus engaged in a

5. As both Meier, *Mentor*, 682; and Funk and the Jesus Seminar, *Acts*, 69, recognize.
6. Funk and the Jesus Seminar, *Acts*, 69; Meier, *Mentor*, 682.

renewal of Israel in opposition to and opposed by the (primarily Judean) rulers and their representatives. Jesus's healings, like his exorcism, are principal manifestations of the renewal of the people over against their rulers. In the sequence of episodes beginning with the healing of the man with skin lesions, the episode of the man with the withered hand makes explicit what is happening in the many healings and exorcisms that are generating such crowds: that is, the renewal of the people that is so threatening to the rulers that their representatives in Judea (Pharisees) as well as in Galilee (Herodians) conspire to destroy Jesus.

Interpreters are also puzzled that in the healing of the man with the withered hand Jesus does not seem to do anything that would violate the Judean prohibitions against working on the Sabbath. But the violation of particular prohibitions is less the issue than the general conflict over Sabbath observance articulated in Jesus's rhetorical question. As should be evident by now in the sequence of episodes—in contrast with the modern separation (for example) of religion or medical practice from politics, economic production and consumption—(Jesus in) the Gospel of Mark does not separate sickness and healing from other aspects of the people's life. Just as sickness and sin, healing and forgiveness, and individual and social bodies are integrally interrelated, so hunger and paralysis are interrelated with observance of the Sabbath. Since the Sabbath was made for people, its observance should not diminish human life but should enhance life. This is the point Jesus makes in the question, "is it lawful to do good or to do harm on the sabbath, to save life or to kill?"[7] Jesus's discourse following his healing of the sick or weak man on the Sabbath in John 5:1–24 makes the same point with considerable elaboration, so it was not idiosyncratic to the Jesus movement in Mark.

Healings in the Second Narrative Step of the Gospel of Mark

In the second narrative step, which follows Jesus's speech in parables, the Gospel of Mark's focus on healings and exorcisms is even more striking (4:35—8:26). The narrative further develops the overall plot of the Gospel, as Jesus continues the renewal of Israel in opposition to and opposed by the rulers of Israel: He commissions the twelve disciples to extend his own

---

7. Thus the rhetorical question in 3:4 is not designed for this particular story only, vs. Funk and the Jesus Seminar, *Acts*, 69.

mission of preaching and exorcism and healing, the prophet John's execution by Herod Antipas prefigures his own execution, and he condemns the scribal and Pharisaic representatives from Jerusalem for violating the basic Mosaic covenantal commandment of God. The episodes of exorcism and healing in this narrative step are integral components of two similar sequences of five "(acts of) power(s)" (*dynameis*) into which these other episodes have been inserted, along with two summaries of his healings or acts of power: sea crossing, exorcism, healing, healing, wilderness feeding.[8] Just as the sea crossings and wilderness feedings are allusions to actions of Moses, the founding prophet of Israel, so the healings are allusions to the actions of Elijah, the great prophet of renewal. Even prior to the recognition of narrative in the Gospels as stories, interpreters had concluded that some healing and exorcism stories were told in such sequences of acts of power prior to or separate from the composition of the Gospel of Mark. This suggests that healing and exorcism stories should not necessarily be taken as separate stories that had been circulating independently. At least some may have been told and retold (not just circulating) as integral components of narratives of Jesus as a prophet like Moses and Elijah, engaged in renewal of Israel. This is certainly the significance the healing and exorcism episodes carry in the narrative of the Gospel of Mark.

In widely read studies of the historical Jesus, however, it was virtually standard that interpreters found elements of "magic" in the healing "miracles" of these sequences. This makes all the more important a critical review and alternative reading of the healing episodes in the second narrative step of the Gospel of Mark.

The Healing of the Hemorrhaging Woman (5:24–34)

As it is usually explained, the episode of the hemorrhaging woman is interwoven with (sandwiched into) the episode of the young woman in the Markan narrative. In their treatment of other healing stories both Meier and Funk often attend to the narrative sequence in the Gospel of Mark. In their respective analyses of these healing episodes, however, in pursuing the standard agenda of isolating the individual stories from the Gospel context,

---

8. These sequences of five stories may have existed prior to the development of the longer Markan story as forms in which Jesus's acts of power were recited in communities of the Jesus movement(s). See the delineation of such "chains" in Achtemeier, "Toward the Isolation"; Achtemeier, "Origin and Function."

they no longer give attention to the narrative sequence. They consequently miss aspects of these stories that separately as well as together convey the deeper and broader significance of these healings, as will emerge in an alternative analysis.

In order to approach these two interwoven episodes it is necessary to lay to rest two misunderstandings that have blocked understanding: the Christian misunderstanding of Jewish purity codes that supposedly stigmatized women, and the imposition of the modern concept of magic.

Meier believes that the woman's hemorrhage would have been "a constant source of ritual impurity according to laws of Leviticus." Hence her touching Jesus "would constitute the brazen act of a ritually unclean woman communicating her uncleanness to a holy man."[9] Funk and the Jesus Seminar find it "surprising" that the story makes no mention of the woman's ritual condition (citing Lev 15:19–25) or that she defiled Jesus with her touch. They find nevertheless that her touching Jesus "must have been considered brazen," the breaking of "a social taboo."[10] In Christian theological interpretation of Jesus and the Gospels in opposition to (the Christian theological construction of) Judaism, it has been standard to understand the hemorrhaging woman, and women generally, as stigmatized by Jewish purity codes and ritual regulations. Such interpretation has involved a serious misunderstanding of what the purity codes were about.[11] In ancient Judea, purity regulations pertained to sacred rituals in the Temple and hence were particularly important for priests. Most ordinary people would have been in a condition of impurity much or most of the time. But the rules in Lev 15:19–30 do not suggest that menstruating women were socially ostracized, excluded from normal social interaction in household and village. Not only does the episode of the hemorrhaging woman give no indication that impurity is an issue, but purity codes that pertained to sacred rituals in the Temple in Jerusalem would not have been applicable to life in Galilean villages.[12]

The second major block to understanding the episode of the hemorrhaging woman is the imposition of the modern construction of ancient

9. Meier, *Mentor*, 709, with no notes or references, which is unusual for him.

10. Funk and the Jesus Seminar, *Acts*, 81.

11. See further Levine, "Discharging Responsibility"; Kraemer, "Jewish Women," 65–66; D'Angelo, "(Re)Presentation," 140; Cohen, "Menstruants."

12. The citation of the Temple Scroll found in the priestly-scribal community at Qumran in Funk and the Jesus Seminar, *Acts*, 81, hardly seems pertinent to stories that arose from life in Galilean villages.

magic. Indeed, as Meier comments, this story is the "star witness" for those who find magic in Jesus's healings and/or elements of magic in the healing stories.[13] Both Funk and Meier exemplify such interpreters. "The reference to power being drained out of Jesus moves the story into the realm of magic."[14] In an ironic projection of the modern scholarly construction, Meier suggests that the woman's belief that "she must physically touch Jesus' cloak" derives from "popular religious ideas that smack of magic." Similarly, the story's portrayal of Jesus as sensing "power streaming from his body" attributes "a magical conception of miracle-working" to him.[15] The function of the final statement about the woman's faith is thus supposedly to "deflect the magical tone of the story."[16] That neither Funk and the Jesus Seminar nor Meier offer any references suggests that touching and power flow had become standard motifs in the modern scholarly construction of ancient magic—a construction simply assumed in interpretation of "miracle stories."[17]

The Markan episode of the hemorrhaging woman's healing is different from other healing stories in the Gospels. The description of the prolonged severity of the woman's condition is more elaborate than that of sicknesses in the other stories. While the persons seeking healing and/or the relatives or friends take initiative in other stories, the hemorrhaging woman takes bolder and more deliberate initiative. In other healing stories, Jesus performs the healing by declaration and/or gesture. By contrast, the healing of the hemorrhaging woman happens through her own aggressive action, while Jesus himself is passive (compare what might be thought of as a correction in Matt 13:21–22, where Jesus speaks before the woman is healed). She herself prescribes how her healing will happen: "If I but touch his clothes I will be made well." And she is right: "Immediately her hemorrhage stopped." She herself, moreover, offers the confirmation of the healing: "She felt in her body that she was healed of her affliction" (*not* "disease"). While Jesus was aware that power had gone forth from him, it was only from the healed woman that he learned of the healing. While other healing stories

---

13. Meier, *Mentor*, 709.
14. Funk and the Jesus Seminar, *Acts*, 81.
15. Meier, *Mentor*, 709.
16. Or its "magical aura" (Meier, *Mentor*, 709).
17. It is puzzling that, after noting how frequent touching is in the healing stories of Jesus and even reifying "touching therapy" as "almost universal in its practice," Funk and the Jesus Seminar, *Acts*, 80–81, nevertheless take the flow of healing energy that goes with it as somehow "magic."

end with onlookers expressing amazement, with the healed person dismissed, and with the healer's fame spreading, this episode closes only with Jesus's confirmation of what the woman already knows: that it was through her trust in the power working through Jesus that she was healed.

Of all the healing episodes, this is the one that most invites, indeed demands, an analysis and interpretation of the importance of the woman's *trust* (faith) and of the role of trust in the healings generally. Funk and the Jesus Seminar reduce the trust/faith to "Mark's own interpretive touch," and Meier takes Jesus's comment about faith as a way of deflecting the magical tone of the story.[18] It is striking, however, that Jesus does not perform, enact, or declare the healing in this case. Healing happens because the woman trusts that it will happen. She had clearly already become aware that healing power was working through Jesus. This healing power, however, was not something that Jesus himself possessed.[19] The healing power working through Jesus, like the healings portrayed in Gospel episodes, was relational. The episodes portray people coming to Jesus expecting healing and trusting that healing can happen, even by touching his garment. The episode of the hemorrhaging woman is the most dramatic portrayal of how the healings were relational—based on a relationship of fame and trust between Jesus, the person seeking healing, and on the network of friends and family who had also heard and who also trusted in the healing power.

The Healing of the Twelve-Year-Old Woman (5:21–24, 35–43)

One of those was the father of the twelve-year-old woman in the interconnected episode. In previous translation and interpretation, he was often misunderstood as a Jewish "ruler," a wealthy and powerful figure. But it is now clear that although an *archon* was a "ruler" (Matt 9:18 has *archon*), an *archisynagogos* was one of the leaders of a local assembly (just as an *archilestes* was a local bandit-chieftan). In the village context in which Mark's Jesus is working, the father was a local leader in the village society in which the people (of Israel) were embodied. Striking in the opening of the episode

---

18. Funk and the Jesus Seminar, *Acts*, 81; Meier, *Mentor*, 709; but neither includes a discussion of faith/trust in treatment of this paradigmatic story of trust.

19. Funk and the Jesus Seminar, *Acts*, 81 offers an unwarranted translation ("power had drained out of him") and peculiar conceptualization of the healing power, as if it belonged to Jesus, was "a limited fund," and the woman somehow "robbed him of power."

is his trust: when he came to Jesus, he fell at his feet, begging him repeatedly to come lay hands on his daughter who was at the point of death.

Funk and the Jesus Seminar find that several features have been added to the story "to heighten the miracle."[20] But this episode, like other healing episodes, does not portray a healing that fits the modern scholarly understanding of "miracle." And the story lowers rather than heightens the stakes. As is often pointed out, the episode begins with a request for healing. A head of a local village assembly begs Jesus to lay hands on his daughter, who, he says, is at the point of death. After Jesus is interrupted on his way by the bold action of the hemorrhaging woman, people from the man's house report that his daughter has died. As Jesus arrives to find the commotion of mourning underway, however, he insists that the child is not dead but sleeping. The episode continues as a healing of the young woman at the point of death, not a raising from the dead. Jesus simply took her by the hand and told her to "get up." The episode gives not a hint of any supernatural force or agency. Rather it reinforces the importance of the human relationship involved in again emphasizing the trust of those seeking healing. As he arrives at the local leader's house, Jesus reinforces the trust that he has already exhibited in begging Jesus to come lay hands on his daughter. Overhearing those who were convinced the girl was dead, Jesus insisted "Do not fear; only trust."[21]

Funk and the Jesus Seminar also find that the Aramaic phrase *talitha koum* ("Little girl, get up.") is reported as though it were a magical formula.[22] As is reported about Jesus and other healers in antiquity, commands in performative speech and actions as performative gestures were instrumental in their healings. In the mix of cultures and languages under the Roman Empire, moreover, the perpetuation of such performative speech in its original language carried an aura that enhanced its effectiveness, perhaps particularly among those for whom it was a foreign (exotic) language. Such foreign words and phrases can be found here and there in the "magical papyri," but they are simply typical of the wider interaction of cultures and languages (discussed in ch. 3, above).

20. Funk and the Jesus Seminar, *Acts*, 83.

21. Not only "believe/belief" but even "faith" is an inadequate translation of *pisteuein/pistis* in modern Western individualistic culture. In the Roman imperial order *pistis/fides* included a political dimension, hence "(exclusive) loyalty to," such that people's loyalty to Jesus meant that they could not be loyal to Caesar as Lord. In the episodes of healing, the best translation would seem to be "trust (in)."

22. Funk and the Jesus Seminar, *Acts*, 83.

The prominence of trust in this episode, in the leader's entreaty and in Jesus's reassuring command, as in the hemorrhaging woman's bold initiative, again emphasizes that the healings are not just actions that Jesus performs my himself, but are fully relational. This is dramatized all the more in the following episode set in Jesus's "hometown." Even though the people are astounded at his "acts of power" when he teaches in the local assembly, his "acts of power" in his hometown are limited to laying hands on a few people and healing them because of some of the locals' lack of trust that he was anything more than the local boy they knew. The healings happen in the relationship between the healer and the people that has Jesus doing acts of power (not as a local boy made good but) in the role of a prophet. Central in that relationship is the trust that the people have in the power working through the prophet.

The relationship of healing is also far more than binary, between healer and healed, but a far wider one between healer, healed, and the support networks that extend in to the village communities and the people (of Israel) as a whole, across multiple village communities. Not only are the healings of these two women woven together. But in the symbolism of the number twelve (the one having been hemorrhaging for twelve years and the other just twelve years old), they are representative of Israel as a whole people (symbolized frequently by the twelve tribes). Not only are these two healings connected, but they are components of the first of two sequences of episodes of "acts of power" that include sea crossings and feedings in the wilderness. Jesus's acts of power in which the people trust are reminiscent of the acts of power performed by Moses, the founding prophet of the people, and of the acts of Elijah, the prophet of renewal. As Moses and Elijah were, or as the new Moses and new Elijah, Jesus is engaged in a renewal of the people of Israel, which is happening through the people's trust in those "acts of power."

Healing of the Deaf-Mute Man (Mark 7:31–37)

It has become standard for interpreters to take numerous ritual-like features in the episode of Jesus's healing of the deaf-mute as elements of magic. Like "the holy man in the ancient world [who] performed his wonders in private" (so others could not "see" the god at work), Jesus took the man aside.[23] Among the "primitive touches" or "bizarre elements," Jesus stuck

---

23. Ibid., 98.

his fingers in the man's ears (symbolic of opening), spat on his fingers and touched the man's tongue (symbolic of loosening the man's tongue), looked up to heaven (in prayer), and groaned ("the inner "arousal" of the charismatic's miracle-working powers"), and pronounced "the magical Aramaic incantation, *ephphatha*, "be opened."[24] Of these it is the spittle that looms most prominent to interpreters of Jesus's "miracles."

The modern construction of "magic," however, is not only inappropriate to the story but unnecessary, as some of the passing observations of both Meier and Funk and the Jesus Seminar suggest.

While Jesus takes the man aside, the healing is nevertheless public and relational. Some other people (again a network of relatives or friends) brought the man to Jesus and (in trust) begged him to lay his hand on him, parallel to the people who brought the paralyzed man to Jesus, and to the head of the assembly, who asked Jesus to lay hands on his daughter. And after the healing, Jesus ordered "them" not to tell anyone.

Interpreters note in passing that in the ancient world saliva was thought to have "medicinal properties" and was used as a "healing agent" and was used in ritual gestures.[25] Pliny the Elder mentions several uses for spitting and saliva in his *Natural History* (28.7.35–39): for healing eyes, as an ointment for neck pain, for healing a numbed limb (by spitting in the bosom), and for throwing back the "infection" from epileptic seizures. If saliva was widely used in healing and related rituals, then there is no reason for classifying it as a mark of magic. Similarly, if putting fingers in ears was a gesture symbolic of opening, it is hardly appropriate or necessary to resort to the concept of "magic" to explain it. It is not clear why interpreters assert, on the one hand, that medicinal plants, animals and animal products, minerals, oils, and spirits (which they think Jesus did not use) are "traditional methods of treatment," while applying saliva and placing fingers symbolically into blocked ears were not traditional.[26] Finally, while retaining the Aramaic word (with intelligible translation, in contrast to the "magical papyri") lent emphasis, Jesus's statement, "Be opened" is a performative command appropriate to deaf ears, parallel to his command appropriate to skin lesions ("Be clean!").[27]

---

24. Ibid.; and Meier, *Mentor*, 712, both repeat what is evidently a standard opinion that it was because the story "smacked too much of magic" that Matthew and Luke both "omitted" it.

25. Funk and the Jesus Seminar, *Acts*, 98; Meier, *Mentor*, 713.

26. Funk and the Jesus Seminar, *Acts*, 98.

27. Meier, *Mentor*, 713, puzzles that this story has a number of words that do not

Healing of the Blind Man at Bethsaida (8:22–26)

The healing of the blind man at Bethsaida is another story in which elements of magic are found. As Meier points out, "the two-stage healing and the use of saliva could be signs of the assimilation of a miracle story about Jesus to the techniques and tools of miracles and/or magic ..., especially as reflected in the magical papyri."[28] Again as in the healing of the deaf-mute, interpreters seize upon the use of spittle on the blind man (both here and in the story in John 9:1–7) as the key indicator of magic. Influenced by the catch-all synthetic construct of Morton Smith (and others), they have come to believe that spittle was among the "techniques ... well-known to both Jewish and Graeco-Roman magical practitioners."[29] Pursuing his primary point about the privacy of magic, Crossan suggests that "the private nature of the cure" of the blind man emphasized the magical features of the story, and "underlines the dangerously deviant nature of magical healing."[30]

As it is in the previous episode of the healing of the deaf-mute, however, here also the construct of "magic" is uncalled for as well as inappropriate. That Jesus led the blind man out of the "village" seems to make the healing act itself private. Yet the healing episode as a whole is again public and relational insofar as it begins with the trusting response of people who brought the man to Jesus and begged for his healing touch.[31] Spittle was commonly used in healing and hardly calls for a resort to the concept of "magic," as mentioned just above. That the healing takes place in two stages contrasts with many of the formulas and rituals in the magical papyri, which (rarely about healing) insist that they are fail-safe and immediately and fully effective. The laying on of hands is the healing touch typical in many of the stories of Jesus's healing. At the end of the episode, Jesus sent

---

appear elsewhere in Mark. Most of those terms, however, are distinctive to the deafness, the speech impediment, and/or the appropriate treatment.

28. Meier, *Mentor*, 692.

29. In the words of Aune, "Magic," 1537, quoted by Crossan, *Historical Jesus*, 325.

30. Crossan, *Historical Jesus*, 325. As noted in ch. 3, above, however, the few (private) formulas in the "magical papyri" that pertain to healing are for minor matters such as headache and fever. "Dangerously deviant" would seem more applicable to the formulas and rituals in the "magical papyri," performed in private, aimed at sabotaging a charioteer or coercing a woman for sex.

31. Meier, *Mentor*, 694, comments that faith is not mentioned. As in many other healing episodes, however, trust is implicit in the action of the people who bring the man to Jesus for healing.

the man (back) into his household—although it is puzzling how he can go to his household without going into the "village" (Bethsaida?).

Healings in the Third Narrative Step of the Gospel of Mark

In the next narrative step in the Gospel of Mark, the focus shifts from healings and exorcisms to the increasing misunderstanding of the disciples about Jesus's agenda of the renewal of the people. The narrative is framed, however, by the episodes of healing of the blind as a pointed contrast with the increasing blindness of the disciples. The healing of the blind man at Bethsaida (8:22–26) functions as the bridge episode from the second to the third step in the narrative. The third step concludes with Bartimaeus regaining his sight, just before Jesus marches up into Jerusalem for direct confrontation with the rulers.

The Healing of Blind Bartimaeus (10:46–52)

Even more than the healing of the blind man at Bethsaida, the healing of Bartimaeus plays a key role in the Gospel narrative, as just indicated. The narrative role of stories of healing of blind men, however, does not lessen their importance in the tradition of Jesus's healing. That there are three stories of healings of blind people included within the Gospels suggests that there may have been a number of healings of blind folks, and that these were significant among the many healings for which Jesus was remembered.[32] While the healing of blind Bartimaeus clearly serves as a counterpoise to the blindness of the disciples in the Markan narrative, however, his hailing Jesus as "Son of David" seems puzzling in the overall story. It does not fit any supposed Markan "Messianic Secret," because the secret in Mark, which Jesus orders the unclean spirits not to reveal, is not that Jesus is "the messiah." When, midway in the story, Peter proclaims that Jesus is "the messiah," but then protests that Jesus must not suffer and die, Jesus rebukes him: "Get behind me, Satan." Peter's so-called confession is a misunderstanding that the story rejects. Moreover, Jesus later teaches that the messiah cannot be the "son of David" (12:35–37). Additionally, not only is Bartimaeus's acclamation of Jesus as "son of David" the only such

---

32. In contrast to the more minimal conclusion that he did at least one healing of a blind person, Funk and the Jesus Seminar, *Acts*, 118.

reference in the Gospel of Mark, but the role of a messiah (descendant or successor of the original king popularly anointed by the people, as in 2 Sam 2:1–4; 5:1–4) did not include healing.[33] In the Gospel of Mark, Jesus is portrayed primarily as a Moses- and Elijah-like prophet engaged in the renewal of Israel, not as a messiah.[34]

In more elite traditions known from the histories of Josephus, however, "son of David" might be a reference to Solomon, who also had a reputation for great wisdom, including herbal medicine and hundreds of psalms and chants—wisdom that might be used in healing and exorcism. Bartimaeus's acclamation could thus be taken as a statement that Jesus had wisdom equal to that of Solomon of old.[35] Or might the Bartimaeus story, not fully adapted into the Markan portrayal of Jesus primarily as prophet, indicate that the healing of Jesus was being related to the role of messiah? The Markan correction of Peter's so-called confession indicates that significant figures in one or another of the Jesus movements understood Jesus as a messiah or as the Messiah, leading resistance to the rulers. And as indicated in the Gospel of John, despite the lack of such a connection in Israelite tradition, it was possible simply to assimilate the healings of Jesus as a prophet into the role (under the title) of Jesus as the messiah.

In other, significant respects, the episode of Bartimaeus resembles the other healing episodes in the Gospel of Mark. Like the hemorrhaging woman, Bartimaeus is persistent and aggressive in his trust in the healing power operative through Jesus and in his drive to be healed. And as in her healing, Jesus confirms in the conclusion to the episode that "your trust has saved/healed you!" In contrast to the modern scholarly concept of "miracle," the episode makes no suggestion that the healing is the result of a special act of God.

---

33. Horsley, "Popular Messianic Movements." See Novakovic, *Messiah*, ch. 3, for how difficult it is to find a link between "the son of David" or "the messiah" and healing in Judean (or later Jewish) texts.

34. Vs. the claim by Funk and the Jesus Seminar, *Acts*, 118, that for Mark "son of David" was almost certainly a "messianic title" since "Mark took Jesus to be the expected Davidic messiah." Numerous critical analyses of the limited occurrence of the term *messiah* and its equivalent in Judean texts suggested that there was no standard Judean expectation of "the Davidic messiah"; see, for example, the essays collected in Neusner et al., *Judaisms and Their Messiahs*; and Charlesworth, *Messiah*.

35. Funk and the Jesus Seminar, *Acts*, 118.

HEALING EPISODES

Healings in Matthew

Healings in Matthew may seem less important than in Mark insofar as Jesus does so much teaching, mainly in five lengthy speeches but also in prophetic instruction interspersed with actions. Yet Matthew has no fewer episodes of healing than Mark. Even though Matthew does not include the episodes of the deaf-mute and the blind man in Bethsaida, the Gospel twice has Jesus heal two blind men (9:27–31; 20:29–34) and has a brief episode of Jesus healing a mute demoniac (9:32–34). The episodes of healing in the Gospel of Matthew are shorter, sometimes much shorter. Most striking is that Matthew consolidates most of the episodes that appear in the first two narrative steps of Mark into the same narrative step (chs. 8–9) following Jesus covenantal speech (the Sermon on the Mount) and leading up to his mission speech. Also in the Matthean summaries of Jesus's healing (and exorcism), the reach of his fame is wider, the range of his healings are specified, and the healings are in done in fulfilment of what was spoken through the prophet Isaiah (8:16–17).

While the healing episodes are shorter than in Mark, they include the same motifs and features. The man with skin lesions, the hemorrhaging woman, the blind men, and the Syrophoenician woman all come to Jesus, implicitly or explicitly with trust that he can heal them. In some cases, such as in the case of the paralytic, the sick person is brought by a support network of friends or family, who also come in the confidence in the healing power working through Jesus. And in several episodes (especially that of the hemorrhaging woman), Jesus declares that they have been healed through their trust. In the actual healing Jesus makes a performative declaration and/or touches the petitioning sick person. In the healing of the paralytic, Matthew has the people glorify God, who had given authority to people to forgive sins (with implications for healing).

Healings in Luke

While the healing episodes are balanced with much more teaching in Luke, as in Matthew, they seem every bit as important in Jesus's agenda of the renewal of Israel as they are in the Markan story. Luke includes nearly all of the healing episodes that were in Mark and adds another five stories. While the stories in Mark are somewhat retold in Luke, they are not shortened nearly as much as in Matthew. And the Lukan healing episodes include nearly all of the key features found in the Markan episodes: people, having heard of his fame as a healer, coming to Jesus in trust; healings taking place in villages and village houses, with supportive networks; and healings happening (partly) because of the trust of the healed.

It has evidently become standard to declare that Luke, like Matthew, deleted the Markan stories of the healings of the deaf-mute and the blind man at Bethsaida (Mark 7:31–37; 8:22–26) because they included unseemly magical elements such as fingers in ears and especially spittle. Evidently interpreters do not notice that Luke does not include any of the second sequence of "acts of power" and other episodes from Mark 6:45—8:26. If anything the healing episodes in Luke seem more ominous than in Mark. In healing Peter's mother-in-law, Jesus "rebuked" the fever, as if it were an unclean spirit or demon. Just before the healing of the paralytic, Luke includes the statement that "the power of the Lord was with him to heal" (5:17). And in one summary, as a great multitude came to be healed, "power came forth from him and healed them all" (6:17–19).

The episodes of the centurion's servant and the son of the widow of Nain serve in the Lukan narrative to set up Jesus's response to the Baptist's question whether he is "the coming one" by pointing to his healings and preaching (7:1–10, 11–17). The centurion, having heard of Jesus's reputation for healing, sends emissaries to plead for the healing of his servant. His confidence that Jesus, as a man under authority, can command that his servant be healed, astounds Jesus as a remarkable expression of trust (with the implication that it is a factor in the healing). The episode of the resuscitation of the son of the widow of Nain makes fully explicit what is implicit in the healing episodes in Mark. For some time those familiar with the cycle of stories of Elijah and his prophet-protégé, Elisha, have noted reminiscences of these great prophets of renewal in the healing stories of Jesus. More recently, interpreters who have attended to the narratives of the Gospels have recognized that the healing and exorcism episodes represent Jesus in the role of (a prophet like) Elijah. The Lukan episode of the healing of the widow of Nain bears a number of close resemblances to particular stories of Elijah and Elisha: the story of Elisha's revival of the son of a woman in the town of Shunem, in lower Galilee near Nain (2 Kgs 4:8–37), and, even more, Elijah's revival of the son of a widow in Zarephath, whom he meets at the gate of the town; after he has revived the boy, Elijah gives him back to his mother (1 Kgs 17:7–24).[36] The witnesses of the revivifica-

---

36. Meier, *Mentor*, 790–95, explores the similarities and differences.

tion in the Gospel episode draw the obvious conclusion: "A great prophet [like Elijah!] has arisen among us," and, in a distinctively Lukan twist, "God has looked favorably on his people" (7:16).

Included in the long journey section of Luke are three further healing stories, all public, distinctive to the Gospel. The episode of the bent-over woman begins like the first exorcism in Mark: as Jesus was teaching in an assembly on the Sabbath, there suddenly appeared a woman with a spirit that had crippled her for years. The healing is effected through Jesus's declaration, "Woman, you are set free from your ailment," and through his laying on of hands. The healing immediately becomes the occasion for Jesus's reply to the objections of the leader of the assembly to his healing on the sabbath. And in this Lukan episode is the only mention of Satan (presumably in apposition to the "spirit") as "binding" someone. Even more is Jesus healing of a man with dropsy simply a foil for yet another assertion by Jesus, this time against the Pharisees: that it is lawful to heal on the sabbath (14:1–6). The story of the ten lepers made clean (only one of whom, a Samaritan, returned to thank Jesus) ends with the repeated point: "your trust has made you well." But it is not clear what the story is about. That the Samaritan is termed a "foreigner" suggests that this story, similar to Jesus's parable of the Good Samaritan, is aimed at sensitivity to, perhaps the inclusion of, Samaritans in the movement, which had not been receptive.

Healings in John

As I noted at the end of ch. 8, the Gospel of John states repeatedly that Jesus performed many "signs" for the people, and it is clear that many if not most of those were healings (see the summary in 6:2). Yet the Gospel includes only three healings, only one of which is explicitly called a sign, and the accounts of the healings are simpler in significant respects than the episodes in the Synoptic Gospels.

The story of the royal official's son's recovery from his severe fever (4:46–54) bears some resemblances to the story of the recovery of the centurion's servant in the somewhat parallel episodes in Matthew and Luke. The story in John resembles healing stories in Mark and the other Synoptics insofar as the officer, knowing of Jesus's reputation as a healer, begs him to heal his son back in Capernaum, implicitly trusting that he can do so. In a short retort (addressed to "you" [plural], and hence not addressed specifically to the officer), Jesus distinguishes what he is doing (in his signs—healings-and-more) from the expectation of signs and wonders (portents); his drawing this distinction seems similar to his rejecting the demand for "signs" in the Synoptics (Matt 16:1–4; Mark 8:11–12; Luke 11:29). Jesus declares simply, "Go, your son will live"; the officer persists in his trust and soon discovers that the fever left his son just at the time of Jesus's declaration, and the whole household comes to trust. It might be modern rationalism to think that the long-distance healing was a mere coincidence of Jesus's declaration to the officer and the fever leaving the boy, but the narrative gives no hint of a special act of God, as in the modern scholarly understanding of "miracle."

The other two healings in John's story also bear certain similarities to stories in Mark, leading some interpreters to conclude that they are variants of those stories. When Jesus encounters the severely crippled ("sick") man at the pool of Bethzatha, he commands him, "Stand up, take your mat, and walk!" and later connects his malady with sinning (5:1–9, 14). This seems similar to the episode of the paralytic in Mark, to whom Jesus declares, "your sins are forgiven," and then "stand up, take your mat, and walk!" (Mark 2:1–12). But key features of the healing episode in Mark and the other Synoptics are missing in this story in John. The man has evidently not heard of Jesus and does not come seeking healing in trust; nor does he express trust afterwards. The healing takes place simply one-on-one. There is no supportive set of friends or family bringing the man to Jesus in the confidence that Jesus can heal him. The healing of the crippled man at the pool of Bethzatha, which turns out to have been done on a Sabbath, serves mainly as a springboard for another of Jesus's confrontations with (the rulers of) "the Judeans" in a discourse about how he is working, including on the Sabbath, to give life to people, in pointed rejection of the Sabbath regulations and (in) their "scriptures." (Moses is even their "accuser.")

The healing of the blind man at the pool of Siloam (9:1–12) is also taken by some interpreters as a variant version another healing story, that of the blind man at Bethsaida in Mark. Commentators are struck by the links in both between a blind man and the use of spittle (with spittle being taken by some as a mark of magic). But, again, the story in John does not have the blind man come to Jesus in trust seeking healing; and only later does he respond positively, declaring that Jesus "is a prophet." Again the healing story serves mainly as a springboard for another in Jesus's series of confrontations with the rulers of the Judeans, in this case with the Pharisees. At the outset, the disciples raise the connection with sins as the cause of sickness. But Jesus's healing on the Sabbath is again the focal issue, the Pharisees charging that it is impossible for a violator of the Sabbath—a sinner—to give life; others insist that a sinner could not perform such signs, and the blind man finally declares that "he [the healer] is a prophet." The healing is a springboard for the confrontation that brings to a head the conflict between Jesus and the rulers of the Judeans, who are now ready to banish from the assembly of the whole people anyone who has become loyal to Jesus (anyone who confesses him to be the messiah; 9:13–23). And the healing serves as the concrete illustration of the broader issue of those who see what is happening in Jesus's mission and those who don't (9:24–41).

Conclusion

As was anticipated in the brief survey of whether the modern concept of miracle is applicable to the Gospel episodes of healing, they display no concern for explanation and do not ascribe agency to God or the supernatural. In contrast to the modern scientific worldview, according to which extraordinary phenomena cannot be explained by human abilities or by other known forces that operate in our world of time and space, the healing episodes happen in the course of social interaction between healer, healed, and other interested and supportive people. Healing often follows upon Jesus's touching the sick person or uttering a command. In many episodes the sick person's and a relative's or a support network's trust is a key factor in the healing. And leading to that trust is evidently the spreading fame of Jesus as a healer. In the healing of the hemorrhaging woman, the trust that drives her initiative is the principal factor, while Jesus himself does nothing. Similarly, in summaries of healings, the sick reach out to touch Jesus or his garment (e.g., Mark 6:53–56). The power that Jesus felt go forth from himself in the healing of the hemorrhaging woman seems to have been operative in his and her world of time and space. The healings happen through the relation and interaction between the sufferer and Jesus, or through the wider relations between the sufferer, the support network, and Jesus. At least since the reflections of Max Weber a hundred or so years ago, it has been recognized that charismatic power can be generated in the relation of leader and followers in certain crisis situations in the world of time and space—or more to the point, in social-historical interaction.

Evident in several of the healing episodes themselves, and not just in their narrative sequence or editorial framing, is the relation of healing and the social-cultural life of the people. Jesus's declaration to the paralytic, "Son, your sins are forgiven," for example, addresses the roots of paralysis in the sense of sin and its reinforcement by self-blame. His declaration to the man with skin lesions that he was "clean," freed him to rejoin ordinary social interaction. This direct relation to other dimensions of personal and social life then fits and reinforces the broader narrative in the first part of the Synoptic Gospels—composed largely of healing stories—that portrays the renewal of Israel as happening in the healings. Most striking in this regard are the healing of the woman who had been hemorrhaging for twelve years and that of the twelve-year-old woman who was near death, obviously figures representative of Israel whose life was being restored and renewed.

10

Exorcism Episodes

FOR CRITICAL ASSESSMENT OF exorcism episodes, far more than for healing episodes, we are dependent on the Gospel of Mark. If the Gospels of Matthew and Luke were following the Markan narrative, then most of the exorcism episodes in those Gospels are adaptations of episodes included in Mark.

Exorcism Episodes in Mark

The four exorcisms in the Gospel of Mark play a special narrative role in the sequence of episodes. In the first narrative step in Mark, Jesus's exorcism in the Capernaum village assembly is the first action of his mission. It is also the action that exemplifies the "authority/power" with which Jesus "teaches," in contrast with the scribes, a theme that runs implicitly through the narrative until it becomes explicit again in his confrontation with the rulers in the Temple: like John the Baptist, Jesus acts/speaks with authority/power as a prophet, in dramatic contrast with the rulers and their representatives. In the second main narrative step in the Markan story, the exorcism of the unclean spirit in Gerasa and that of the Syrophoenician woman's daughter precede and set up the healing episodes that follow in the two sequences of five "acts of power."

Partly because there are fewer exorcism stories than healing stories, it is all the more important to examine them carefully in the context of the overall Markan story in historical political-cultural context. And partly because these stories have been read with key Christian theological concepts in mind, as well as taken as "miracles" or "magic," it is important to discern the key features that are present in the stories.

The Exorcism in the Capernaum Village Assembly (1:22–30)

Contrary to previous assumptions and assertions, this episode cannot be said to be the beginning of some sort of messianic secret. On the contrary. Although Jesus commands the unclean spirit to "be silent," that is in response to the spirit's aggressive vocal resistance to what is about to happen and part of the statement of exorcism: "Be silent, and come out of him." Christology and christological titles are much later Christian theological concepts. In fact, it may be a stretch to claim that the spirit's identification of Jesus as "the Holy One of God" is a messianic title or role, insofar as the Gospel of Mark resists identification of Jesus as "the messiah."[1] "Holy one of God" could refer rather to a prophet whose healing role in Israelite tradition may have expanded from healing (Elijah, Elisha) to exorcism of spirits in the new circumstances of imperial rule.

The exorcism does not fit the modern construct of ancient magic in virtually any respect. Exorcism was not included in the ancient accusatory discourse of magic, and its few appearances in the "magical papyri" are late texts dependent on Jewish and/or Christian tradition. Strikingly different from the construct of magic as expanded by Smith and Crossan is that this exorcism is so public, in the midst of the Sabbath gathering of the Capernaum village assembly (the meaning of *synagoge*),[2] to the amazement of the people—and "at once his fame began to spread throughout . . . Galilee."

After Jesus had been teaching in the assembly, the problem erupted suddenly ("immediately"): there was a man "with an unclean spirit" who confronted Jesus in a wild, bizarre way. This is anything but normal interaction, the man is not himself, the unclean spirit is the agent of confrontation. In an ensuing summary passage, such phenomena are called "those who are spirit possessed" (*daimonizomenous*) and Jesus is said to cast out many "spirits/divine powers" (*daimonia*). In the episode itself, however, the agent of the agitated behavior is termed "an unclean spirit." And the unclean spirit is evidently one of many unclean spirits: "what have you to do with *us*?" Perhaps modern interpreters should not be too hasty to "demonize" these spirits. Although the bizarre behavior of the man and the unclean

---

1. Explained in Horsley, *Hearing the Whole Story*, ch. 10.
2. Horsley, *Galilee*, ch. 10.

spirit erupts suddenly in the assembly, evidently evoked by the presence of Jesus, the man is known to have exhibited odd or wild behavior previously, explained in the culture as due to possession by a spirit.

Jesus's response is to "subdue" the unclean spirit. The term in Greek is stronger than conveyed by "rebuke," and seems to have corresponded to a term used in performative commands in Israelite tradition, as when God would "conquer" or "subdue" a hostile enemy[3]—although this episode has no hint of some special action by God. And Jesus's command evokes a violent struggle as the unclean spirit "convulsed" the man and "cried out in a great loud voice" as he came out of the man. The amazed people exclaim that he has manifested new teaching. (Powerful actions were understood as rooted in wisdom, with authority/power [*exousia*].)

The Exorcism in Gerasa/Gadara (5:1–20)

Again this episode is not part of some messianic secret; there is not even a command of silence. The unclean spirit's address of Jesus as "Son of the Most High God" is not a recognizable messianic title.[4] And again the scholarly construct of magic does not fit. The episode is not something private and individual but something public and socially, even politically, interactional.

The episode takes place in the countryside. Again a man "with an unclean spirit" encounters Jesus. And again the unclean spirit is (among) "many" unclean spirits (5:9, 11). The man, later referred to as "the spirit-possessed one" ("demoniac"), utterly controlled, driven, by the unclean spirit, has done extreme violence to himself and others in the community. Attempts to restrain him with shackles and chains could not control his superhuman strength. Possession by (an) unclean spirit(s) had extreme social manifestations. It is in the encounter between the possessed man and Jesus that the difference between the unclean spirit and the man who has become possessed becomes evident. It is the spirit who addresses Jesus, and Jesus utters the command: "Come out of the man, you unclean spirit!" Distinctive in this exorcism episode is Jesus's attempt to identify the unclean spirit: "What is your name?" Unclean spirits evidently (could) have distinctive identities. And the answer, "Legion," indicates unmistakably that the identity of the spirit(s) was the Roman military. The imagery of the subsequent

---

3. Kee, "Terminology."

4. For perspective on lack of evidence for "Jewish expectations" of "the messiah," see the essays in Neusner et al., *Judaisms and Their Messiahs*; Charlesworth, ed. *Messiah*.

events in the episode confirms this identity. Jesus gave permission for the unclean spirits to enter the "battalion" of swine, who "charged" down the bank into the Sea (as in Mediterranean Sea, not a large inland lake) to their own self-destruction by their own violence.

In this episode it is thus revealed that the identity of the force that has invaded and possessed the man is the Roman military. The community had tried extreme measures to control the extreme violence that the spirit had caused the man to wreak against himself and against others. The exorcism having revealed the heretofore unrecognized identity of the cause of the violence, the people in the community beg Jesus to leave. Whatever *modus vivendi* had been achieved by the community in adjusting to the impact or trauma from Roman military violence had been disrupted.

The Exorcism of the Syrophoenician Woman's Daughter (7:24–30)

This exorcism has become the occasion for the breakthrough in which Mark's Jesus (the Jesus movement) becomes open to participation by other (non-Israelite) peoples. There is no description of the problem or any strange behavior other than the statement that the daughter "had an unclean spirit." The encounter between the woman and Jesus is public, in a house in a village under the rule of Tyre, with the girl in another house in the village. In this case, there is no encounter between the demon and Jesus, who simply tells the bold woman who begged his help and forced the issue of acceptance, "the spirit has left your daughter." Only on the basis of the previous episodes and summaries would we assume that an exorcism had taken place.

The Exorcism of the Father's Son (9:14–29)

This exorcism has become an occasion on which the disciples fail in exorcism that Jesus had commissioned them to perform. In this case "a spirit" possesses a boy, making him unable to speak, and causing a "seizure" in which it "dashes him down and he foams and grinds his teeth and becomes rigid." It had also cast him into the fire and into water, and other such self-destructive behavior. When the spirit sees Jesus, it again convulses the boy—that is, again the encounter with Jesus evokes the symptoms of the possession. In a fully public context, in front of a crowd, Jesus rebukes the spirit: "You spirit . . . , I command you, come out of him, and never enter him again!" Again as in the first exorcism in Mark, so here the spirit comes out with a violent struggle: crying out and convulsing the boy, so that he is left like a corpse.

Exorcism Episodes in Matthew and Luke

The Gospel of Matthew omits the first exorcism episode found in Mark (1:22-28) and shortens the other episodes (Matt 8:28-34; 17:14-21). But Matthew has two demoniacs coming out of the tombs to confront Jesus (in Gadara) and adds other references to exorcisms: of a demoniac that was mute and of a demoniac that was blind and mute (8:28-34; 9:32-34; 12:22-23). While the exorcism episodes are more concise in Matthew, they include all of the same key features found in their counterparts in Mark. They are public; the spirit possession has affected others, and the people witnessing the exorcism are affected (either asking Jesus to leave or responding positively). The effects of the possession are severe. The episodes in Matthew refer to *daimonia* rather than "unclean spirits," and the brief episodes distinctive to Matthew refer to "demoniacs" (the "demon-possessed"). Jesus ("rebukes" and) "casts out" the "demon" (spirit) by a command and/or heals the demoniac.

The Gospel of Luke includes all four of the exorcism episodes in Mark and, while retelling them, retains all of the key features. The spirit possession and the exorcism are public, involving other people. The effects of possession are severe, violent for people in the community as well as especially for the possessed. The episodes use both "unclean spirits" and "demons" in reference to the possessing agents. Jesus utters a command to "come out," and the spirit's exit may be a struggle. In a few healing episodes the portrayal in the Gospel of Luke suggests that the sickness is due to spirit possession and/or that Jesus's healing is exorcism-like. In the healing of Peter's mother-in-law, immediately following his rebuking the spirit in the Capernaum assembly, "Jesus stood over her and rebuked the fever [as if it were a spirit], and it left her" (4:38-39). Aspects of both sickness and possession and of healing and exorcism are portrayed in the episode of the crippled woman (in which the main issue is healing on the Sabbath; Luke 13:10-17). "A spirit had crippled her for eighteen years" is restated as "Satan had bound her"; this is the only appearance of Satan in Gospel exorcism episodes. Jesus heals her by laying hands on her and by the performative declaration, "Woman, you are set free from your ailment."

Although there are far fewer exorcism episodes in the Gospels than there are healing stories, the presence of unclean spirits and exorcism is if anything more prominent in the summary passages and in Jesus's speeches commissioning the disciples to extend his own mission. All of the Gospels include periodic summaries referring to Jesus's casting out spirits, and in the mission speeches he gives the disciples "authority over the unclean spirits."

Spirit Possession and Jesus's Exorcisms as Portrayed in the Gospels

Further analysis and clarification of the portrayal of spirit possession and exorcism in the Gospels is called for in response to the scholarly concepts that have been projected onto them. A close examination of the Gospel portrayals of the exorcisms of Jesus shows that they do not seem to fit the modern conception of miracle as involving a special intervention by God; they do not fit the modern scholarly discussion of ancient magic as involving adjuration of and gaining power from/over spirits; and they do not fit readily into Christian theological generalizations of a struggle between God and Satan.

Scholarly investigation of the exorcisms, as well as of the historical Jesus in general, focuses on separate "miracle stories" one by one, looking for particular elements that might go back to Jesus. Little attention is thus given to the picture that the exorcism episodes considered together in the narrative context of the Gospels might offer of spirit possession more generally, and of Jesus's exorcism more generally, in their historical cultural context. Interpreters avoid this via one or another of two routes. Interpreters of Jesus who have been refining the form-critical approach that found parallels to the form of "miracle stories" in (mostly later) Hellenistic texts have generally given little attention to the Israelite cultural tradition and context in which both Jesus and the Gospel stories are deeply rooted.[5] Interpreters working from a Christian theological construction of Jesus's ministry in a context of the supposed apocalyptic dualism of (early) Judaism find that both spirit possession and Jesus's exorcism were part and parcel of an almost cosmic struggle between God and Satan for the control of the world and people's lives. The first route seems not to recognize that Jesus, Jesus-traditions, and the Gospel episodes and stories are rooted in

---

5. Exemplified by Funk and the Jesus Seminar, *Acts*.

(popular) Israelite culture. The second route, still working within Christian theological constructs such as apocalypticism, has not recognized the considerable diversity of texts, figures, and movements in late second-temple Judea. And neither line of interpretation seems to have recognized the cultural division between the scholarly, scribal circles (who produced nearly all texts except the Gospels) and the ordinary people in village communities—that is, the difference between reflective scribal Judean culture and ad-hoc popular Israelite culture.

One would expect that after the discovery of the Dead Sea Scrolls, discussion of spirits in Gospel stories would involve some reference to and comparison (or contrast) with striking passages in the *Community Rule* and the *War Scroll*.[6] Particularly striking in connection with God and the loyal heavenly forces ("angels") and the renegade heavenly forces in Daniel 10–12 and the Book of Watchers and the Animal Vision (*1 Enoch* 1–36; 85–90) is a sweeping statement in the *Community Rule*, evidently a charter for the life of the priestly-scribal community at Qumran. All of history since the creation, and especially the life of the community, was happening under the struggle between two forces, the Prince/Spirit of Light and the Angel of Darkness/Belial (1QS 3:18—4:24; 1QM 13, 15–19). Human lives are happening according to the dominance of one or another of these Spirits, the Qumran community itself being determined by the Spirit of Light. And God has appointed a time in the future when the conflict would be ended as God and the forces of Light would prevail over the forces of Belial. In this connection, members of the Qumran community enjoyed close association with heavenly spirits. And just to ward off any counterinfluences of dangerous spirits, (leaders of) the community recited certain apotropaic psalms that reinforced divine protection. No possession by hostile spirits seems evident in the Qumran texts, presumably because the whole community was, in effect, under the influence of (possessed by) the Spirit of Light. Highly significant may be the passages in the *War Scroll* from Qumran that insist that the actions of "the Kittim," who are identified with the Romans, are determined by Belial (the hostile Spirit of Darkness). Indeed, the *War Scroll* expresses the anticipation that at some point in the future the community, acting in the power of the Spirit of Light, will be engaged in battle with the Kittim, acting under the influence of Belial.

---

6. Missing in Meier, *Mentor*; Funk and the Jesus Seminar, *Acts*; Crossan, *Historical Jesus*.

This understanding of current history, including particularly the life of the Qumran community as caught up in a struggle between opposing Spirits, was used to reinforce (and explain) Christian theological understandings of the Gospels as involving a struggle between God and Satan and of Jesus himself as the agent of God in the struggle against Satan. It is unwarranted, however, to generalize from these striking Qumran texts to what modern scholars have understood as Judaism in general. Historically there was no such thing as Judaism in whose supposed general worldview Jesus, his followers, and the Gospels were rooted. Rather there was a diversity of groups and movements, including the temple-state headed by the high priests, all rooted in Israelite tradition, but in different ways. The Qumran texts were produced by one small community of the tiny percentage of Judeans who were literate, of the scribes who served in the temple-state in Jerusalem. The Qumranites, moreover, were dissident scribes and priests who had withdrawn from the temple-state into the wilderness and hence developed views that differed from those of other scribal circles, such as the Pharisees (whom they attack as "smooth interpreters").[7] In the apocalyptic texts produced by other scribal circles (particularly in the mid-second century BCE), such as Daniel 7; 8; 10–12 and *1 Enoch* 1–37; 85–90, it is difficult to find the supposed apocalyptic dualism or dualistic cosmology of two opposing kingdoms, that of God and that of Satan.[8]

The understanding of life as caught in a conflict between the Spirit of Light/Angel of Truth and the Angel of Darkness/Belial, however, may serve as a schematic scribal worldview in comparison with which we can more adequately discern how spirit possession and exorcism are understood in the Gospels. There are certain similarities that may illumine both the spirit possession and the exorcism portrayed in the Gospels. But there are also significant differences, which are probably rooted in and explained by the differences between intellectuals, such as the Qumran scribes, and villagers, among whom Jesus worked and among whom the Gospel traditions of Jesus originated.

---

7. See, for example, Horsley, *Revolt of the Scribes*, ch. 7.

8. This has been a standard generalization in New Testament studies for much of the last century, but it is virtually unattested in Judean texts outside the Dead Sea Scrolls. As an example of how terms and phrases from a variety of New Testament texts become lumped under the assumed kingdom of God versus the kingdom of Satan, see Sorenson, *Possession and Exorcism*, 118–19, esp. n. 1. For a detailed survey of how late second-temple Judean so-called apocalyptic texts do not attest the modern scholarly concept of apocalypticism, see Horsley, *The Prophet Jesus*, chs. 1–5.

EXORCISM EPISODES

Spirit possession is a widespread phenomenon among peoples of the world, and is particularly prevalent and striking among those who are under the domination of others, as has been studied long since.[9] The articulation of spirit possession, however, is determined by particular cultures. In attempting to understand spirit possession in the Gospel episodes, therefore, it make sense to investigate sources for the Israelite culture in which Jesus and the Gospels were deeply rooted rather than to turn first to generalizing comparative studies and surveys.[10]

Israelite culture is different from cultures of many other peoples in having a long tradition of resistance to domination by outside rulers, resistance led by prophetic figures, (and) inspired by a god who stood in judgment against domination. When the domination seemed so powerful and severe that it could not be explained simply as God's punishment for sins (for breaking the covenantal commandments), scribal circles produced texts that explained the violence and other distress as due to heavenly forces who had rebelled against God's heavenly governance of earthly affairs, whether the life of the people themselves or the imperial rulers who had subjugated them (Daniel 10–12; The Book of Watchers, *1 Enoch* 1–36).

This is where Crossan begins in his broad, general discussion of spirit possession and exorcism. But his discussion illustrates the potential pitfalls of interpretation in which the standard dualistic reading of apocalyptic texts persists, on the one side, and we rely on comparative studies that do not attend sufficiently to particular cultures, on the other. He draws on only one Judean scribal text, the Similitudes of Enoch (*1 Enoch* 37–71) and reads it through the standard dualism of God, God's heavenly agents, and God's people, on the one hand, and "the chief demon, Azazel, his angels, and the kings and the mighty," on the other.[11] Semihazah and other rebel heavenly forces play a central role in the scribal explanation of the origin of imperial military violence and exploitation in the earlier Enoch text, the Book of Watchers (*1 Enoch* 1–36). In the later Similitudes, however, the role of Azazel and other rebel forces recedes considerably, and the focus becomes more explicitly political—on God's judgment (not the destruction) of "the kings

---

9. E.g., Lewis, *Ecstatic Religion*; Boddy, *Wombs and Alien Spirits*; Behrend and Luig, *Spirit Possession*; Crapanzano and Garrison, *Case Studies*; Goodman, *How about Demons?*

10. The approach in Crossan, *Historical Jesus*; Craffert, *Galilean Shaman*.

11. Crossan, *Historical Jesus*, 313, relying on Nickelsburg, *Jewish Literature*, 215, 223. See also Horsley, *Jesus and the Spiral*, 184–86.

and the mighty" (imperial rulers), along with the problematic forces.[12] The text, however, does not suggest at all that "God's people were possessed by demons on the social level." The text articulates rather how the people have been suffering under "the kings and the mighty and those who possess the earth" as a result of the rebel heavenly forces having taught them metallurgy for the manufacture of weapons, and so forth. The ancient Judean intellectuals' explanation of imperial rule is a good bit more complicated than modern intellectuals' dualistic scheme. Crossan, however, then shifts immediately to a psychological explanation of the supposed demon possession: schizophrenia; the self desires or seeks the power of the possessing demon now inside the self in order to destroy it.[13] But the Similitudes of Enoch is not about possession; it focuses rather on the people's historical suffering under imperial rule and looks to the judgment of "the kings and the mighty" by the Chosen One.

When Crossan moves to "the Little Tradition," of which he takes the story of the Gerasene demoniac as representative, he draws upon older comparative studies such as that by the anthropologist I. M. Lewis.[14] Many of the cultures he studies in which possession (and exorcism) occurred, however, do not appear to have had an equivalent to the God of Israelite tradition, who is concerned about the people and prepared again to inspire leadership for their deliverance, as in acts of liberation in the past. Even the possession of Algerians under French colonial rule by *djinn*, at least in Frantz Fanon's (political-)psychological analysis that finds a Manichean dualism, does not appear to have involved the concern of the divine or some sort of benign spirit(s).[15]

The conflict between the two Spirits in the Qumran *Community Rule* is a schematic overview of historical life from dissidents in the scribal version of Israelite tradition. It both explains the domination that seems out of control and articulates the trust that deliverance will surely come in the future. At the popular level, on the other hand, from the histories of Josephus, we know of movements among the villagers of Judea, Galilee, and/or Samaria led by popular prophets who were caught up in the trust that new

---

12. See the analysis of Enoch texts in historical contexts in Horsley, *Scribes, Visionaries*, 157–63; Horsley, *Revolt of the Scribes*, chs. 3, 9.

13. Crossan, *Historical Jesus*, 313–14.

14. Ibid., 313–17.

15. Ibid., 317, drawing on Hollenback's discussion of Fanon: Hollenback, "Jesus, Demoniacs," 573, 575–77.

acts of deliverance were about to happen. Given that peasants generally do not leave textual sources, however, we do not happen to have any portrayals of spirit possession and exorcism among people of Israelite heritage outside of the Gospels.

The Gospel portrayals of spirit possession and exorcism, however, can be understood as parallel to the Qumran texts in Israelite tradition, yet as far more ad hoc and less schematic, as we would expect of ordinary people. Judging from the exorcism episodes in the Gospels, people of Israelite heritage in Galilee (and perhaps other peoples) attributed a whole range of bizarre behavior to superhuman spirits that took possession of people: violence to oneself and others in the family and community, seizures, blindness, speech difficulties, and other forms of disability. Some spirits were identified as causing a particular behavior or disability. Some were identified by their apparent character or source. Particularly noteworthy, given the frequency of spirit possession among people who live under certain forms of domination, and given the Qumran *War Scroll*'s assertions that the Kittim (the Romans) were acting under the influence or control of Belial, is the identification of the unclean spirit or spirits that were causing such extreme violence with Legion, the Roman military and the military behavior of the spirits once they possessed the swine.

There is nothing in the exorcism episodes, however, that suggests that all of the spirits are somehow part of the same great company or coordinated or under the authority or command of an overarching Spirit. Contrary to assertions one finds, for example, that the overarching conflict in the Gospel of Mark is (determined by) that between God and Satan, Satan makes only rare appearances in the story, and usually as the tempter (1:13; 8:33) and equally rare and similar appearances in Matthew and Luke (only in the episode of the crippled woman, Luke 13:10-17, does "Satan" appear in parallelism with a possessing spirit). Nor does the representation of Satan in the Beelzebul controversy (to be discussed just below) suggest such an overarching role in conflict with God. The conception of the spirits in the exorcism episodes is quite ad hoc and particular, evidently, to the behavior of the people they have possessed.

The casting out of spirits by Jesus in the exorcism episodes is understood as under the ultimate sovereignty of God and implicitly as manifestation of the rule of God, just as the ultimate sovereignty belongs to God, who has appointed a time for the resolution of the controlling conflict between the opposing Spirits. But Jesus's exorcisms, like the spirits that he casts out, are ad hoc. There were no particular exorcisms at Qumran because the whole community was (already) under the influence of or guided by the Spirit of Light. The Spirit of God or Holy Spirit does not play a role in the exorcism episodes of Jesus—or in the healing or other episodes. The (Holy or divine) Spirit plays a prominent role in the beginning of the Gospel narratives: in Jesus's baptism and wilderness preparation in Mark, and in the infancy narratives and baptism narratives in Matthew and Luke. John the Baptist's announcement in Matthew and Luke and even more so Jesus's coming to Galilee "filled with the power of the Spirit" and the application of the prophecy in Isa 61:1 to himself in Luke (4:14, 18–21), may be particularly influential in modern readers' sense that the Holy Spirit is involved in Jesus's actions. Yet the Spirit hardly plays any role in the rest of the episodes of Luke's narratives of Jesus's mission.

Accusation and Response in the "Beelzebul Controversy"

The principal episode on which interpreters of Jesus and the Gospels may have based their sense that Jesus's exorcisms are manifestations of a general conflict between God (and/or Jesus) and Satan is the Beelzebul controversy. Mark includes this accusation of Jesus and his response, and Matthew and Luke appear to have known a parallel episode in the series of Jesus's speeches they have in common (Q). The importance and influence of this episode warrant a closer critical examination, particularly once we recognize the portrayal of Jesus's mission in the overall Gospel narratives, and also recognize the distinctive social location and political role of the scribes and Pharisees in late second-temple Judea.

The Gospel of Mark states explicitly that it was "the scribes who came down from Jerusalem" who accused Jesus of being "possessed by Beelzebul" and "casting out demons by the ruler of demons." This fits with the overall portrayal in Mark of Jesus engaged in the renewal of Israel in opposition to and opposed by the rulers and their scribal and Pharisaic representatives. In the parallel tradition of the episode evident in both Matthew and Luke, the episode begins with an exorcism of a demon that was dumb (Matthew adds "blind"), after which the man spoke. In Matthew it is then "the Pharisees" who make the accusation that "he casts out demons by Beelzebul the ruler of the demons." Again this fits the overall narrative of the Gospel in which Jesus works in opposition to and opposed by the scribes and Pharisees, as representatives of the high-priestly rulers. Luke has the indefinite "some of them" (i.e., some of the crowd that marveled at the exorcism). This fits less with the overall narrative in Luke, in which, while Jesus eats with the Pharisees, he is nevertheless in sharp conflict with the scribes and Pharisees through most of the story.[16]

The name Beelzebul was evidently derived from and a continuation from ancient Canaanite society, in which the executive god was Baʻal (Lord Storm). In second-temple Judea, as is known from texts later included in the Hebrew Bible and from other texts, polemic against Baʻal and other deities of rival regimes was at home in scribal culture, in which rival gods were demonized. Fitzmyer concluded from the sources he analyzed that Beelzebul preserves "the name of an old Canaanite god, meaning 'Baal, the Prince,' or 'Baal of the Exalted Abode'"[17]—that is, the name Beelzebul came from scribal tradition preserved in written texts, not from popular tradition.[18] In any case, as Mark and Matthew both have it, the accusation that Jesus was himself possessed by Beelzebul, a rival god utterly unacceptable and rejected in the ideology of the temple-state, was made by the scribes or Pharisees, the professional representatives (and in the Gospels the social enforcers) of the high-priestly rulers. This is parallel to what happens in other societies where the establishment attempts to repress or demonize possession as hidden protest or exorcism.[19] More familiar perhaps, it is parallel to the condemnation of peasant healers and midwives as witches by both Catholic and Protestant authorities in the great European witch hunts.[20] Although the scribes and Pharisees would not have shared the two-Spirits scheme articulated in the Qumran *Community Rule*, the latter may help us imagine the kind of dualistic scribal thinking that viewed whatever

---

16. In the Gospel of Mark the Beelzebul controversy, a component episode in the wider conflict between Jesus and the scribes and Pharisees as representatives of the temple-state, is framed more immediately by Jesus's family's concern that he is *exeste*. The Greek term occurs frequently in the healing and exorcism stories, usually translated "astounded/astonished." In the framing of the Beelzebul episode it means something more like "out of his mind." Following his response to the charge of being possessed by Beelzebul, Jesus (implicitly at least) rejects their concern. While Funk and the Jesus Seminar were persuaded that some of the authorities thought Jesus demon possessed, they do not assemble the evidence in the next section (72–73). They rather level out the family's concern and the scribes' charge to the conclusion that some thought Jesus was demon possessed.

17. Fitzmyer, *Gospel according to Luke*, 2:920.

18. Cf. Crossan, *Historical Jesus*, 319.

19. Lewis, *Ecstatic Religion*.

20. Horsley, "Who Were the Witches?"; Horsley, "Further Reflections."

did not agree with and support the established order of the temple-state as alien and dangerous.

In interpretation of this controversy it has often been assumed—in a field that reduces particular names, images, and metaphors to key concepts of a synthetic Judaism and early Christianity—that Beelzebul (the ruler of demons) and Satan (the devil) are synonyms, referring to the same figure. But this cannot be simply assumed in a controversy in which a charge is brought by representatives of the rulers against a peasant healer/exorcist, and in which the peasant appeals to his own audience of ordinary people on the basis of the (Israelite) popular tradition that he shares with them. In Mark's version of the exchange, the scribes level two charges: "he is possessed by Beelzebul," and "he casts out spirits/demons by the ruler of spirits/demons." It is at least possible that it is the scribes who (are understood to) make the connection, implying that the alien god/force Beelzebul that they are demonizing is "the ruler of the demons," who is, in Jesus's exorcisms, attacking the established order of which they are the enforcers. In the other version of the accusation, in both Matthew and Luke, Beelzebul stands in apposition to, equated with "the rulers of the demons," although of course the Pharisees could be the ones (understood to be) making the equation.

In the Markan version Jesus presents two related arguments in response. The first is paralleled in the somewhat different version evident in Matthew and Luke. Jesus draws on the traditional image, in Israelite culture, of house, which has a range of reference and meaning, from a patriarchal household through the lineage that rules in that household to a kingdom and the dynasty that rules.[21] This image hardly originates with Jesus and would not have its force without the deep cultural tradition in which it is rooted. Best known in biblical studies is surely "the house of David," which rose from a local household to imperial kingship and then became divided against itself in the rebellion led by David's son Absalom; again it was dramatically reduced in its rule when the majority of Israelites withdrew in insurrection after the death of Solomon. Jesus refutes the scribes' charge by drawing an analogy between a house/kingdom divided against itself, and Satan risen up against himself. In the rhetorical situation, however, it is not quite clear whether Jesus is arguing that surely Satan would not be so foolish as to rise up against himself. Perhaps he is arguing, more subtly and cleverly, that on the scribes' (or Pharisees') assumption that he is casting out demons through Beelzebul, the latter's rule is collapsing; the scribes

---

21. Oakman, "Rulers' Houses."

should be pleased at that collapse and the exorcisms through which it is happening.

Jesus's second argument in the Markan episode, following on both the focal image and the conclusion of the first, shifts the focus to the house or palace of a powerful man (suggesting Satan): it is not possible to plunder a strong man's goods without first tying up the strong man. This leaves it to the audience to draw the analogy: Satan's goods (or goods belonging to the ruler of the demons)—that is, the demons or the people they have possessed—are being plundered, so Satan must have been bound.

In Jesus's response in the Markan version and in its partial parallel in the Matthean and Lukan episode, it is not clear to what Satan's kingdom or house refers. What is its extent? What does it include? Interpreters have often projected some sort of apocalyptic dualism, in which Satan and his minions were imagined to be in control of life or history, with the people desperately hoping that God would soon intervene, overthrow Satan's rule, and establish the kingdom of God. But this hardly seems warranted by the references to Satan (or the devil) in the rest of the Gospel stories, or by Judean texts, which are sources from scribal circles, but which might also be used critically and carefully as indirect sources that might suggest what ordinary people may have been thinking.

Other than in the Beelzebul episode, Satan appears rarely in the Markan story, as the tester in Jesus's wilderness preparation for his mission as a prophet, as the agent who blocks the effectiveness of the word sown by the sower, and as the tempter who makes Peter misunderstand Jesus as the messiah. In Matthew Satan appears only in the Beelzebul episode, in Peter's confession, and as a synonym for the devil in the temptation episode. Satan has more varied if still minimal roles in Luke: as tempter of Judas and other disciples, as the agent (spirit) who had bound the crippled woman, and as a heavenly power whom Jesus beholds "fall from heaven." "The devil" appears mainly as the tempter in the temptation episode in Matthew and Luke (4:2–22; 4:1–13), then as the sower of the weeds in the parable (Matt 13:39), and as taking the seed in the parable of the sower (Luke 8:12). In sum, in the Gospel stories Satan (the devil) pops up occasionally as an agent of temptation and of obstruction for the mission of Jesus, but this figure can hardly be said to be locked in a cosmic conflict with God that is controlling earthly affairs. In no episode other than the Beelzebul controversy is Satan even associated with (other) spirits/demons, much less identified as the ruler of demons. Just as spirit possession and exorcisms are ad hoc and particular, so Satan's activity is ad hoc in the Gospel stories that have developed from the basis of Jesus movements in Israelite popular culture. And in Jesus's response to the charge of casting out demons by the ruler of the demons, the kingdom or house of Satan is not similar, not even comparable, to Belial or the Angel of Darkness in the scribal scheme from the Qumran *Community Rule*.

The image of Jesus's having seen Satan fall from heaven in Luke (10:17–20) seems at least somewhat similar to the disarray and division among the heavenly forces (angels) in the divine governance of the world in certain Judean (scribal) texts. In the much earlier Book of Watchers (*1 Enoch* 1–36), "the watchers, the sons of heaven," rebel against the heavenly governance, led by their chief, Shemihazah (clearly the forces behind Hellenistic imperial violence), and are expelled from the heavenly governance and bound. The more contemporary Parables of Enoch (*1 Enoch* 37–71) repeat the apparently standard scribal lore about how powerful inhabitants of the earth have learned "the secrets of the angels and the violence of the satans." Again these rebel heavenly forces are condemned and punished in the judgment of the Most High. Most of the contents of these visionary books is clearly scholarly, scribal lore. In these scribal texts Shemihazah is one among many rebel heavenly forces with particular functions in the heavenly governance that they have disrupted, but nothing comparable to Belial in the grand scheme of the two Spirits in the Qumran *Community Rule*. It is easily imaginable that some of the images of rebel heavenly powers may have been shared by people on the popular level as well. "Satan" in Jesus's response may have been understood as "the ruler of the demons" but was hardly understood as a heavenly force that controlled earthly affairs generally.

The other version of the Beelzebul controversy, upon which Matthew and Luke draw, includes an argument in Jesus's response to the charge that does not appear in Mark, one that is virtually verbatim in the two Gospels: "And if I cast out demons by Beelzebul, by whom/what do your sons cast [them] out?" The argument clearly implies that Jesus is not alone in casting out demons. In the episode in Luke, where "some of them" bring the charge, this could refer more broadly to "their offspring"—to other people who are also engaged in exorcism. In Matthew, "your sons" would presumably refer to the disciples (students were often called "sons") of the Pharisees, that is, some of them who were doing exorcism. This fits with references elsewhere in the Gospels that others were doing exorcism. It may be difficult

EXORCISM EPISODES

for modern intellectuals to imagine that their ancient predecessors could have been engaged in "casting out demons." But it should not be imagined that ordinary people were the only ones vulnerable to spirit possession, or that intellectuals in service of the rulers did not have rituals by which they attempted to exorcise possessing spirits. Of course if addressed to a charge by the Pharisaic enforcers of the threatened established order, this argument of Jesus may have been a rhetorical ploy to the effect that, since others are also performing exorcisms, why are you singling me out for attack?

Again in both Matthew and Luke this episode concludes with a remarkable assertion by Jesus. Having effectively responded to (refuted) the charge of casting out demons by Beelzebul, the ruler of demons, Jesus now asserts his (movement's) understanding of what is happening in his exorcisms: "If it is by the finger/spirit of God that I cast out the demons, then the (direct) rule of God has come upon you." It has been argued that "finger of God" must have been the phrase in their common source, since if it had been "spirit of God," Luke would surely have retained it. Of course "spirit of God" is very unusual in Matthew and nearly as unusual in Luke. But "finger of God" stands out in a way that fits well with the overall story in all of the Synoptic Gospels and with the agenda of the Jesus speeches paralleled in Matthew and Luke, which portray Jesus as a prophet like Moses, engaged in the renewal of Israel. It is an unmistakable reference to the exodus story, in which Moses is engaged in a contest of feats and ritual performance with the learned scribes at the court of Pharaoh in Egypt. (The modern concept of magic has of course been projected onto the so-called pagan courts of the Pharaoh and of the Babylonian emperors, in standard translations of biblical narratives in Exodus and Daniel.) When Moses performs a feat that they cannot match, the learned scribes of Egypt exclaim, "It is by the finger of God." With the image of "finger of God" Jesus is thus suggesting that his mission, in the exorcisms at least, is a new exodus, a new liberation of the people from bondage under imperial rule. And that would mean life under the direct rule of God—which would fit with other statements about the direct rule of God in the Gospels. For example, "the direct rule of God is *among* you" (Luke/Q 17:20), that is among the people who are undergoing renewal in (as a result of) the mission of Jesus.

The episode of accusation that Jesus casts out demons by Beelzebul and his response is not about and is not controlled by a schematic, dualistic struggle between God and Satan. The image of a ruler of the demons, like the figure Beelzebul, is (part of) the charge leveled by the scribes or

Pharisees. That Satan is the ruler of the demons is not attested in any other episode in the Gospels. And Jesus's statement, in the Matthean and Lukan episodes, "if it is by the finger/spirit of God that I cast out spirits/demons, the rule of God has come upon you," is not an assertion about a dualistic struggle between God and Satan, and is not about a schematic struggle like that between the Spirit of Light and the Angel of Darkness in the Qumran *Community Rule*.

Agency in the Exorcism Episodes

From these critical considerations, it seems questionable that either references to the Spirit toward the beginning of the Synoptic Gospel stories or Jesus's statements in the Beelzebul controversy can be claimed to attest the agency of God or the (Holy) Spirit in Jesus's exorcisms. The references to the Spirit descending upon Jesus at his baptism and the reference especially in Luke to Jesus's being filled with the power of the Spirit apply to Jesus's mission of renewal of the people in general. His statements in the Beelzebul episode are responses to the charge of the scribes and Pharisees, and cannot be transformed into a theological or cosmological scheme similar to that articulated by the dissident scribes and priests at Qumran. It must remain striking that the exorcism episodes themselves do not point to God or the Spirit as agents, or suggest a general opposition of God/Spirit versus Satan. In this connection it should also be noted that references in the Gospel story to divine power, to God as "Power," pertain to future fulfilment of the kingdom of God, to the completion of deliverance (Mark 9:1; 14:62; cf. Jesus or the Son of Man coming in deliverance, Mark 13:26–27).

Finally, it is striking that except for the accusation of "having Beelzebul," there is no specific reference in the exorcism episodes or elsewhere in the Gospels stories to Jesus as having been possessed by the Spirit or a spirit. The story of Micaiah ben Imlah (1 Kings 22) and a scene at the beginning of the long poem in Isaiah 40–55—along with the stories of their predecessors, the liberators (judges), also known as prophets (as in the Song of Deborah, Judges 5)—suggest that Israelite prophets were inspired in ecstatic experiences, even received their visions/prophecies in being caught up to the heavenly court of Yahweh. Nothing like this appears in the Gospels even though Jesus is clearly portrayed in the tradition and role of an Israelite prophet, and even though his healings are taken to mean that he is a prophet. Interaction with heavenly powers, spirits, or angels was

EXORCISM EPISODES

cultivated in scribal circles, as evident in Enoch texts and Daniel 10–12 as well as in various texts from Qumran. But were Jesus and other popular figures in Galilee or Judea who performed exorcisms (e.g., the implications of Mark 9:38–41), including the disciples (implied in the mission speeches; see esp. Luke 10:17), also interacting with spirits or possessed by a spirit?

Two references might be taken to point in this direction, but by no means say as much. When the seventy report after their mission that "even the demons submit to us in your name," Jesus declares, "I saw Satan fall from heaven like lightning" (Luke 10:18). As noted above, this is a unique location and role for Satan in the Gospel stories. Is it a piece of or a reference to scribal lore that has been picked up among ordinary people? Or did ordinary people, particularly those caught up in a movement of renewal, have a sense, even an experience, of (various) heavenly forces allied with or opposed to God that transcended the spirits or demons they were casting out? Earlier Israelite tradition of the prophets (for example, the story of Micaiah ben Imlah) knows of multiple voices in the heavenly court. But when it comes to these prophets' inspiration, it is by "the spirit of Yahweh."

The other reference that might point to Jesus himself having been possessed is the framing of the accusation of Beelzebul by the scribes in Mark, as "those around him" being concerned that he is "out of his mind." Yet this is not comparable to the scribes' charge of his being possessed by Beelzebul. Moreover, their concern would seem to be part of a subplot (or one of several subplots) in the Gospel of Mark: "those around him" (his family?) are suspicious about the prophetic role and mission in which he has become caught up (3:19–21, 31); they and others in his hometown—who know him simply as a local carpenter, and know his mother and brothers and sisters—do not share the excitement and trust that have grown up around him (6:1–6); and only later does his (brothers') mother come to trust (15:41–47; 16:1); and only much later does his brother James join the movement and emerge as a key leader (Acts 12:17; 15:13).

One of the principal Gospel texts from which scholars (and readers generally) would derive the idea that God—alongside or in synergism with Jesus—was an active agent in the healings and exorcisms comes from the Gospel of John, particularly Jesus's discourse following his healing of the paralyzed man at the pool of Bethzatha. As the issue becomes defined as healing on the Sabbath, Jesus declares that, as he has just illustrated in the healing, "my Father is still working, and I am also working" in giving life to people. This discourse in John, of course, is reinforced by other discourses in which Jesus declares his close synergistic "working" relationship with the Father.

What remains striking, considering the exorcism episodes (stories) in the context of the Synoptic Gospel stories as a whole, is that in the stories themselves, Jesus does not call upon or appeal to any higher agent or authority: God or the Spirit.[22] If the phrase in Jesus's response to the charge of having Beelzebul—"if it is by the Spirit or finger of God that I cast out demons"—is an assertion that he has been exorcizing by the power or authority of the Spirit or of God, then it seems remarkable that in the course of composition and performance of the Gospel stories some reference or appeal to the Spirit of God does not appear in the exorcism episodes themselves. The exorcism episodes in the Gospels, parallel to the episodes of healing, portray Jesus as having the authority or power to cast out spirits himself in his performative commands: "Be silent, and come out (of him)!"

---

22. So also Twelftree, *Jesus the Exorcist*, 160–61.

Conclusion

JESUS WAS NOT PERFORMING miracles or practicing magic. To apply these concepts to the healing and exorcism (stories) of Jesus is to modernize him. The investigations in these chapters indicate that the concepts of miracle and magic under which the healing and exorcism (stories) of Jesus have been classified and interpreted are the products of Enlightenment Reason shaped by (natural and social) scientific perspective. The concept of miracle and especially the concept of magic were also influenced by colonial and Orientalist attitudes. Interpretation of Jesus and the field of New Testament studies in general somehow became stuck in these modern constructs. Most books in the recent wave of scholarly interpretation of the historical Jesus give little or no attention to "miracle stories"; this neglect applies to the healings and exorcisms of Jesus as well. But the most influential scholars who have devoted considerable attention to the healing and exorcism stories have simply perpetuated the modern constructs in which New Testament studies have been stuck for at least the last century and more.

There is remarkable agreement among New Testament scholars on their understanding of miracles as extraordinary events that find no explanation in the ordinary world of time and space (nature) and hence must be caused by God or some supernatural agency. A survey of ancient Judean, Hellenistic Jewish, and Greco-Roman sources, however, finds no evidence for or concept that corresponds to the modern concept of miracle. The Judean and Hellenistic elite who produced the texts that are extant simply did not make a distinction between nature and the supernatural, a distinction that became standard in modern Enlightenment thinking. Nor do the Gospel accounts of Jesus have any concept of or term for miracle. Modern interpreters simply impose the concept onto the Gospel accounts, sweeping the healing and exorcism stories along with other phenomena up into this vague, general category.

The discovery of the "magical papyri" in Egypt became a stimulus to revival of scholarly interest in and construction of ancient magic a century ago. Interest revived again in the 1970s and 1980s as the attendant conceptual confusion continued. Interested scholars seem to have ignored the eminent scholar Arthur Darby Nock's clear survey of the ambiguity of the use of the term *magos/magoi*, which often referred to the Persian priests-sages who cultivated a wide-ranging wisdom and those who continued it in Hellenistic culture. That other usage was polemical and accusatory, however, did not appear to have registered with those who took *mageia* and *magoi* as references to magic and its practitioners. Scholars used the "magical papyri," most of which were from late antiquity, to fill out their construction of ancient magic, and simply assumed that it, like earlier polemical statements about "magicians," referred to actual practice and practitioners in earlier centuries.

Interpreters of the miracle(s) (stories) of Jesus, looking for the significance of particular words and phrases, declared that there were elements of magic in some of the healing and exorcism stories. As they gave further attention to motifs of magic in the miracle stories, they assumed that healing and exorcism loomed large in the practice of magic. With no critical review of the "magical papyri," however, they did not notice that healings and exorcisms were rare in the papyri and that the few references to exorcism exhibited features of having been borrowed from earlier Jewish and Christian tradition. In the Gospels, moreover, Jesus is not accused of practicing magic. Nevertheless, starting on the basis of later charges against Jesus, Morton Smith presented a seemingly well-documented argument that Jesus had been, basically, a magician. Building on Smith's highly synthetic (and often uncritical) construction, but dependent on the abstract functionalist sociological typology of Bryan Wilson, Crossan widened the concept of ancient magic/magician still further—as a deviant, individualistic healer and exorcist. Wilson's discussions in *Magic and the Millennium* only serves to illustrate the Western intellectual baggage that is projected onto Jesus's healing and exorcism with the modern scholarly construction of ancient magic.

Only in the last decade or so have some classics scholars and historians of antiquity presented more critical analyses of some of the texts and earlier construction thought to provide evidence of ancient magic.

CONCLUSION

Recognizing that many if not most of the references to "magic" or "magicians" are polemical and accusatory, some scholars now discuss them as ancient "discourse" about "magic." Others have recognized that a variety of distinctive ritual practices (e.g., *defixiones* or protective amulets or hymns/chants) had become classified under the broad general construct of ancient "magic," and that it would be more appropriate historically to investigate the evidence for such distinctive types of ritual practice. Finally, historians of ancient Egypt began to explain historically how the combination of elite Greek and especially Roman fascination with and suspicion of ancient Egyptian wisdom and ritual practices resulted in the production of papyri such as those collected in the "magical papyri." Scholarly belief in ancient magic and magicians is beginning to dissipate before our eyes. But this opens the promising possibility of investigating ancient healing practices, including (the portrayal of) Jesus's healings and exorcisms, as stories of healing and exorcism.

One of the principal problems with the standard investigation of healing and exorcism in interpretation of Jesus was the isolation of healing and exorcism stories from their narrative context, which offered the only indication of the historical context. Now that the Gospels have been recognized as sustained stories of Jesus's mission, it is evident that the Gospel stories (not the isolated, individual "miracle stories") are the sources for Jesus's healings and exorcisms, and for how they were understood. Investigation of the healing and exorcism episodes as stories of healing and exorcism (not as "miracles") in the context of the over narratives of the respective Gospels offers an approach that is appropriate to the ancient historical interaction in historical context.

Perhaps the most striking feature of the healing episodes is their portrayal of the interaction of Jesus and those seeking healing and their local supporters in a historical context of considerable conflict and distress. The relational character of the healings includes the reputation or fame of Jesus that had been spreading among Galilean villages, the local and cultural context of the healings, and the implicitly or explicitly stated trust with which people approached Jesus. Addressing the question of agency depends on recognizing the interaction portrayed in the healing stories. Jesus is the principal agent. But the healings happen in interaction (not just from the trust of those who are healed), which involves the spreading fame of Jesus, which then evokes people's expectation and the sick person's support network before and after the healing.

CONCLUSION

These aspects of the interaction of healer and healed and supporters in village communities points to what will be perhaps the most important agenda for future investigation of the healing episodes in the Gospels and the healings of Jesus: that is, more careful and precise investigation and understanding of the historical context of conflict and of the popular Israelite culture in which Jesus and his interactors were living and working, including the social-polilitical-religious roles given in the popular cultural tradition (e.g., by popular prophets, in the tradition or social memory of Elijah and Elisha). Information from similar societies in similar historical situations will be important as well. But it seems clear that the investigation of the all-important popular Israelite culture depends on breaking free of other broad, vague scholarly constructs that have obscured information from the sources and limited historical investigation, such as the general concepts of *Judaism* and *apocalypticism*.

Episodes of Jesus's exorcism as well can be adequately understood only in the context of the overall Gospel stories in the historical context that they presuppose and from which they emerged. Because there is such a paucity of information on spirit possession and exorcism (stories) in Galilee and Judea, as well as in the early Roman Empire in general, and since extant texts give information mainly for elite culture, it should not be assumed that those texts offer information about popular culture. Careful analysis of exorcism episodes in the Gospel stories, which evidently do originate in popular Galilean Israelite culture, becomes all the more important—without imposing the synthesizing scholarly construct of (early) Judaism that is based on a synthesis of texts produced by the intellectual elite.

As in the healing episodes of the Gospel sources, so in the exorcism episodes agency belongs to Jesus, and not to God. Depending on how one reads the Beelzebul controversy in Matthew and Luke, it might point to the agency of (the finger or Spirit of) God. And the Gospel of Luke represents Jesus (toward the outset) as working in the power of God in his mission in general (not just in the exorcisms and healings). It thus seems all the more significant, for a fresh approach to Jesus's exorcism, that the exorcism episodes in the Gospels do not suggest the agency of God.

Even more than interpretation of his healing, interpretation of Jesus's exorcisms has been closely linked with, even explained as part of the apocalypticism that was supposedly prominent, even dominant, in late second-temple Judaism. Belief in spirit possession and the conflict between Satan and God have been assumed and explained as part of the apocalyptic

CONCLUSION

worldview that scholars for the last century and more have constructed from selected text fragments and from motifs of texts that they classified as apocalyptic. But it now seems questionable that the late second-temple Judean texts classified as apocalyptic actually attest the highly synthetic scholarly construction of apocalypticism. Thus a careful, critical investigation of the exorcism (stories) of Jesus depends on breaking free of the synthetic construct of Jewish apocalypticism. Then it may be possible to discern, among other important matters, the differences between the portrayal of Jesus's exorcisms in the Gospel episodes (on the one hand) and (on the other hand) scribal portrayals of the conflict between the governance of the world or of history by the Most High and his loyal heavenly forces (angels) and the rebel heavenly forces behind imperial violence.

Fuller and more precise understanding of (the Gospels' portrayal of) Jesus's healing and exorcism depend upon fuller and more precise investigation of how sickness and healing, how spirit affliction and spirit possession, and how protection from or exorcism of spirits may have been understood in Israelite tradition and, if possible, in first-century Judea and Galilee. Attaining this fuller understanding will also entail gaining clear awareness that there may be differences between popular culture (out of which the Gospel portrayals arose) and the scribal culture (attested in most sources).

The Gospel stories present healing and exorcism as the principal activity in Jesus's mission of renewal of Israel in village communities. Once free of the modern constructs of miracle and magic in the ancient world, present-day interpreters of Jesus's interactive mission can focus on healing and exorcism portrayed in the Gospel sources in the historical context of Roman Palestine and Israelite tradition.

Bibliography

Aberle, David F. "Religio-Magical Phenomena and Power, Prediction, and Control." *Southwestern Journal of Anthropology* 22 (1966) 221–30.

Achtemeier, Paul J. *Jesus and the Miracle Tradition.* Eugene, OR: Cascade Books, 2008.

———. "The Origin and Function of the Pre-Markan Miracle Catenae." *JBL* 91 (1972) 198–221. Reprinted in Achtemeier, *Jesus and the Miracle Tradition*, 87–116.

———. "Toward the Isolation of Pre-Markan Miracle Catenae." *JBL* 89 (1970) 265–91.

Alexander, Philip S. "Incantations and Books of Magic." In *The History of the Jewish People in the Age of Jesus Christ* 3/1, by Emil Schuerer, 342–80. Edited by Geza Vermes et al. Edinburgh: T. & T. Clark, 1986.

———. "*Sepher ha-Razim* and the Problem of Black Magic in Early Judaism." In *Magic in the Biblical World: From the Rod of Aaron to the Ring of Solomon*, edited by Todd E. Klutz, 170–90. JSNTSup 245. London: T. & T. Clark, 2003.

———. "'Wrestling with Wickedness in High Places': Magic in the Worldview of the Qumran Community." In *The Scrolls and the Scriptures: Qumran Fifty Years After*, edited by Stanley E. Porter and Craig A. Evans, 318–37. JSPSup 26. Sheffield: Sheffield Academic, 1997.

Alkier, Stefan. "'For Nothing Will Be Impossible with God' (Luke 1:37)." In *Miracles Revisited: New Testament Miracle Stories and Their Concepts of Reality*, edited by Stefan Alkier and Annette Weissenrieder, 5–22. Studies of the Bible and Its Reception 2. Berlin: de Gruyter, 2013.

Alkier, Stefan, and Annette Weissenrieder, eds. *Miracles Revisited: New Testament Miracle Stories and Their Concepts of Reality.* Studies of the Bible and Its Reception 2. Berlin: de Gruyter, 2013.

Attridge, Harold W. *The Interpretation of Biblical History in the "Antiquitates Judaicae" of Flavius Josephus.* HDR 7. Missoula, MT: Scholars, 1976.

Aune, David. "Magic in Early Christianity." In *ANRW* II:23/2 (1980) 1507–57.

Becker, Michael. "*Magoi*—Astrologers, Ecstatics, Deceitful Prophets." In *A Kind of Magic*, edited by Michael LaBahn and Bert Jan Lietaert Peerbolte, 87–106. T. & T. Clark Library of Biblical Studies. LNTS 306. European Studies on Christian Origins. London: T. & T. Clark, 2007.

———. *Wunder und Wundertäter im frührabbinischen Judentum.* WUNT 2/144. Tübingen: Mohr/Siebeck, 2002.

BIBLIOGRAPHY

Behrend, Heike, and Ute Luig, eds. *Spirit Posession, Modernity & Power in Africa*. Madison: University of Wisconsin Press, 1999.

Betz, Hans Dieter. "The Formation of Authoritative Tradition in the Greek Magical Papyri." In *Self-Definition in the Greco-Roman World*, edited by B. F. Meyers and E. P. Sanders, 161–70. Jewish and Christian Self-Definition 3. Philadelphia: Fortress, 1982.

———, ed. *The Greek Magical Papyri in Translation, Including the Demotic Spells*. Chicago: University of Chicago Press, 1986.

———. "Introduction." In *The Greek Magical Papyri in Translation, Including the Demotic Spells*, edited by Hans Dieter Betz, xli–liii. Chicago: University of Chicago Press, 1986.

Betz, Otto. "Das Problem des Wunders bei Flavius Josephus im Vergleich zum Wunderproblem bei den Rabbinen und im Johannesevangelium." In *Josephus-Studien: Untersuchungen zu Josephus, dem antiken Judentum, und dem Neuen Testament, Festschrift Otto Michel*, edited by Otto Betz et al., 23–44. Göttingen: Vandenhoeck & Ruprecht, 1974.

Blau, Ludwig. *Das Aljüdische Zauberwesen*. Budapest: 1897–98; Berlin: Lamm, 1914.

Bloomquist, L. Gregory. "The Role of Argumentation in the Miracle Stories of Luke-Acts: Toward a Fuller Identification of Miracle Discourse for Use in Sociorhetorical Interpretation." In *Miracle Discourse in the New Testament*, edited by Duane F. Watson, 85–124. Atlanta: Society of Biblical Literature, 2012.

Boddy, Janice. *Wombs and Alien Spirits: Women, Men, and the Zar Cult in Northern Sudan*. New Directions in Anthropological Writing. Madison: University of Wisconsin Press, 1989.

Bokser, Baruch M. "Wonder-Working and the Rabbinic Tradition: The Case of Hanina ben Dosa." *JSJ* 16 (1985) 42–92

Brashear, W. "The Greek Magical Papyri: An Introduction and Survey; Annotated Bibliography (1928–1994)." In *ANRW* II:18/5 (1995) 3380–684.

Brooke, George J. "Deuteronomy 18:9–14 in the Qumran Scrolls." In *Magic in the Biblical World: From the Rod of Aaron to the Ring of Solomon*, edited by Todd E. Klutz, 66–84. JSNTSup 245. London: T. & T. Clark, 2003.

Brown, Peter. "The Rise and Function of the Holy Man in Late Antiquity." *Journal of Roman Studies* 61 (1971) 80–101. Reprinted in Brown, *Society and the Holy in Late Antiquity*, 103–52. Berkeley: University of California Press, 1982.

———. "Sorcery, Demons, and the Rise of Christianity from Late Antiquity Into the Middle Ages." In *Witchcraft Confessions and Accusations*, edited by Mary Douglas, 17–45. London: Tavistock, 1970. Reprinted in Brown, *Religion and Society in the Age of Augustine*, 119–46. New York: Harper & Row, 1972.

Bultmann, Rudolf. *The History of the Synoptic Tradition*. Oxford: Blackwell, 1963; original German, 1921.

———. *Jesus and the Word*. New York: Scribner, 1958. German orig., 1926.

———. "New Testament and Mythology." In *Kerygma and Myth*, edited by Hans Werner Bartsch, 1:1–44. 2 vols. London: SPCK, 1957.

Burridge, Kenelm. "Review of *Magic and the Millennium: A Sociological Study of Religious Movements of Protest among Tribal and Third-World Peoples*, by Bryan R. Wilson. *HR* 14 (1975) 228–30.

Cadbury, Henry J. *The Peril of Modernizing Jesus*. Lowell Institute Lectures. New York: Macmillan, 1937.

BIBLIOGRAPHY

Chadwick, Henry. *Origen: Contra Celsum*. Cambridge: Cambridge University Press. 1953.

Charlesworth, James H., ed. *The Messiah: Developments in Earliest Judaism and Christianity*. The First Princeton Symposium on Judaism and Christian Origins. Minneapolis: Fortress, 1992.

Cohen, Shaye J. D. "Menstruants and the Sacred." In *Women's History and Ancient History*, edited by Sarah B. Pomeroy, 271–99. Chapel Hill: University of North Carolina Press, 1991.

Cotter, Wendy. *The Christ of the Miracle Stories: Portrait through Encounter*. Grand Rapids: Baker Academic, 2010.

———. *Miracles in Greco-Roman Antiquity: A Sourcebook*. London: Routledge, 1999.

Craffert, Pieter F. *The Life of a Galilean Shaman: Jesus of Nazareth in Anthropological-Historical Perspective*. Matrix: The Bible in Mediterranean Context 3. Eugene, OR: Cascade Books, 2008.

Craig, William Lane. "The Problem of Miracles: Historical and Philosophical Perspective." In *The Miracles of Jesus*, edited by David Wenham and Craig Blomberg, 9–48. Gospel Perspectives 6. Sheffield: JSOT Press, 1986.

Crapanzano, Vincent, and Vivian Garrison, eds. *Case Studies in Spirit Possession*. Contemporary Religious Movements. New York: Wiley, 1977.

Crossan, John Dominic. *The Historical Jesus: The Life of a Mediterranean Jewish Peasant*. San Francisco: HarperSanFrancisco, 1991.

D'Angelo, Mary Rose. "(Re)Presentation of Women in the Gospels: John and Mark." In *Women & Christian Origins*, edited by Ross Shepard Kraemer and Mary Rose D'Angelo, 129–49. New York: Oxford University Press, 1999.

Deissmann, Adolf. *Light from the Ancient East*. New York: Doran, 1927. German orig. 1908.

Delling, Gerhard. "Josephus und das Wunderbare." *NovT* 2 (1958) 291–309.

Dickie, Matthew W. *Magic and Magicians in the Greco-Roman World*. London: Routledge, 2001.

———. "Magic in the Roman Historians." In *Magical Practices in the Latin West*, edited by Richard L. Gordon and Francisco Marco Simón, 79–104. Religions in the Graeco-Roman World 168. Leiden: Brill, 2010.

Duling, Dennis C. "The Eleazar Miracle and Solomon's Magical Wisdom in Flavius Josephus's *Antiquitates Judaicae* 8.42–49." *HTR* 78 (1985) 1–25.

Eliade, Mircea. *Shamanism: Archaic Techniques of Ecstasy*. Bollingen Series 76. Princeton: Princeton University Press, 1964.

Eshel, Esther. "Genres of Magical Texts in the Dead Sea Scrolls." In *Die Dämonen: Die Dämonologie der israelitisch-jüdischen und frühchristlichen Literatur im Kontext ihrer Umwelt*, edited by Armin Lange et al., 395–415. Tübingen: Mohr/Siebeck, 2003.

Eve, Eric. *The Healer from Nazareth: Jesus' Miracles in Historical Context*. London: SPCK, 2009.

———. *The Jewish Context of Jesus' Miracles*. JSNTSup 231. London: Sheffield Academic, 2002.

Faraone, Christopher A., and Dirk Obbink. "Preface." In *Magika Hiera: Ancient Greek Magic and Religion*, edited by Christopher A. Faraone and Dirk Obbink, v–vii. New York: Oxford University Press, 1991.

Fitzmyer, Joseph A. *The Gospel according to Luke*. 2 vols. AB 28–28A. Garden City, NY: Doubleday, 1981–1985.

Frankfurter, David. *Religion in Roman Egypt: Assimilation and Resistance.* Princeton: Princeton University Press, 1998.

———. "Ritual Expertise in Roman Egypt and the Problem of the Category 'Magician.'" In *Envisioning Magic: A Princeton Seminar and Symposium,* edited by Peter Schäfer and Hans G. Kippenberg, 115–35. Studies in the History of Religions 75. Leiden: Brill, 1997.

Frazer, James George. *The Golden Bough: A Study in Magic and Religion.* New York: Macmillan, 1922.

Funk, Robert W., and the Jesus Seminar, eds. *The Acts of Jesus: The Search for the Authentic Deeds of Jesus.* San Francisco: HarperCollins, 1998.

Gager, John G., ed. *Curse Tablets and Binding Spells from the Ancient World.* New York: Oxford University Press, 1992.

———. "Introduction." In *Curse Tablets and Binding Spells from the Ancient World,* edited by John G. Gager, 3–41. New York: Oxford University Press, 1992.

Gallagher, Eugene V. *Divine Man or Magician? Celsus and Origen on Jesus.* SBLDS 64. Chico, CA: Scholars, 1982.

Goodman, Felicitas D. *How about Demons? Possession and Exorcism in the Modern World.* Folklore Today. Bloomington: Indiana University Press, 1988.

Gordon, Richard L. "Religion in the Roman Empire: The Civic Compromise and Its Limits." In *Pagan Priests: Religion and Power in the Ancient World,* edited by Mary Beard and John North, 233–55. London: Duckworth, 1990.

———. "Reporting the Marvelous: Private Divination in the Greek Magical Papyri." In *Envisioning Magic: A Princeton Seminar and Symposium,* edited by Peter Schäfer and Hans G. Kippenberg, 65–92. Studies in the History of Religions 75. Leiden: Brill, 1997.

Gordon, Richard L., and Francisco Marco Simón. "Introduction." In *Magical Practices in the Latin West,* edited by Richard L. Gordon and Francisco Marco Simón, 1–49. Religions in the Graeco-Roman World 168. Leiden: Brill, 2010.

Graf, Fritz. *Magic in the Ancient World.* Translated by Franklin Philip. Revealing Antiquity 10. Cambridge: Harvard University Press, 1997.

Green, William Scott. "Palestinian Holy Men: Charismatic Leadership and Rabbinic Tradition." *ANRW* II:19/2 (1979) 619–47.

Hadas, Moses, and Morton Smith. *Heroes and Gods: Spiritual Biographies in Antiquity.* Religious Perspectives 13. New York: Harper & Row, 1965.

Heinrichs, A., ed. *Papyri Graecae Magicae: Die Griechischen Zauberpapyri.* 2 vols. Stuttgart: Teubner, 1973–1974. Revision and republication of Preisendanz.

Hengel, Martin. *The Charismatic Leader and His Followers.* Studies of the New Testament and Its World. Edinburgh: T. & T. Clark, 1981.

Hollenbach, Paul. "Jesus, Demoniacs, and Public Authorities: A Socio-Historical Study." *JAAR* 49 (1981) 567–88.

Hopfner, Theodor. *Griechisch-ägyptischer Offerbarungszauber.* 2 vols. Leipzig: Hässel, 1921–24.

Horsley, G. H. R. *New Documents Illustrating Early Christianity.* North Ryde, New South Wales, Australia: The Ancient History Documentary Research Centre, Macquarie University, 1981.

Horsley, Richard A. "Further Reflections on Witchcraft and European Folk Religion." *HR* 19 (1979) 71–95.

———. *Galilee: History, Politics, People.* Valley Forge, PA: Trinity, 1995.

———. *Hearing the Whole Story: The Politics of Plot in Mark's Gospel*. Louisville: Westminster John Knox, 2001.

———. *Jesus and the Politics of Roman Palestine*. Columbia: University of South Carolina Press, 2014.

———. *Jesus and the Spiral of Violence: Popular Jewish Resistance in Roman Palestine*. San Francisco: Harper & Row, 1987.

———. "Oral Communication, Oral Performance, and New Testament Interpretation." In *Method and Meaning: Essays on New Testament Interpretation in Honor of Harold W. Attridge*, edited by Andrew B. McGowan and Kent Harold Richards, 125–56. SBLRBS 67. Atlanta: Society of Biblical Literature, 2011.

———. "Popular Messianic Movements around the Time of Jesus." *CBQ* 46 (1984) 471–95.

———. *The Prophet Jesus and the Renewal of Israel: Moving beyond a Diversionary Debate*. Grand Rapids: Eerdmans, 2012.

———. *Revolt of the Scribes: Resistance and Apocalyptic Origins*. Minneapolis: Fortress, 2010.

———. *Scribes, Visionaries, and the Politics of Second Temple Judea*. Louisville: Westminster John Knox, 2007.

———. *Sociology and the Jesus Movement*. New York: Crossroad, 1989.

———. *Text and Tradition in Performance and Writing*. Biblical Performance Criticism Series 9. Eugene, OR: Cascade Books, 2013.

———. "Who Were the Witches? The Social Role of the Accused in the European Witch Trials." *Journal of Interdisciplinary History* 9 (1979) 689–715.

Horsley, Richard A., with Jonathan Draper. *Whoever Hears You Hears Me: Prophecy, Performance, and Tradition in Q*. Harrisburg, PA: Trinity, 1999.

Horsley, Richard A., and John S. Hanson. *Bandits, Prophets, and Messiahs: Popular Movements in the Time of Jesus*. 1985. Reprinted, Harrisburg, PA: Trinity, 1999.

Horsley, Richard, and Tom Thatcher. *John, Jesus, and the Renewal of Israel*. Grand Rapids: Eerdmans, 2013.

Hull, John M. *Hellenistic Magic and the Synoptic Tradition*. SBT 2/28. London: SCM, 1974.

Janowicz, Naomi. *Magic in the Roman World: Pagans, Jews, and Christians*. Religion in the First Christian Centuries. London: Routledge, 2001.

Kee, Howard Clark. *Miracle in the Early Christian World: A Study in Sociohistorical Method*. New Haven: Yale University Press, 1983.

———. *Medicine, Miracle, and Magic in New Testament Times*. SNTSMS 55. Cambridge: Cambridge University Press, 1986.

———. "The Terminology of Mark's Exorcism Stories." *NTS* 14 (1967/1968) 232–46.

Keener, Craig S. *Miracles: The Credibility of the New Testament Accounts*. 2 vols. Grand Rapids: Baker Academic, 2011.

Kelber, Werner. *Imprints, Voiceprints and Footprints of Memory: Collected Essays of Werner H. Kelber*. SBLRBS 74. Atlanta: Society of Biblical Literature, 2013.

———. *Mark's Story of Jesus*. Philadelphia: Fortress, 1979.

Kloppenborg, John S. *The Formation of Q: Trajectories in Ancient Wisdom Collections*. Studies in Antiquity and Christianity. Philadelphia: Fortress, 1987.

Koskenniemi, Erkki. "The Function of the Miracle Stories in Philostratus's *Vita Apollonii Tyaenensis*." In *Wonders Never Cease: The Purpose of Narrating Miracle Stories in the New Testament and Its Religious Environment*, edited by Michael Labahn and Bert

Jan Lietaert Peerbolte, 70–83. LNTS 288. European Studies on Christian Origins. London: T. & T. Clark, 2006.

Kotansky, Roy. "Incantations and Prayers for Salvation on Inscribed Greek Amulets." In *Magika Hiera: Ancient Greek Magic and Religion*, edited by Christopher A. Faraone and Dirk Obbink, 107–37. New York: Oxford University Press, 1991.

Kraemer, Ross S. "Jewish Women and Women's Judaism(s) at the Beginning of Christianity." In *Women & Christian Origins*, edited by Ross S. Kraemer and Mary Rose D'Angelo. New York: Oxford University Press, 1999.

Labahn, Michael, and Bert Jan Lietaert Peerbolte, eds. *Wonders Never Cease: The Purpose of Narrating Miracle Stories in the New Testament and Its Religious Environment*. LNTS 288. European Studies on Christian Origins. London: T. & T. Clark, 2006.

Lange, Armin. "The Essene Position on Magic and Divination." In *Legal Texts and Legal Issues: Proceedings of the Second Meeting of the International Organization for Qumran Studies, Cambridge 1995: Published in Honour of Joseph M. Baumgarten*, edited by Moshe Bernstein et al., 377–435. STDJ 23. Leiden: Brill, 1997.

Leppin, Hartmut. "Imperial Miracles and Elitist Discourses." In *Miracles Revisited: New Testament Miracle Stories and Their Concepts of Reality*, edited by Stefan Alkier and Annette Weissenrieder, 233–48. Studies of the Bible and Its Reception 2. Berlin: de Gruyter, 2013.

Levine, Amy-Jill. "Discharging Responsibility: Matthean Jesus, Biblical Law, and Hemorrhaging Woman." In *Treasures New and Old: Recent Contributions in Matthean Studies*, edited by David R. Bauer and Mark Allan Powell, 379–97. SBLSymS 1. Atlanta: Scholars, 1996.

Lewis, Ioan M. *Ecstatic Religion: An Anthropological Study of Spirit Possession and Shamanism*. Pelican Anthropology Library. Harmandsworth, UK: Penguin, 1971.

Luig, Ute. "Constructing Local Worlds: Spirit Possession in the Gwembe Valley, Zambia." In *Spirit Possession, Modernity & Power in Africa*, edited by Heike Behrend and Ute Luig, 124–41. Madison: University of Wisconsin Press, 1999.

Luke, Trevor Stacy. "A Healing Touch for Empire: Vespasian's Wonders in Domitianic Rome." *GR* 57 (2010) 77–106.

MacRae, George. "Miracle in the *Antiquities* of Josephus." In *Miracles: Cambridge Studies in Their Philosophy and History*, edited by C. F. D. Moule, 127–47. London: Mowbray, 1965.

Malinowski, Bronislaw. *Magic, Science, and Religion, and Other Essays*. Selected with an introd. by Robert Redfield. Boston: Beacon, 1948.

Margalioth, Mordechai. *Sepher Ha-Razim: The Book of Mysteries*. Translated from 1966 Hebrew edition by Michael Morgan. SBLTT 25. Pseudepigrapha Series 11. Chico, CA: Scholars, 1983.

Martin, Dale B. *Inventing Superstition: From the Hippocratics to the Christians*. Cambridge: Harvard University Press, 2004.

Meier, John P. *A Marginal Jew: Rethinking the Historical Jesus*. Vol. 2, *Mentor, Message, and Miracles*. 4 vols. ABRL. New York: Doubleday, 1994.

Meyer, Marvin, and Paul Mirecki, eds. *Ancient Magic and Ritual Power*. Religions in the Graeco-Roman World 129. Leiden: Brill, 1995.

Miller, Patricia Cox. "In Praise of Nonsense." In *Classical Mediterranean Spirituality: Egyptian, Greek, and Roman*, edited by A. H. Armstrong, 481–505. World Spirituality 15. New York: Crossroad, 1986.

BIBLIOGRAPHY

Moore, Stephen D. *Literary Criticism and the Gospels: The Theoretical Challenge*. New Haven: Yale University Press, 1989.

Morgan, Gwyn. *69 AD: The Year of Four Emperors*. Oxford: Oxford University Press, 2006.

Moyer, Ian. "Thessalos of Tralles and Cultural Exchange." In *Prayer, Magic, and the Stars in the Ancient and Late Antique World*, edited by Scott Noegel, et al., 39–56. Magic in History. University Park: Pennsylvania State University Press, 2003.

Naveh, Joseph, and Shaul Shaked. *Amulets and Magic Bowls: Aramaic Incantations of Late Antiquity*. Jerusalem: Magnes, 1985.

Neusner, Jacob. *A History of the Jews in Babylonia*. 5 vols. Studia Post-Biblica 9, 11, 12, 14, 15. Leiden: Brill, 1965–70.

———. *The Wonder Working Lawyers of Talmudic Babylonia: The Theory and Practice of Judaism in Its Formative Age*. Lanham, MD: University Press of America, 1987.

Neusner, Jacob, et al., eds. *Judaisms and Their Messiahs at the Turn of the Christian Era*. Cambridge: Cambridge University Press, 1987.

Nickelsburg, George W. E. *Jewish Literature between the Bible and the Mishnah: A Historical and Literary Introduction*. Philadelphia: Fortress, 1981.

Nock, Arthur Darby. "The Greek Magical Papyri." In *Essays on Religion in the Ancient World*, edited by Zeph Stewart, 1:176–94. 2 vols. Cambridge: Harvard University Press, 1972.

———. "Paul and the Magus." In *Essays on Religion in the Ancient World*, edited by Zeph Stewart, 1:308–30. 2 vols. Cambridge: Harvard University Press, 1972.

Novakovic, Lidija. *Messiah, the Healer of the Sick: A Study of Jesus as the Son of David in the Gospel of Matthew*. WUNT 2/170. Tübingen: Mohr/Siebeck, 2003.

Oakman, Douglas E. "Rulers' Houses, Thieves, and Usurpers: The Beelzebul Pericope." *Forum* 4/3 (1988) 109–23. Reprinted in Oakman, *Jesus and the Peasants*, 118–31. Matrix: The Bible in Mediterranean Context 4. Eugene, OR: Cascade Books, 2008.

Ogden, Daniel. *Greek and Roman Necromancy*. Princeton: Princeton University Press, 2001.

Peel, J. D. Y. "An Africanist Revisits *Magic and the Millennium*." In *Secularization, Rationalism, and Sectarianism: Essays in Honour of Bryan R. Wilson*, edited by Eileen Barker, et al., 81–100. Oxford: Clarendon, 1993.

Penner, Hans H. "Rationality, Ritual, and Science." In *Religion, Science, and Magic: In Concert and in Conflict*, edited by Jacob Neusner et al., 11–24. New York: Oxford University Press, 1989.

Penney, D. L., and Michael O. Wise. "'By the Power of Beelzebul': An Aramaic Incantation Formula from Qumran (4Q560)." *JBL* 113 (1994) 627–50.

Philostratus. *Life of Apollonius*. Translated by Frederick Cornwallis Conybeare. 2 vols. LCL 116–17. Cambridge: Harvard University Press, 1960.

Pilch, John J. *Healing in the New Testament: Insights from Medical and Mediterranean Anthropology*. Minneapolis: Fortress, 2000.

Porterfield, Amanda. *Healing in the History of Christianity*. Oxford: Oxford University Press, 2005.

Preisendanz, Karl, ed. *Papyri Graecae Magicae: Die Griechischen Zauberpapyri*. 3 vols. Stuttgart: Teubner, 1928–1931. Revised and republished, edited by A. Heinrichs. Stuttgart: Teubner, 1973–1974.

Rea, John. "A New Version of P. Yale Inv 299." *ZPE* 27 (1977) 151–56.

Remus, Harold. "Miracle: New Testament." In *ABD* 4:856–69.

———. *Pagan-Christian Conflict over Miracle in the Second Century.* Patristic Monograph Series 10. Cambridge: Philadelphia Patristic Society, 1983.

Rhoads, David, and Joanna Dewey, and Donald Michie. *Mark as Story: An Introduction to the Narrative of a Gospel.* 3rd ed. Minneapolis: Fortress, 2012. 1st ed., 1982.

Ricks, Stephen D. "The Magician as Outsider in the Hebrew Bible and the New Testament." In *Ancient Magic and Ritual Power*, edited by Marvin Meyer and Paul Mirecki, 131–44. Religions in the Graeco-Roman World 129. Leiden: Brill, 1995.

Ritner, Robert Kriech. *The Mechanics of Ancient Egyptian Magical Practice.* Studies in Ancient Oriental Civilization 54. Chicago: Oriental Institute of the University of Chicago, 1993.

———. "The Religious, Social, and Legal Parameters of Traditional Egyptian Magic." In *Ancient Magic and Ritual Power*, edited by Marvin Meyer and Paul Mirecki, 43–60. Religions in the Graeco-Roman World 129. Leiden: Brill, 1995.

Rives, James B. "Magic in Roman Law: The Reconstruction of a Crime." *Classical Antiquity* 22 (2003) 313–39.

———. "*Magus* and its Cognates in Classical Latin." In *Magical Practices in the Latin West*, edited by Richard L. Gordon and Francisco Marco Simón, 53–77. Religions in the Graeco-Roman World 168. Leiden: Brill, 2010.

Robbins, Vernon K. "Sociorhetorical Interpretation in the Miracle Discourse in the Synoptic Gospels." In *Miracle Discourse in the New Testament*, edited by Duane F. Watson, 17–84. Atlanta: Society of Biblical Literature, 2012.

Robinson, James M., et al., eds. *The Critical Edition of Q.* Hermeneia Supplements. Minneapolis: Fortress, 2000.

Sanders, E. P. *The Historical Figure of Jesus.* New York: Penguin, 1993.

———. *Jesus and Judaism.* Philadelphia: Fortress, 1985.

Schiffman, Lawrence H. *Reclaiming the Dead Sea Scrolls: The History of Judaism, the Background of Christianity, and the Lost Library of Qumran.* ABRL. New York: Doubleday, 1995.

Schiffman, Lawrence H., and Michael D. Swartz. *Hebrew and Aramaic Incantation Texts from Cairo Geniza: Selected Texts from Taylor-Schechter Box K1.* Semitic Texts and Studies 1. Sheffield: JSOT Press, 1992.

Scott, James C. "Protest and Profanation: Agrarian Revolt and the Little Tradition; Part 1." *Theory and Society* 4/1 (1977) 1–38.

———. "Protest and Profination: Agrarian Revolt and the Little Tradition; Part 2." *Theory and Society* 4/2 (1977) 211–46.

Smith, Jonathan Z. "The Temple and the Magician." In *Map Is Not Territory*, 172–89. SJLA 23. Leiden: Brill, 1978.

———. "Trading Places." In *Ancient Magic and Ritual Power*, edited by Marvin Meyer and Paul Mirecki, 13–27. Religions in the Graeco-Roman World 129. Leiden: Brill, 1995.

Smith, Morton. *Jesus the Magician.* San Francisco: Harper & Row, 1978.

Sorenson, Eric. *Possession and Exorcism in the New Testament and Early Christianity.* WUNT 2/157; Tübingen: Mohr/Siebeck, 2002.

Stark, Rodney. "Reconceptualizing Religion, Magic, and Science." *RRelRes* 43 (2001) 101–20.

Stratton, Kimberley B. *Naming the Witch: Magic, Ideology, & Stereotype in the Ancient World.* Gender, Theory, & Religion. New York: Columbia University Press, 2007.

Swartz, Michael D. "Magical Piety in Ancient and Medieval Judaism." In *Ancient Magic and Ritual Power*, edited by Marvin Meyer and Paul Mirecki, 167–83. Religions in the Graeco-Roman World 129. Leiden: Brill, 1995.
Tambiah, Stanley J. *Magic, Science, Religion and the Scope of Rationality*. Lewis Henry Morgan Lectures 1984. Cambridge: Cambridge University Press, 1990.
———."The Magical Power of Words." *Man*, n.s. 3/2 (1968) 175–208.
Theissen, Gerd. *The Miracle Stories of the Early Christian Tradition*. Translated by Francis McDonagh. Studies of the New Testament and Its World. Edinburgh: T. & T. Clark, 1983.
Tieleman, Tuen. "Miracle and Natural Cause in Galen." In *Miracles Revisited: New Testament Miracle Stories and Their Concepts of Reality*, edited by Stefan Alkier and Annette Weissenrieder, 101–13. Studies of the Bible and Its Reception 2. Berlin: de Gruyter, 2013.
Toner, Jerry. *Homer's Turk: How Classics Shaped the Ideas of the East*. Cambridge: Harvard University Press, 2013.
Trachtenberg, Joshua. *Jewish Magic and Superstition: A Study in Folk Religion*. New York: Behrman House, 1939.
Trocme, Etienne. *La formation de l'Evangile selon Marc*. Université de Strasbourg. Faculté de théologie protestante. Études d'histoire et de philosophie religieuses 57. Paris: Presses Universitaires de France, 1963.
Tuckett, Christopher, ed. *The Messianic Secret*. Issues in Religion and Theology. London: SPCK, 1983.
Twelftree, Graham H. *Jesus the Exorcist: A Contribution to the Study of the Historical Jesus*. WUNT 2/54. Tübingen: Mohr/Siebeck, 1993.
Tylor, E. B. *Primitive Culture*. n.p., 1871.
VanderKam, James C. *Enoch and the Growth of an Apocalyptic Tradition*. CBQMS 16. Washington DC: Catholic Biblical Association of America, 1984.
Veltri, Giuseppe. *Magie und Halakha*. TSAJ 62. Tübingen: Mohr/Siebeck, 1997.
Vermes, Geza. *Jesus the Jew: A Historian's Reading of the Gospels*. New York: Macmillan, 1974.
Wallis, R. T. "The Spiritual Importance of Not Knowing." In *Classical Mediterranean Spirituality: Egyptian, Greek, and Roman*, edited by A. H. Armstrong, 460–80. World Spirituality 15. New York: Crossroad, 1986.
Watson, Duane F., ed. *Miracle Discourse in the New Testament*. Atlanta: Society of Biblical Literature, 2012.
———. "Miracle Discourse in the Pauline Epistles: The Role of Resurrection and Rhetoric." In *Miracle Discourse in the New Testament*, edited by Duane F. Watson, 189–96. Atlanta: Society of Biblical Literature, 2012.
Wax, Murray, and Rosalie Wax. "The Notion of Magic." *Current Anthropology* 4 (1963) 495–518.
Wilson, Bryan R. *Magic and the Millennium: A Sociological Study of Religious Movements of Protest among Tribal and Third-World Peoples*. New York: Harper & Row, 1973.
———. *Religious Sects*. London: Weidenfeld and Nicolson, 1970.
———. *Sects and Society: A Sociological Study of Three Religious Groups in Britain*. Heinemann Books on Sociology. London: Heinemann, 1961.

BIBLIOGRAPHY

Wire, Antoinette Clark. *The Case for Mark Composed in Oral Performance*. Biblical Performance Criticism 3. Eugene, OR: Cascade Books, 2011.

Worsley, Peter. *The Trumpet Shall Sound: A Study of "Cargo" Cults in Melanesia*. 2nd ed. New York: Schocken, 1968.

Yalman, Nur. "Magic." In *International Encyclopedia of the Social Sciences*, edited by D. L. Sills, 9:521–28. 19 vols. New York: Macmillan, 1968.

Young, Allan. "The Anthropology of Illness and Sickness." *Annual Review of Anthropology* 11/2 (1982) 257–85.

Zachman, Randall C. "The Meaning of Biblical Miracles in Light of the Modern Quest for Truth." In *Miracles in Jewish and Christian Antiquity: Imagining Truth*, edited by John C. Cavadini, 1–18. NDST 3. Notre Dame, IN: University of Notre Dame Press, 1999.

www.ingramcontent.com/pod-product-compliance
Lightning Source LLC
Chambersburg PA
CBHW020848160426
43192CB00007B/837